SAGE was founded in 1965 by Sara Miller McCune to support the dissemination of usable knowledge by publishing innovative and high-quality research and teaching content. Today, we publish over 900 journals, including those of more than 400 learned societies, more than 800 new books per year, and a growing range of library products including archives, data, case studies, reports, and video. SAGE remains majority-owned by our founder, and after Sara's lifetime will become owned by a charitable trust that secures our continued independence.

Los Angeles | London | New Delhi | Singapore | Washington DC | Melbourne

Advance Praise

Combining nuanced ethnographic insights with rich theoretical perspectives, this book represents the contradictory positioning of India's youth as either 'population dividend' or as masses of troublemakers. As Maithreyi explicates, 'life-skills' training for disadvantaged youth entails attempts to fit them into the dominant class and cultural capital apparatus and the subsequent rendering of life-skills training as meaningless to their life-worlds. The book will be a landmark study that provides insights into the trajectories of mainstream education, the misplaced orientation that overlooks the agency of youth and the personal disorientation and systemic distortions that ensue. A must-read for all educationists and education policymakers.

—**Professor A. R. Vasavi**
Social Anthropologist

In this brilliant new study, Maithreyi develops a compelling argument about the role of education in the formation of youth identities. The book charts with extraordinary sophistication and clarity the changing context shaping young people's actions as well as youth efforts to reinterpret and, sometimes, transform what it means to be young and successful. A tour de force.

—**Professor Craig Jeffrey**
Director of the Australia India Institute and
Professor of Geography, University of Melbourne, Australia

EDUCATING YOUTH

EDUCATING YOUTH

Regulation through Psychosocial Skilling in India

R. MAITHREYI

Los Angeles | London | New Delhi
Singapore | Washington DC | Melbourne

Copyright © R. Maithreyi, 2021

All rights reserved. No part of this book may be reproduced or utilised in any form or by any means, electronic or mechanical, including photocopying, recording, or by any information storage or retrieval system, without permission in writing from the publisher.

First published in 2021 by

SAGE Publications India Pvt Ltd
B1/I-1 Mohan Cooperative Industrial Area
Mathura Road, New Delhi 110 044, India
www.sagepub.in

SAGE Publications Inc
2455 Teller Road
Thousand Oaks, California 91320, USA

SAGE Publications Ltd
1 Oliver's Yard, 55 City Road
London EC1Y 1SP, United Kingdom

SAGE Publications Asia-Pacific Pte Ltd
18 Cross Street #10-10/11/12
China Square Central
Singapore 048423

Published by Vivek Mehra for SAGE Publications India Pvt Ltd and typeset in 10.5/13 pt Adobe Caslon Pro by AG Infographics, Delhi.

Library of Congress Control Number: 2021941446

ISBN: 978-93-91370-03-9 (HB)

SAGE Team: Amrita Dutta, Satvinder Kaur, Shivani Anupkumar Damle and Kanika Mathur

In the question lies the answer.

—Raja P. K.

To my family.

Thank you for choosing a SAGE product!
If you have any comment, observation or feedback,
I would like to personally hear from you.

Please write to me at **contactceo@sagepub.in**

Vivek Mehra, Managing Director and CEO, SAGE India.

Bulk Sales

SAGE India offers special discounts
for purchase of books in bulk.
We also make available special imprints
and excerpts from our books on demand.

For orders and enquiries, write to us at

Marketing Department
SAGE Publications India Pvt Ltd
B1/I-1, Mohan Cooperative Industrial Area
Mathura Road, Post Bag 7
New Delhi 110044, India

E-mail us at **marketing@sagepub.in**

Subscribe to our mailing list
Write to **marketing@sagepub.in**

This book is also available as an e-book.

Contents

Acknowledgements		ix
List of Abbreviations		xiii
1	Introduction: Framing Youth in Contemporary Times	1
2	The Skilling Economy and Youth at Risk	29
3	Cultures of Schooling in India	58
4	Schooling, Skilling and a Range of Actors Redefining 'Educated Youth'	89
5	Life Skills Education as Pedagogies of 'Discipline'	130
6	Ends of Discipline: Curricular Transactions and Social Reproduction of Identities	150
7	Cultural Disconnects and the Possibilities for Subject Formation	183
8	Conclusion	232
Appendices		240
Bibliography		247
About the Author		270
Index		271

Acknowledgements

Every book stands as a testimony not just of the work put in by the author but also of the train of conversations and experiences through which it is built—the willing cooperation of research participants, the love and support of mentors and peers and the thoughtful responses of reviewers and editors. This book is no different, and I have a lot of people to thank for their kindness and generosity in helping me see this manuscript through.

First, let me start by thanking all my research informants, without whom this book just wouldn't be. I'm grateful to every one of them—the life skills organizations, their field staff, students and their families, the teachers and the officials of the education department—all of whom so willingly let me into their lives and allowed me to weave a story from their narratives. It is they who have given me the 'stuff' that this book is made of.

I am very grateful for the generosity and encouragement received from several mentors. Specially, I would like to thank Professor A. R. Vasavi, who has over the years become a well-wisher and a friend, having started as a teacher from whom I've learnt to read and write critically. I'm also very grateful to Professor T. S. Saraswathi, whose dynamism is inspiration and kindness comforting, for pushing me relentlessly to work on the book; and to Professor Vimala Ramachandran, who set me off on this journey first by introducing me to the world of publishing and for always having an encouraging word.

I'm also extremely grateful to have received the friendship and intellectual support and feedback from several others—Dr Arathi Sriprkash and Dr Manish Jain, friends whose sharp minds and comments have helped me strengthen the manuscript; and Professor Aradhana Sharma and Professor Craig Jeffrey, whose works I greatly admire and whose kind words of support and feedback have helped me soldier through. A special thanks to Dr Savitha Suresh Babu who has been the most generous with her time in providing a thorough feedback on the first draft. Thanks is also in order to the reviewers who have provided valuable feedback to improve upon the original manuscript.

The list would not be complete without recalling the stimulating environment at the National Institute of Advanced Studies (NIAS), from where I began this journey, and the many people there, from faculty to administrative and support staff who have contributed to this journey. A special thanks to my advisor Dr B. K. Anitha and doctoral committee members—Dr Shivali Tukedeo, Dr Rajesh Kasturirangan, Professor Sundar Sarukkai and Professor Shekar Seshadri (from NIMHANS)—for all their support and guidance during the course of this research. In addition, I am extremely grateful to Professor Carol Upadhya for her invaluable support during my tenure at NIAS and for her generosity with respect to her time, resources and networks that she shared with me freely. A special thanks to Ms Sandhya J., Ms Hamsa Kalyani, Ms Vijaylakshmi and the canteen staff, whose administrative assistance, library assistance and the wholesome food provided the strength to see the doctoral days through.

A special thanks to the members of the Foucault Reading Group—Dr Madhuri Ramesh, Dr Vasanthi Mariadass and Dr Rashmi M—for being compatriots in exploring the challenging works of Michel Foucault and for the engaging discussions that have helped me develop my understanding of his works. To Rashmi, I owe much more, for all the long conversations not just on work but also on life, many of which figure, in one way or the other, in many of the arguments I make in the book.

In the end, a big and heartfelt thank you to my family that has been a pillar of strength and unconditional support, without whom this book and the PhD journey before it would have just not been possible. I am very grateful to my parents-in-law, my husband, Raja P. K., who has been the driving force behind the book, and my parents and sister for giving me the moral and emotional strength to see my dreams through. Thanks to amma also for so willingly taking up not just the first round of copy-editing but also offering to do so a second time (!), despite her demanding everyday routine and despite finding academic literature a taxing read. Last but not least, heartfelt thanks to Amrita Dutta from SAGE for the enormous professional support and patience she has lent in seeing this work through.

List of Abbreviations

AEP	Adolescence Education Programme
BEOs	Block education officers
CBSE	Central Board of Secondary Education
CSR	Corporate social responsibility
D.Ed.	Diploma in Education
DSERT	Department of State Educational Research and Training
EFA	Education for All
GES	Government elementary school
HM	Headmaster
HR	Human resources
IP	Imagine Possibilities
IT	Information technology
KV	Kendriya Vidyalaya
LSE	Life Skills Education
LSP	Life Skills Programme
MD	Managing director
MES	Millennium Education Society
MFCL	Media for Change Limited
MoSDE	Ministry of Skill Development and Entrepreneurship
MoSPI	Ministry of Statistics and Programme Implementation
MoYAS	Ministry of Youth Affairs and Sports
NCERT	National Council for Education Research and Training
NCF	National Curriculum Framework
NEP	National Education Policy
NGOs	Non-governmental organizations
NIAS	National Institute of Advanced Studies
NIEPA	National Institute of Educational Planning and Administration

NIMHANS	National Institute of Mental Health and Neurosciences
NLP	Neuro-linguistic programming
NPM	New Public Management
NVS	Navodaya Vidyalaya Samiti
NYP	National Youth Policy
PAHO	Pan American Health Organization
SADPI	Sub-assistant director of public instruction
SAP	Structural adjustment programme
SDGs	Sustainable Development Goals
SEAL	Social and Emotional Aspects of Learning
SEL	Social and Emotional Learning
SEZs	Special Economic Zones
SMH	School mental health
SSLC	Secondary School Leaving Certificate
TTP	Teacher training programme
UNESCO	United Nations Educational, Scientific and Cultural Organization
UNICEF	United Nations International Children's Emergency Fund
UNPFA	United Nations Population Fund Activities
USP	Unique selling point
VYB	Viveka Youth Brigade
WCEFA	World Conference on Education for All
WHO	World Health Organization

CHAPTER 1

Introduction
Framing Youth in Contemporary Times

This book discusses the regulation of youth through educational and training programmes. Although the focus on young people is not a new one, the book contributes to an under-examined area of research on the negotiated production of youth as a category to be known and managed. Interest in youth in the present (as in the past) stems from the hope they offer to nations and societies as current or future workers, leaders and productive citizens. Additionally, fears and concerns about the deviation of youth from these 'positive' developmental trajectories, and the consequences this may have for the social and economic order, have further contributed to the increased interest in and surveillance and management of young people (Cieslik, 2003; Dev & Venkatnarayana, 2011).

Contemporary research on youth comes from several disciplines including sociology, anthropology, geography, education, economics, psychology, criminology, development and media studies and has contributed to making youth more comprehendible to a range of authorities and policymakers. These different disciplines have contributed to an understanding of youth cultures, youth transitions, geographical and generational experiences of youthhood as well as provided an understanding of what constitutes 'normal' developmental trajectories, 'risks' and deviations from expected timetables of development between late childhood to early adulthood (or the period that is roughly characterized as 'youth').

Few studies, however, have examined the construction of 'youth' as a distinct social category, in part through the production of knowledge across these various disciplines (Cieslik, 2003). Few have sought to examine how disciplinary accounts have set the normative frameworks through which youth can be comprehended and fewer still have examined how these knowledges are tied to key goals of national and international development, particularly in the Global South. The discursive production of frameworks around youth have also significantly contributed to the structuring of developmental and educational interventions that have come to be positioned as urgent and necessary to ensure 'positive youth development' and well-being (Coppock, 2011; Wyn & White, 1997) under structural conditions of uncertainty and risk (Beck, 1992; Giddens, 1991).

Examining the last point, in particular, the book presents an account of developmental interventions as regulation, while also demonstrating how such interventions are productive of the normative frameworks through which youth can be understood. Specifically taking the example of Life Skills Education (LSE), the book demonstrates how developmental interventions such as LSE work as 'technologies of self' (Foucault, 1988) that produce the discourses and practices by which youth come to know themselves and align themselves with the expectation of authorities. However, rather than providing a monolithic and deterministic account of how discourse and governmental interventions operate, the book draws attention to the negotiated production of subjectivities in the context of interactions between local, provincial settings, international developmental agendas, progressive pedagogic interventions and youth agencies that nevertheless also feed into the neoliberal project.

Before discussing the LSE programme in more detail in the subsequent chapters, the remainder of this chapter first sets up the context by examining the production of knowledge on youth from several perspectives. Specifically, it examines how social and psychological explanations regarding young people's lives and experiences have shaped discourses and practices in relation to youth and have contributed to the regulation of marginalization or marginalized youth. Further, the chapter sets up the theoretical framework that informs this research, and how this can be used to understand the disciplinary technologies of research and developmental interventions, then briefly describes the methodology used in this study, before discussing life skills programmes (LSPs) observed in government and aided schools in Bengaluru in the following chapters.

1.1. The Emergence and Categorization of Youth as a Distinct Category

Youth (as recognized by the UN, consisting of individuals between 15–24 years) make up 1.2 billion and comprise 17 per cent of the world's population (Population Reference Bureau, 2017; United Nations, 2019), though these estimates may vary based on who is categorized as 'youth' and for what purposes across different nations.[1] In total, 45 per cent of the youth population is located in Asia alone, which is witnessing a youth bulge (Wyn, 2015), while 84 per cent of all youth in the world live in developing countries (UN, 2007). According to the UN, about a quarter of the world's youth also live in extreme poverty (UN, 2007).

What is evident from just this statistical information is that young people rarely ever constitute a homogenous category developmentally, culturally or geographically (Holland, 1990), though they come to the notice of authorities in numbers (Cohen, 1990). Not only does 'youth' represent a 'fluid' category that gets variously constituted based on social, cultural, political, institutional, locational, governmental and

---

[1] For example, contradicting the above definition of youth, the United Nations Convention on the Rights of the Child recognizes child as up to the age of 18 years, in order to protect and ensure basic provisions for a larger group of persons. Similarly, the Indian government identifies youth as persons between 15 and 35 years. Further, the age brackets constituting child and youth groups differ based on the purposes of identification of this groups—for example, in relation to labour laws, legal rights for voting and even with regard to the age of consent in matters related to sexual choices and preferences.

economic contexts, but experiences of youth also differ according to place and time (Wyn, 2015). New research on youth located within non-traditional departments—such as geography, childhood and youth studies, women's studies and cultural studies, and in universities of the Global South—have raised questions over the ontological basis and social status accorded to youth by theories of psychology, sociology and anthropology. These theories that have largely been produced within the Global North, particularly within Anglophone countries, have contributed to an understanding of 'youthhood' as a fixed and universal stage of development. Scholarship in the newer disciplines has however highlighted the performative aspects of youth identities in relation to their ecological contexts, through which young people negotiate the fixed categories of 'childhood' or 'youth' applied to them and the expectations around education, employment, marriage and transitions this sets for them (e.g., see Lesko, 1996; Morrow, 2013; Ruddick, 2007). These newer accounts have also drawn attention to how social and personal histories of caste, class, race, religion, gender, development and geography complicate experiences of youthhood.

Historically, attention to 'youth' as a distinct category of individuals, requiring separate attention and services, emerged during the period of modernization that had started in the 17th century in some Western societies of Europe and America. The development of an industrial society, which replaced agriculture and its economic modes of production and social relations, along with other changes such as the rapid urbanization and growth of cities that were distinctly different in character from rural economies and societies, the displacement of a large number of young persons from gainful employment and/or apprenticeship, changes in social relations within and outside families, and increasing poverty and inequality brought attention to the vulnerability of the young, caught up in these transitions (Stearns, 2005). This resulted in not just the identification of the displaced/unemployed young as a distinct group but also initiated the establishment of new relations of authority, protection and regulation through institutionalized spaces of secular and/or religious education (Hunter, 1996; Rose, 1999; Wyn & Cahill, 2015). Further, as Austin (2019) argues, concentration of young people, away from families, in schools and other exclusive centres, created the conditions for the formation of peer groups and associated 'youth cultures' that allowed youth to set themselves apart from the larger adult society.

By the 19th century, a particular 'portrait' of youth had been captured for the first time in Anglo-American literature with J. D. Salinger's novel *The Catcher in the Rye*, which was further epitomized through movies, songs, magazines and television programmes (Danesi, 2019). A more 'scientific' account about the idea of what constituted 'youthhood' had been introduced even earlier by G. Stanley Hall in 1904, in his book *Adolescence: Its Psychology and its Relations to Physiology, Anthropology, Sociology, Sex, Crime, Religion, and Education* (Vols. I & II). Attempting to resolve the contradictory accounts of youth within biological, psychological and social research, Hall's work positioned adolescence as a period of 'storm and stress'. Hall's work identified the adolescent period as susceptible to increased influence of media and peers, depressed mood, heightened pleasure seeking (which could result in temporary or more permanent expression of problem/criminal behaviours) and relational aggression (Arnett, 2006). The work, which was later criticized, anticipated much of the later discussions within psychology and sociology (Arnett, 2006), beginning in the 1950s–1970s, when youth as a category became a distinct field of study (Fiexa & Nofre, 2012; Wyn, 2015).

During this period, a growing body of research within psychology set up the 'logic of childhood and youth as discrete developmental phases' (Wyn, 2015), with specific timetables and developmental tasks. Locating the phenomenon of 'youth' within the biology of individuals, and newer scientific discoveries made possible through the latest digital imaging technologies have, in fact, produced more concrete evidence on topics such as brain development and its associations with youth behaviours. For example, as Wyn (2015) and McLeod (2012) point out, reliance on the latest research in the neurosciences that have demonstrated continued development of the frontal cortex (linked to the development of capacities for judgement and decision-making) up to the late 1920s have fuelled theories about the probable causes of impulsive and risk-taking behaviours during adolescence. This new evidence has also lent support to earlier hypotheses regarding youth and their associations with criminality and risk.

Within sociology, the earliest frameworks of structural functionalism attempted to explain the role of youth within society, which was seen as a system geared towards maintaining homeostasis (Kingsbury & Scanzoni, 2009). Central to the maintenance of this homoeostasis was the culturally assigned role to each member and the shared values between them (Kingsbury & Scazoni, 2009). Scholarly work within this tradition such as by Talcott Parsons established youth/youth culture as 'irresponsible', performing the important function of easing youngsters from the security of childhood into the difficult tasks of learning adult responsibilities revolving around work and establishment of families, within the structural context of transition from traditional to modern societies and, thus, contributing to the maintenance of social order (Cohen, 1997; Fiexa & Nofre, 2011). Consequently, not only did such theories mark youth as an immanent category but, as with psychological theories, served to establish normative functions of youthhood, any deviation from which was understood to lead to a disorganization of society.

Critics of the structural-functionalist accounts have pointed to the lack of adequate attention paid to factors such as class that significantly contribute to young people's experiences. Marxist frameworks, particularly emerging from the Centre for Contemporary Cultural Studies at the University of Birmingham, brought attention to youth cultures, particularly amongst working-class youth, as an expression of class revolt against the dominant expectations of a capitalist society and middle-class cultures of respectability. As Cohen (1997) argues, the new body of work emerging in the 1960s, particularly within British sociology, began paying attention to the changing class structure in post-Second World War Britain, which disrupted the older reproduction of class structures, manifest in the form of differences that working-class youth presented in terms of language, dress, music and territory. Comprising what came to be known as theories of resistance (replacing earlier theories of reproduction), these new frameworks were also extended to an analysis of gender and ethnicity.

Analysis of youth cultures in the 1960s–1970s took three main forms. In the 1970s, Stanley Cohen paying attention to these separate sub-cultures proposed a 'moral panic theory', arguing that youth cultures were regarded as the signal of impending dangers and threat to social integration by adult society. Another perspective put forth by cultural theorist Mikhail Bakhtin (1986) argued that youth cultures appeared to challenge adult authority by profaning the sacred and serious work of adult life, while representing no serious political challenge to society. A third strand of theorization offered by Thomas Frank (1997) presented youth culture as the default culture of all of American and European society, as commodification of youth came to be seen as a profitable avenue through which music, fashion and culture could be sold (Danesi, 2019).

Theorizations of youth cultures and sub-cultures undoubtedly provided a way forward from the deterministic accounts of structural functionalism and maturational theories of psychology, paying attention to the cultural expressions of agency among young people. Despite bringing attention to issues of class, race and gender, however, they also continued to circulate the problematic view of youth as 'spectacle', particularly highlighting how a sub-group of youth, mainly working class and male, deviated from 'normal' adult society (Clarke, 1982; Cohen, 1997; Gough, Langevang, & Owusu, 2013; Wallace & Cross, 1990; Wyn, 2015). Specifically, critics point to how attention within this tradition remained focused on a few 'authentic' members, while sidelining the majority whose 'normalcy' or 'straightness' was considered indistinguishable or unremarkable (Clarke, 1982; Cohen, 1997). Thus, critics of these cultural accounts drew attention to how these works continued to reproduce the same moral divide between classes (despite identifying structural reasons for this) that has formed the basis for state and philanthropic policies towards youth since the 1880s (Cohen, 1997). Specifically, such a divide valourized the moral values and behaviours of dominant economic classes, thus marking working class culture as deviations from the norm.

1.2. Understanding Youth in Contemporary Times

Limitations of earlier theorizations on youth have given rise to new approaches (Cieslik, 2003), complex metaphors (see Cahill, 2015) and explanations. For example, Chisholm (1990) has argued for the need to examine youth experiences as a 'Rubic cube' in order to fully understand their experiences. Beneath the superficial aspects of cultural and media consumption that commonly affect and influence young people's lives today and render them similar, it is recognized that young people's experiences are multiple and unequally marked by class, caste, race, gender, geography and religion (Wyn & White, 1997; Wyn, 2015). Further, new research is paying attention to both continuity and changes in experiences of youthhood, which may align young people with others from across generations. For example, when seeking to understand the continuities in gender reproduction, youth from across different generations may be compared, while such constitutions may change when examining changes in gender production as a result of deeper, historical influences of individualization and progressive liberalism of the current times on youth as a group constituted across geographical boundaries (see Lesko, Chacko & Khoja-Moolji, 2015; Wyn, 2015). Others have pointed to structural contexts of uncertainty under which the period of youth itself has been extended, as young people are forced to spend more time within education and training, delay family formations and remain highly mobile, under conditions of globalization, shrinking labour markets and 'failed promises' of education and high skills training (Brown, Lauder & Ashton, 2011; Bynner, 2001; Chauvel, 2010; Cieslik, 2001, 2003; Cieslik & Pollock, 2002; Evans & Furlong, 1997; Palmer, 2006; Wyn, 2015).

Under these circumstances, Holland (1990) has argued for the need to consider youth a 'real social category', albeit not one based on universal stages of biological maturation, but as a transitional phase held in place by specific practices, goals and institutional structures within contemporary capitalistic societies, with specific associated social, cultural and economic meaning. He argues that it is these goals and values that together determine the transition from child or adolescent to the specific adult identities of a 'manual labourer', 'white-collar professional', 'housewife', 'working mother' and so on. Wyn and White (1997) have argued for the need to shift from viewing 'youth' as a category to considering youth as a 'social process' through which the meanings and experiences of becoming adult are socially mediated. Further elaborating on how this perspective can be brought to the study of youth, Wyn (2015) has put forth the 'triple helix' that must form the framework of inquiry into youth, consisting of an interest in understanding individual transition, social change and personal identity.

Other recent literature has challenged the idea of youth as a transitional phase itself. The diversity of experiences that are beginning to be recognized within research have cast questions over the idea of capturing young people's lives as in 'transition', as this sets up a false binary between child and adult, school and work, leaving home and getting married; while young people in the Global South and/or in difficult circumstances may experience all of these expectations at once. As several studies have shown, youth from non-elite and non-White backgrounds and marginalized social groups more frequently encounter deviations from these 'normal' trajectories that are based on White, middle-class lives that often involve taking on adult responsibilities earlier, including that of work, managing families and caregiving (see Morrow, 2013; Wyn, 2015). Instead, the concept of 'vital conjectures' has been put forward to explain the uneven challenges that young people face, which can be understood by attending to the structural configurations that are pertinent to the context (Jeffrey, 2010; as cited in Morrow, 2013). As Morrow (2013) has also pointed out, studying youth may also involve paying attention to the contexts they are located in, which might also be undergoing transitions, encountering rapid social change and emerging forms of modernity, experiencing uneven economic development, uncertain labour markets and global pressures on national policy priorities. Thus, the need to examine youth located at the 'vital conjectures' (Jeffrey, 2010; as cited in Morrow, 2013) of individual–personal developments and structural socio-economic changes has been recognized (Cieslik, 2003; Wyn, 2015).

Contemporary research traditions in the social sciences have opened the pathways to understanding youth more relationally and contextually, compared to earlier ahistorical, decontextualized and deterministic accounts of young people's lives. Yet, dominant accounts of youth and youth culture continue to undergird functionalist accounts of family sociology and youth development theories that have a powerful influence on policy and practice (Kingsbury & Scazoni, 2009; Wyn &

White, 1997). It is these latter accounts that have shaped and legitimated the institutional and systemic practices of youth intervention that I now turn attention to, drawing upon conceptual frameworks of governmentality to explain it.

1.3. Youth and Regulation: Theoretical Accounts of Governmentality

Despite a large majority of youth enjoying good health and persisting despite the odds, reports in the media and policy discourses have constructed youth at large to be 'at risk' (Coppock, 2011; Gough et al., 2013). Over 2,500 research papers on risks among youth and families have been produced since 1989 (Kelly, 2001), indicating the intensive attention that the topic has received. Current estimates on mental and behavioural disorders among youth vary widely (see Ecclestone & Hayes, 2009), with the United Nation's International Children's Emergency Fund's (UNICEF, 2011) *The State of the World's Children Report* stating that as high as 20 per cent of all adolescents worldwide have a mental health or behavioural disorder.

Others such as the World Health Organization (WHO) note that 'all young people today face significant stresses in their lives' and identify a range of stressors—biological, socio-cultural and environmental as contributing to mental health and behavioural disorders among youth. The WHO report on *Mental Health Programmes in Schools* states:

> Some changes are part of normal growing up, e.g., growth and hormonal changes, as well as the changes in relationships that young people experience with parents and society. Other stresses are more individual, involving pressures to advance in school and to earn a living, peer pressure, family moves, school changes, parental fighting and divorce, or pressures to engage in substance use. Sexual and physical mistreatment, AIDS, natural catastrophes and severe or chronic physical illnesses and hospitalizations may also cause significant stresses. Young people negotiate these stresses with varying degrees of resilience and mastery. (Hendren et al., 1994, p. 1)

To address these conditions, the WHO advocates for individual skills to be built via universal school-based mental health programmes that can teach children and adolescents how 'to counter environmental stress and disadvantages with which they have had to cope up in growing up' (Hendren et al., 1994, p. 3).

The construction of youth within reports of developmental agencies such as the UNICEF and WHO merits further discussion and discursive attention. Within these accounts, adolescence and youth continue to be presented as stressful periods, re-characterized in new ways to incorporate external risks as problems of individual management. As McLeod (2012) argues, adolescence is explained using a 'neo-developmental and socio-biological conception of identity', showing it to be a 'tumultuous time in the life course during which behaviour and decisions can have significant and potentially negative consequences in adult life'. Within such policy texts, young people are discursively positioned as 'broken' and needing 'to be fixed' (Butterwick & Benjamin, 2006). Everyday experiences—from that of 'growing up' to taking part in social life—are all characterized as potentially stressful and, therefore, potentially placing all young people at risk, and the phases of childhood and adolescence itself as 'risky'. Further, the aetiology of such risks is placed within the innate biologies and capacities of individuals, despite the structural contexts of disadvantage and uncertainty through which these risks may be produced.

Drawing on the framework of governmentality in analysing such youth risk discourses, Kelly (2000) argues that this presents a 'historically novel development' in the regulation of youth wherein the perpetuality of risk allows for the regulation of youth to be 'endless' (Tait, 1995; as cited in Kelly, 2000). Tait (1995) similarly points out that the framing of young people's life in this manner leaves 'nothing' beyond the purview of 'governmental intervention', since risk 'can be legitimately found anywhere'.

In drawing upon frameworks of governmentality, scholars such as Kelly and Tait reference social theorist and philosopher Michel Foucault's works to explain how power operates through the specific constructions of subjects using a genealogical approach. Examining the new modes of control of populations since the modern period that coincided with the rise of the nation state, Foucault (1991) argued that power operates relationally and not centrally through the bureaucratic apparatus of an all-pervading state. Foucault and other Foucauldian scholars have drawn attention to the distributed networks and practices of power through which the modern nation state is governed (see Barry et al., 1996; Foucault, 1991; Kelly, 2000; Rose, 2004; Rose & Miller, 1992) through the application of a series of 'individualizing' and 'totalizing' practices (Rabinow, 1984). Such effects, they argue, are made possible through the objectivization of the individual subject through categories (e.g., 'at risk', 'youth', 'third world', 'excluded' and so on) produced by various discourses of expertise (i.e., academia, development agencies, state bureaus, teachers, medical professional, media and so on), by which individuals come to know themselves (Rabinow, 1984) as well as come to the notice of authorities (Rose, 1999). Thus, for Foucault and other Foucauldian scholars, power succeeds in enforcing its ends through distributed modes that not only include relations between individuals and authorities but also by setting up relations between individuals and their selves, through which they work upon themselves to align their behaviours, mannerisms and attitudes in line with the ends of power (e.g., to become resilient and cope in the face of stress) (Foucault, 1977, 1982; Rose, 1999).

The important distinction that Foucault made through this conceptualization is with regard to how power is productive, rather than repressive or negative; in that it produces the individual and the social conditions under which s/he can think and operate. Extending Foucault's work on subjectification, other scholars such as Dean (1999), Parker (2007) and Rose (1999) have attempted to show how this is made possible through disciplinary discourses, such as that of the 'psy complex'.[2] Producing knowledge about the individual, the psy-sciences function as technologies of discipline and power, in that they set the norms and conditions for freedom, desire and self-realization by which we come to identify ourselves (Rose, 1999). This has, in fact,

---

[2] Disciplines of psychology, psychiatry, psychiatric social work and allied disciplines that work together in producing knowledge about the individual.

been extended even further in the current context through the linkages that have been established between 'positive psychology' and self-regulation in everyday life, coinciding with the neoliberal economic turn (Peters, 2001). Calling this the 'therapeutic culture', others, such as Ecclestone and Hayes (2009), Furedi (2004), Lau (2012), Nolan (1998), as well as Rose (1999), have drawn attention to how, within the advanced liberal contexts of Western Europe and North America, a new understanding has been established in which greater freedom is linked to individuals' own efforts at self-control. Lau (2012) has drawn attention to how, within this culture, 'positive therapy' gains significance as a means to enhance well-being and engulfs even those who are 'non-users' of therapy. Within this culture, he argues that the qualitative aspects of life such as development of self-esteem and emotional management come to be presented as formalistic processes of 'skills acquisition' that can be gained through education and training, linking up a non-clinical population more firmly with 'expertise' that determines their responses and reactions.

Thus, a 'clinical language' pervades these discussions, putting forth the assumption that once 'scientifically identified, objectively measured and quantified', risks emerging from 'manufactured uncertainities' (Giddens, 1991) and the 'unsettling and disintegrating effects of modernity' can be rendered manageable by making 'prudent, choice-making subjects' more responsible for the consequences of their own behaviours and dispositions (Kelly, 2000). Early diagnosis and interventions, particularly during points of transition, targeting youth to prevent escalation of problems and to bring them back on track is seen to be most useful (Kelly, 2000), thus prompting policymakers and development agencies such as WHO to argue for greater investments in programmes such as LSE to promote 'school mental health'. Kelly argues that such policy discourses are structured through 'competing concerns' of 'humanism' and 'economic rationality'. Policies and programmes for youth regulation are justified on the grounds of the prevention of harm and trauma and provision of support for vulnerable and at risk youth, as well as in terms of the savings to be had on the costs of treatment and loss of potential for not just families but communities and nations (Kelly, 2000).

More importantly, as Ecclestone and Hayes (2009) point out such discourses of benevolent interest in youth serve to reconstitute problems of social exclusion, through an identification and re-writing of 'institutionally structured relations of class, gender, ethnicity, (dis) ability and geography as complex, but quantifiable, factors which place certain youth at risk' (Kelly, 2000). As McLeod (2012, p. 13) notes, 'the designation of vulnerability', within youth policies,

> reflects neo-liberal processes of individualisation and an accompanying self-responsibility for demonstrating, claiming and enacting citizenship. Further, even though it appears to evoke a compassionate disposition for all citizens, the notion of vulnerability is currently mobilised in youth and educational policy discourse as an attribute that signifies 'otherness', as a marker of the non-citizen and the dysfunctional community and simultaneously as constitutive of the robust and virtuous (youth) citizen.

Ecclestone and Hayes (2009) argue that under these circumstances, education has come to be positioned as a key tool to address 'diverse material, personal and psychological disadvantages', while exclusion has wholly come to be represented as a psychological state. Recognizing this as a process of 'individualisation of resilience and the marginalisation of social and welfare responses', Ecclestone and Lewis (2013, p. 17), have argued for the need to urgently challenge these powerful discourses on youth risks that positions youth in the service of various ideological ends of the state and market.

While agreeing with these scholars regarding the need to critically interrogate youth risk discourses and the governmental interventions deployed to address this, in the book I also aim to demonstrate the workings of youth agencies and the ways in which these counter the governmental strategies and reasons of neoliberal empowerment programmes. As Aradhana Sharma (2011a, p. 73) notes, '...empowerment is 'dangerous' in that it is laden with risks and unexpected possibilities (Foucault 1982: 231; Sharma 2008)', which belies the possibility for individuals to be wholly determined. In this, she draws upon Foucault's own articulations on power in his later works. For example, in 'The Subject and Power' (1982, p. 790), he states,

Power is exercised only over free subjects, and only insofar as they are free. By this we mean individual or collective subjects who are faced with a field of possibilities in which several ways of behaving, several reactions and diverse comportments, may be realized'.

Thus, Sharma is cautions against 'unequivocally depoliticizing the effects of empowerment' and instead suggests engaging with the 'subaltern politics that are enabled by the governmentalization of empowerment in the age of neoliberalism' and its limits too (Sharma, 2011a, p. 73). Drawing on these understandings of governmentality and workings of power, in the final analytical chapter, I therefore examine the possibilities for resistance within the context of skilling and empowerment interventions, and its implications for youth formations.

1.4. Youth Discourses in the Indian Context

While there is a strong tendency to classify youth as 'risky' worldwide, frameworks of governmentality and youth risk discourses cannot be directly applied to understand youth in the Indian context. Youth constitute the largest demographic segment in India, comprising 34.8 per cent of the total population.[3] They have also been identified as a 'demographic dividend' based on macroeconomic projections that have shown India to continue enjoying a youthful population in the coming decades, when globally populations across developed countries are aging (Ministry of Skill Development and Entrepreneurship, henceforth MoSDE, 2015; Ministry of Statistics and Programme Implementation, henceforth MoSPI, 2017). Public discourses on youth in India are therefore mostly characterized by an urgency around 'harnessing' this 'dividend' against worrying indicators of literacy, education and employment for youth. As per the 2011 census, literacy rates for persons above 15 years still remains 69.3 per cent in the country, with a 20-point difference between male and female literacy rates (MoSPI, 2017). While India has taken steps to improve access to and completion of primary schooling, gross enrolment ratios considerably

---

[3] The *National Youth Policy* (NYP; Ministry of Youth Affairs and Sports, 2014) defines youth as individuals between the ages of 15–29 years.

decline between primary and secondary education and further at higher-secondary and higher-education levels. Unemployment rates remain the highest for individuals between 15–29 years compared to the total population, with women between 15–29 years having a much higher unemployment rate (15.8%), compared to men (8.9%) (MoSPI, 2017). Thus, with systematic inequalities present in educational and employment outcomes for youth, the state's vision of capitalizing on India's youthful demographic has largely been unrealized.

Youth in India are marked by a significant divide, mapping on in some ways to the differences in the social and cultural makeup of the rural, provincial and vernacular context of *Bharat* and that of the globalized urban spaces of *India* that are more deeply tied to the transnational circuits of capital and consumerism (Upadhya, 2019). Access to and participation within these two very different spheres remains contingent upon factors of caste, class and gender, which have produced different forms and trajectories of modernity. As Kaviraj (2003) and Dattatreya (2016) note, the uneven spread of 'western' modernity in India, fostered through selective access made available to colonial education and rule has produced 'asymmetries' that have, in fact, sustained and re-inserted themselves into modern economic and political institutions of industry and electoral democracy and through new caste–class complexes within state administration and governance (Fernandes, 2006; Kaviraj, 2003). A significant marker of these differences among populations has been the formation of divergent subjectivities, much of which do not align with modern ideas of the individualistic and atomistic subject of liberalism (Kaviraj, 2003). Rather, as Kaviraj argues, it has produced a state–citizen relationship of dependency, wherein the large majority of those without equitable access to wealth make demands for the extension of the bureaucratic state. Aradhana Sharma (2011b), in her analysis of state–citizen relationships, has further elaborated on this point, arguing that subalterns in modern India reference a different time and moral economy, articulating citizenship from their positions of inequality by holding the paternal state ethically accountable for care towards its subject. Such enactments of citizenship, Sharma (2011b) argues, differ significantly from that of the Enlightenment's subject within Western democracies—who are rational, secular, sovereign and autonomous in enacting the 'equality of citizenship'—offered by a liberal–democratic state.

It is within this context that state–youth relationships in India have to be examined. 'Youth risks' in this context appear to be largely framed in relation to state provisions and access for marginalized populations (Ministry of Youth Affairs and Sports, henceforth MoYAS, 2014). The NYP (MoYAS, 2014,) identifies five thrust focus areas of the state concerning youth, of which the first objective is the 'creation of a productive workforce' (Table 1.1). This is followed by objectives for 'developing a strong and healthy generation', 'instilling social values and promoting community service', 'facilitating participation and civic engagement' and 'supporting youth at risk and creating equitable opportunity for all'. The last objective particularly merits attention. Rather than identifying youth 'at risk' as a population in deviation from the norm, youth 'at risk' within the NYP has been framed as populations facing significant structural disadvantage, who require 'special attention' to ensure social justice and equitable opportunities (MoYAS, 2014, p. 22). This is clearly seen in the NYP which states:

> A few segments of the youth population require special attention. These include economically backward youth, women, youth with disabilities, youth living in conflict affected regions including left wing extremism, and youth at risk due to substance abuse, human trafficking or hazardous working conditions. It is essential that government policies are inclusive and provide equitable opportunities to all. It is also important to ensure these youth do not suffer from stigma or discrimination, and have equitable access to justice to ensure a dignified life to all segments amongst the youth. (p. 22)

What is evident from an examination of the objectives of the policy is the strong language of responsibility adopted by the state towards harnessing the youth population who are seen as a vital economic, social and political resource for the nation. Rather than viewing youth as 'entrepreneurial citizens' responsible for their own outcomes through participation in markets enabled by the state, a paternalistic

Table 1.1 Objectives for Youth Development Identified in the National Youth Policy, 2014

Objective	Priority	Future Imperatives
1. Create a productive workforce that can make a sustainable contribution to India's economic development	Education	• Build system capacity and quality • Promote skill development and lifelong learning
	Employment and skill development	• Targeted youth outreach and awareness • Build linkages across systems and stakeholders • Define role of government vis-à-vis other stakeholders
	Entrepreneurship	• Targeted youth outreach programmes • Scale-up effective programmes to build capacity • Create customized programmes for youth entrepreneurs • Implement widespread monitoring and evaluation systems
2. Develop a strong and healthy generation equipped to take on future challenges	Health and healthy lifestyle	• Improve service delivery • Awareness about health, nutrition and preventive care • Targeted disease control programme for youth
	Sports	• Increase access to sports facilities and training • Promotion of sports culture among youth • Support and development for talented sports person

3. Instil social values and promote community service to build national ownership	Promotion of social values	• Formalize values of education system • Strengthen engagement programmes for youth • Support NGOs and for-profit organizations working towards spreading values and harmony
	Community engagement	• Leverage existing community development organizations • Promote social entrepreneurship
4. Facilitate participation and civic engagement at all levels of governance	Participation in politics and governance	• Engage youth outside of the political system • Create governance mechanisms that youth can leverage • Promote youth engagement in urban governance
	Youth engagement	• Measure and monitor effectiveness of youth development schemes • Create a platform for engagement with youth
5. Support youth at risk and create equitable opportunity for all disadvantaged and marginalized youth	Inclusion	• Enablement and capacity building for disadvantaged youth • Ensuring economic opportunities for youth in conflict-affected regions • Develop a multi-pronged approach to supporting youth with disability • Create awareness and opportunities to prevent youth being put at risk
	Social justice	• Leveraging youth to eliminate unjust social practices • Strengthen access to justice at all levels

Source: National Youth Policy 2014, MoYAS, Government of India.

character is evident in the youth policy's characterization of state–youth–citizen relationships, through which it nevertheless seeks to achieve its own goals of national productivity and competitiveness within international markets.[4]

Yet the language of care of the national youth policy appears deceptive when seen in relation to young people's struggles and everyday negotiations with the state. Despite articulations of responsibility for the marginalized in the youth policy, as Krishnan (2020) has pointed out, the 'liveability' of lives for minority and disadvantaged youth has in fact increasingly come under threat in recent times against the context of ascendant Hindu nationalism and neoliberalism. Within this context, it is specific youth (e.g., Muslim, as de Geest's work shows, but also lower caste, liberal and left-supporting) that are seen as 'risks' for the nation state, criminalized and targeted through political and media campaigns on and off university campuses, and wrested of their rights to democratically and peacefully express themselves on a range of issues—from citizenship to welfare policies and practices (de Geest, 2020; Pathak, 2020; Singh, 2014; Tahir, 2017). Young people's deaths that have resulted on university campuses from these encounters with the state and mounting caste violence, such as Rohith Vemula's, Payal Tadvi's and Fathima Latheef's (to name just a few), and that have rendered life 'non-viable' (Dyson & Jeffrey, 2020) for marginalized youth, however, do not merit concern or attention within this framework of youth risks. Rather, 'risks' remain largely moral or developmental, as with the concern around young people's sexual and reproductive health (Santhya & Jejeebhoy, 2007) and substance use (Boradia, 2009), or that which comes to be perceived as 'terror' or threat to the integrity of the Indian state. Thus, youth risk discourses appear largely political than benign and caring.

---

[4] See former Prime Minister, Manmohan Singh's (2012) speech on reaping the demographic dividend by skilling and educating youth of India and Prime Minister Narendra Modi's speeches on making youth 'job creators' through innovation (2018), and giving youth the capabilities to make it an 'Indian century' (2016).

Alongside this, significantly, the 'hyper-masculine religious nationalism' (Pathak, 2019) that has come to dominate the state's policies and practices also deeply embeds a neoliberal ethic of 'responsibilization' and entrepreneurialism in strangely novel ways. Nowhere is the ideology of entrepreneurialism more clearly seen than in the calls for skill development to harness India's youth demographic, in order to make them 'employable' (Ministry of Labour and Employment, 2009; MoSDE, 2015). With entrepreneurialism tightly wedded to nationalism, as seen through the prime minister's clarion calls on 'Atmanirbhar Bharat', 'Make in India' and 'Skill India', the ideal young person is called upon to unquestioningly and productively engage themselves, through education and employment, and demonstrate a resilience by pulling themselves up by the bootstrings, even under worsening structural conditions of unemployment (Mitra & Singh, 2019) and heightened insecurities related to jobs, security, citizenship and everyday life. As Vasavi (2008) has noted, within a largely exclusive education system, opportunities for vocational education and training have long remained under addressed but have recently received focused attention. Fears of a growing population of unemployed youth and their 'dangerousness' and the imminent potential to absorb them (Vasavi, 2008) within the expanding service economy has seen massive state investments in skilling. While some basic training in technical skills in fields such as IT, automobile, retail and health have been offered through these programmes, the predominant focus of such training remains on soft skills and English, and to adapt to the language, mannerisms and comportment required to serve the elite customer (Gooptu, 2013; Vasavi, 2008). An analysis of policies and programmes on skilling and workforce preparation reflect the divergence from the paternalistic approaches of the state seen within the youth policy and reflect the global emphasis on 'employability', which, critiques have argued, shifts responsibility for employment from the state to individuals (Gibb & Walker, 2011).

The emphasis on 'employability', which demands not just a set of technical skills but psychological and affective skills as well, has more strongly been affected by industry, which has played a critical role in shaping youth-related policies on education and employment in recent times.[5] Alongside this, there has been a proliferation of 'skilling' programmes, offered by a range of actors, from corporate agencies, charitable organizations, psychologists, educationists and other educated persons belonging to the middle classes, often drawing funding from international donor organizations or corporate social responsibility funds of multinational companies. In the chapters that follow, I take up a fuller discussion of this, drawing attention to how this focus on skilling youth for work glibly conflates skills with working upon one's self and associates poor social and economic outcomes with a lack of specific skills. But before turning to the political economy of skilling and the formation of youth subjectivities, which is the main substance of this book, I briefly describe the research and methodology upon which this book is based in the remainder of this chapter.

1.5. Methodology

The book is based on an ethnographic study of LSE programmes in Bengaluru, India, mainly for high-school students between 13–15 years and some primary-school students between 10–12 years. Though this group does not strictly classify as 'youth' according to certain official categorizations of youth, I bring this group into a discussion on youth regulation for two reasons: first, to draw attention to the differing social norms that mark childhood, youth and adulthood for young people from disadvantaged communities in the Global South, who take on adult responsibilities of work and care early. As Meenakshi Thapan (2005) argues, 'Cultures of adolescence are complex in a

---

[5] A clear signal of this was the appointment of S. Ramadorai, Chairman of Tata Consultancy Services, as the Skills Advisor to the prime minister in 2011, with the rank of a Cabinet Minister (Chenoy, 2013). In education, corporate participation in policy making is now almost two decades old, with representatives of India's largest industrial houses, Mukesh Ambani and Kumar Mangalam Birla constituting the prime minister's 'special subject group on policy framework for private investments in education, health and rural development' in the 2000s (Sharma, 2005; Vijayan, 2016) and more recently with members such as Anurag Behar, CEO of Azim Premji Foundation, participating in the formulation of National Education Policy, 2020.

heterogenous, pluralist and changing society like India where they are shaped by class, gender and educational status and mediated by the peer group, marriage and childbearing.' The second important reason to bring this age group into the discussion of youth is to draw attention to how discourses and programmes for young people 'at risk' target younger and younger populations, who are identified even as they enter adolescence in anticipation of the youth 'risk' behaviours and attitudes that they will potentially display in the future. Finally, though focused on a programme for young people between 10–15 years of age, the subjects of this study included the facilitators (i.e., those who conducted these programmes in schools) and the conceptualizers and managers of these LSP also, who also mostly fell within the category of youth (i.e., were between mid to late 20s and late 30s).

Belonging to a Tamil Brahmin family of professionals, socialized with the very same material and immaterial cultural capital symbolized by LSPs, and a master's degree in psychology, my foray into the field was equally marked by an uncritical acceptance of the power of such 'education-cum-empowerment' programmes offered by many of my field informants. Exposed to these skills of appropriate communication, emotional regulation and self-management, within the elite, private, English medium schools that I had attended; through the network of family and friends that brought the influences and culture of the modern, corporate multinational workplace into the home; and the wide access to self-help literature and training programmes, such as *Chicken Soup for the Soul*, Stephen Covey's *Seven Habits of Highly Effective People*, I had imbibed this culture of constantly working upon the inner aspects of the self in order to become more socially acceptable and 'presentable'. The cosmopolitan spaces of Mumbai and Bengaluru—where I grew up in the late 1980s–1990s, characterized by a peer culture defined by MTV, Levis jeans and veg burgers at KFC—were strong influences that shaped my ideas of self, success and modernity.

Entering my field—government and aided high schools in Bengaluru—however, offered a foil to my uncritical, middle-class modernity, devoid of an understanding of how caste–class positions are central to educational success. Experiences within these schools strongly countered my understanding of self-help skills and programmes like LSE. Here, discourses of the modern, autonomous self and practices of 'self-making' were absent not just in students' behaviours and discourses but also that of teachers, who, despite belonging to the forward castes (Sriprakash, 2013) and embodying a middle-class status and lifestyle (Mooij, 2008; Morarji, 2014; Sriprakash, 2013), jointly upheld (along with the local communities) a set of patriarchal values. Caste positions as well as traditional hierarchical patterns of social organization, highly valued within the communitarian social set-up in the Indian context (Clarke, 2003), rendered teachers the final authority over students and knowledge (Sarangapani, 2003a). Students, mostly in their early adolescence, from classes 8–10, belonged to disadvantaged and migrant communities for whom government schools have become the last refuge and hope (Batra, 2013; Chavan, 2009; De, Noronha & Samson, 2002–2003; Dyer, 2009; Mooij, 2008; Velaskar, 2010).

Within this context, children were primarily seen as requiring 'discipline', and it is within this strong culture of 'disciplining' that LSE found relevance within schools, as interviews with the LSE providers showed. Schools and LSE classes remained sites for culturally disciplining the child, by preparing them to comply with established norms, roles and expectations of society, rather than spaces for the cultivation of autonomous, self-managing individuals.

The stark contrast observed between government and aided schools, within which self-help programmes were applied to the regulation of conduct, albeit somewhat differently from Western psychology's thrust on the creation of the self-managing individual, helped me realize how it is within specific circuits (that map on to the modern India, described earlier) that discourses and practices around the cultivation of the entrepreneurial self travel. Thus, adopting *Institutional Ethnography* as an approach to examine how the practice of LSE is situated within larger frameworks and processes of globalization and uncover the '…empirical linkages among local settings of everyday life, organisations, and translocal processes of administration and governance', I situated the local LSPs observed on field in relation to '…broader visions, policies and practices (of education and economic development) within the global imaginative space' (Madsen & Carney, 2011, p. 116). As Madsen and Carney (2011, p. 116) note, it is by bringing a 'critical' focus to these relations and '...not only the usual bedrocks of educational ethnography (e.g. physical space, teacher, pupil, text and content)' that it may become possible to question the 'unsaid' goals of education (and economic development), which otherwise, uncritically 'continue(s) to identify itself as a project of progress and enlightenment'. I thus examine LSE as discursively-constituted practice and see it in relation to other discourses that constitute it and that are constituted by it, and how these are tied together in the production of 'modern', 'self-managing' and 'flexible' subjects, in the present context (Houtman & Wright, 2004).

The 'field' of study thus consisted of not only the physical locations of the schools and organizations visited in order to gather the data about LSE, but also the broader discursive realm consisting of literature, theory, policies, programmes, practices and individual and institutional narratives, experiences and accounts of LSE. The primary field work was conducted in Bengaluru and focused on obtaining 'thick' ethnographic descriptions of the local school sites, organizations and social contexts in which the LSPs were observed. The ethnographic 'field', framed in this manner, consisted mainly of three organizations (two NGOs—Imagine Possibilities [IP] and Viveka Youth Brigade [VYB], and one private limited company called Media for Change Limited [MFCL]), which will be described in more detail in Chapter 4.[6] From here, it extended outwards to include other sites and individuals who formed a part of these organizations' networks such as schools, corporate and non-corporate partner organizations, children's homes and communities, and other training agencies that interfaced with them. Four other organizations conducting LSPs in Bengaluru were also covered, less briefly, through interviews with management and a few visits to their school sites to understand how their programmes and activities were structured. The data collected in this manner consisted of observations,

---

[6] All names of organizations, schools and individuals mentioned in the book have been changed in order to maintain confidentiality.

interviews, informal conversations and interactions that emerged from an 'immersion' into the routines and culture of the organizations (Hammersly & Atkinson, 2007). As a 'participant-observer', I became a volunteer with two of the organizations and was simultaneously considered an 'insider' as well as an 'outsider'.[7] This had certain advantages, since, as an 'insider', I was able to become a part of the routines, activities and the social world I was studying. This, then, allowed me access to certain important details such as organizational rationales, goals, strategies, and networks that I would otherwise not have been able to access. The latter status, of an 'outsider', awarded as a result of not being a full-time, formal employee with a defined role in the organizations, allowed me to flexibly move between them (i.e., the different organizations). Further, it also allowed me to take on the role of a 'handy-man', who was expected to help as and where required, thus, allowing me to move between the various groups within each organization. This also created certain difficulties, namely that of having to carefully balance my affiliations with the different interest and power groups in the organizations, making sure that I did not lean to any one side that would render me an 'other' to opposite groups. Second, it also made it difficult for me to access organizational space and events, which were largely open to me only as per the organizations' discretion. This meant that I missed out on certain events or information, when members 'forgot' to inform me or did not see it as related to my work. Information about budgets, human resource (HR) management and day-to-day internal problems were, for example, considered inconsequential to my work, and were kept away, and I had to mainly rely on informal conversations and sources to access these.

[7] While IP and VYB engaged me as a volunteer and gave me a considerably larger access to their office, programme, curriculum, schools and other official events, MFCL restricted access and was extremely guarded in interactions with me. This may have been due to concerns in sharing their copyrighted and proprietary material. Access to MFCL was only based on scheduled appointments and invitations to limited events of their choice, though encounters with staff from this organization and observations of their programmes became opportunistically available on certain occasions when I visited a school or event as part of the other two organizations.

Data gathered in this manner over multiple sites (i.e., offices, schools, partner organizations, corporate offices and so on) across one year (from February 2012 to April 2013) was put together in the form of field notes. Field work conducted in this manner comprised of over 600 hours of data collection. A large part of this time was spent within schools, attending life skills classes. Based on the programme model adopted by each organization, classes spanned across the whole school day and, thus, I attended the entire school day, at least once a week. In addition, at least two days were spent, most weeks, at one of the organizations, participating in their meetings, organizational work and/or trainings.

As with any ethnographic research, the data was thematically coded and recursively analysed using a Foucauldian Discourse Analytic framework. Chapters 3–7 present observations from the field, which includes a thick description of the school context (Chapter 3) and organizational and programme structures and rationalities (Chapter 4). Chapter 5 presents a detailed account of the psychological–pedagogic format of LSE, identifying how it closely resembles Christian theological practices, through which individual subjects are brought to reshape themselves. The chapter also identifies the limitations of these pedagogical practices, pointing to how these limitations in fact map onto the understanding of the subject within liberalism, which informs the discipline of psychology.

Chapter 6 describes the ends to which LSE programme seeks to 'discipline' their subjects. These pedagogical ends of disciplining, while serving the local ends of schools, seeking the 'disciplined' students and improved academic outcomes, also contribute to the larger goals of developmentalism in education, which desires the self-regulating, entrepreneurial student subject and 'skilled' worker. Further, the chapter also discusses how the lessons and programme structures of the LSE interventions bring together middle-class cultures, neoliberal values of enterprise as well as patriarchal values of obedience, compliance and gendered norms in shaping marginalized youth subjectivities.

Chapter 7 then discusses how cultural differences between the middle-class organizers of the LSPs, and the non-elite facilitators and youth receiving the programmes contributes to the formation of new subjectivities, which nevertheless also embeds aspects of entrepreneurialism. Instead of a straightforward reproduction of class, caste and gendered subjectivities through the programme, and regulation of youth in line with the expectations of governmental visions, the chapter shows how young people negotiate local and global pressures in producing themselves.

The final chapter concludes by drawing out the implications of the study. It discusses how dominant discourses and production of knowledges on youth, to control and harness their productivity, remain contingent. Discussing the LSPs that target youth within neoliberal economies to take on entrepreneurial roles and thus reduce dependency on the state, I present how an examination of the LSPs in India neither show a straightforward reproduction or transformation of these neoliberal agendas. Rather, I attempt to show how the reading of the life skills discourse in the Indian context allows us to see both the appropriation and rejection of neoliberal values by young people, who actively participate in the reproduction and remaking of their (class and caste) identities. Thus, I conclude on an optimistic note about the nature of social regulation and transformation, pointing to the critical role that agents (in this case youth) play in determining outcomes as well.

CHAPTER 2

The Skilling Economy and Youth at Risk

What can we not achieve if we believe in ourselves and work hard?.... We are working hard to increase the self-confidence of the poor, the deprived and the underprivileged. The impact of this can be seen in the confidence of our young people and our daughters. Recently in the Asian games our players have shown that no matter how poor you are, no matter what kind of family you come from, with confidence and hard work you can make your country proud of you.

Keeping in mind the aspiration of youth the government is bringing a new work culture and a new approach .... Even after 70 years of freedom, while literacy may have increased, many of our young people lack the skills to make them employable. Sadly, our education system has not given enough emphasis to skills. Recognising the importance of skill development for youth the government has created a dedicated ministry for skill development. Besides our government has opened the doors of the banks for youth who want to achieve their dreams on their own.'

—PM Narendra Modi, 11 September 2018.[1]

[1] https://www.youtube.com/watch?v=liQd6EqGk2c

In 2018, speaking at the valedictory function of the 125th anniversary of Swami Vivekananda's Chicago speech organized by the Sri Ramakrishna Math at Coimbatore, India's Prime Minister Narendra Modi emphatically articulated the importance of developing skills, confidence and entrepreneurialism in India's youth. The speech, a signpost of the times, reflects the global culture within which skills and individual personalities have come to be seen as the appropriate developmental solutions. In this chapter, focusing on skilling discourses and the multiple training programmes available for youth, I draw attention to how skilling has become the new 'training gospel' (Swift, 1995). Some of these programmes target the development of specific technical or vocational knowledges, while others focus on the cultivation of new personalities, attitudes and mannerisms.

The chapter sets the context for the LSE skilling programmes described in the remainder of the book. It presents a rationale for why skilling programmes of all kinds—technical–vocational or psycho-educational; for personality development; 'high skills' and 'low skills'; for working youth, youth in the transitional phase from school to work or higher education, young people still within education and unemployed youth—must all be seen as part of the same continuum of skilling.

The acquisition of skills and knowledge has been seen as both a challenge and an opportunity to achieve full employment in many countries of the Global North (Crouch et al., 2004). Skills have been equated with a number of other social and economic outcomes as well—from poverty alleviation and national productivity to individual mobility and 'employability' (see Ashton et al., 1999; Crouch et al., 2004; Gibb & Walker, 2011; Keep & Mayhew, 1999; Taylor, 1998).

In India, too, skilling has come to be accepted as an important educational intervention. Since 2004, a national strategy for skill development has been available in the country.[2] Along with 120 other

---

[2] Though there is a longer history to vocational education and training available in the country, since the 1950s, I refer to 2004 to signal the new outlook and urgency with which skill development has become a priority area in India. While vocational education and training were introduced to address the large

countries from across the globe (Allais, 2012), India has also reorganized its existing educational and training structures along internationally recognized formats of National Qualifications Frameworks. The National Skills Qualifications Framework (NSQF, as it is called in India) integrates all forms of education (general, technical, vocational, long-term and short-term) under one system, based on the identification of core competencies and skills related to all levels and types of courses (Lauder, 2013; Young, 2013), signalling a trend at 'policy borrowing' (Philip & Ochs, 2004). The seriousness with which this strategy has been pursued in India is reflected in the delineation of an entire chapter on skilling for the first time, identified as part of its 'Education Plan', in the 11th Five-Year Plan document (King, 2012; Planning Commission, 2008) as well as by the creation of a MoSDE by 2015. Alongside this, the latest National Education Policy (Ministry of Human Resource Development [MHRD], 2020) has similarly laid emphasis on the importance of a range of skills for youth—from 21st century skills to life skills, for developing well-rounded, thinking and self-reliant individuals. Simultaneously, there is also an emphasis placed within the policy on the early introduction of vocational educational and training to bring vocational skills on par with general education, to be able to 'tap our demographic dividend and address skill-deficits of the economy'.[3]

Simultaneously, a growing body of critical work has begun tracing these shifts to the expanding influences of neoliberalism and the development of an 'enterprise culture'. Within policy, justification for skilling has been put forth using arguments about the transparency and objectivity this offers educators and employers in understanding the specific resources that individuals possess. Critical scholars, on the other hand, have drawn attention to the processes of commodification of the self and its subjectification through skilling programmes,

---

populations for whom higher education remained inaccessible, the thrust on skilling is mainly driven by an urge to harness the demographic dividend and make India globally competitive by addressing the specific kinds of demands for skills made by industry.

[3] As expressed in an opinion piece in *Outlook* Magazine by Sanjay Dhotre, Minister of State for Human Resource Development (August 15, 2020).

identifying it with technologies of neoliberal governmentality.[4] Analysing various forms of skilling, going beyond narrow conceptualizations of skilling as vocational or technical skills, the chapter presents a semiology of skilling and identifies how skilling interventions include several ways of managing the self for work and the economy. Such forms of management include learning personality, learning confidence, as well as a set of personal ethics such as that of hard work (Bloom, 2017; Weber, 2001), as reflected in the prime minister's speech above.

The production of an enterprise culture by skilling young people in general behaviours, mannerisms and attitudes calls for a more critical examination and mapping of the skills discourse. It calls for an analysis of the different forms, levels and linkages through which skilling discourses circulate and operate in producing the productive, global subject of neoliberalism. While the large volume of available critical literature on skilling has examined skill development in relation to the new economy and the production of a flexible workforce (Ainley & Corbett, 1994; Butterwick & Benjamin, 2006; Jackson & Jordan, 1999; Upadhya, 2019; Vasavi, 2008), few—particularly in the Indian context—have paid attention to the continuities between employment and training programmes for working-age populations and various forms of psycho-education, including life and social skills programmes deployed within schools, particularly for 'at risk' youth. Identifying the continuities between the two sets of programmes is important in order to understand how together these sites of skilling serve as the grounds upon which youthhood is psychologically reconstructed, along neoliberal lines, through the dual discourses of 'employability' and 'risks'. Though psycho-education programmes are supposedly deployed towards very different ends, of preventing psychological

---

[4] The idea of 'neoliberal governmentality' draws upon Foucauldian analyses of modes of governance, which explains how individuals are indirectly intervened upon from a distance to shape themselves according to the rationalities of governance, which, under conditions of neoliberalism, desire the 'entrepreneurial' subject who can be encouraged to become more responsible and enterprising in managing their own selves and lives. (See Collier & Ong, 2005; Ferguson & Gupta, 2002; Kipnis, 2008; Ong, 2006; Rose, 2004)

breakdown and teaching young people to 'cope', the chapter presents a genealogical analysis of one form of psycho-education, that is, LSE and identifies its continuities with other forms of training for workforce preparation, such as 'soft skills' training, technical and vocational education and training and 'employability' skills. Identifying a common discourse that runs through both sets of programmes, the chapter discusses the ideological work of skills education and the ways in which it seamlessly integrates different sets of populations towards a common end of cultivating the neoliberal citizen with an understanding of his/her role within an enterprise culture.

2.1. The 'Skills Turn' and the New Economy

> In the emerging global economy, everything is mobile: capital, factories, even entire industries. The only resource that's really rooted in a nation—and the ultimate source of all its wealth—is its people. (*Putting People First,* Bill Clinton and Al Gore; as cited in Crouch et al., 2004)

Why skill development and training have become so central to national strategies of economic planning in the present can be gleaned from the statement of the former President of the USA, Bill Clinton, and Vice-President, Al Gore, given above. As Clinton and Gore note, the high degree of flexibility associated with capital, technology and the means of production in the current economic context and the economic uncertainty that this produces for nations has increasingly pushed states to rely on their people or the productive workforce. Skill development in this context has particular relevance—its function is to adapt labour to the constantly and rapidly changing conditions of capitalist production, which has become flexible and temporally dislocated (Kirpal & Brown, 2007). Thus, as Brown (1999, p. 234) argues, 'The study of skills in the twentieth century is essentially a study of post-industrial changes in our understanding of the global, national, local and personal'.

Though the term 'skills' seems to simply imply 'learned abilities to do something well'(University of Waterloo Career Services, n.d.; as cited in Urciuoli, 2008, p. 211), it in fact marks the complex history of its own metonymic development, as well as offers a genealogical account of the political–economic changes emerging around the 1960s–1980s. Skills discourses trace the shifts from liberalism to neoliberalism, Fordist to post-Fordist modes of production and the emergence of a post-industrial, information society across advanced liberal countries of the West (Brown, 1999). They also signal the changes witnessed by conservative and closed economies of the Global South, such as that of India and China, since the 1990s following economic globalization (Brown & Lauder, 2010; Harvey, 2005). As such, skills discourses map onto several broad, simultaneously-occurring changes seen across these varied contexts and the specific study of the rise of skills economy can reveal the diversity of ends that are sought to be achieved through it.

What current skilling discourses more commonly reflect is the global rise of neoliberalism as the underlying rationale of government, despite the variations in histories, cultures, privileges and wealth across nations (Bloom, 2017), as well as the different forms in which neoliberal ideologies are increasingly being adopted across these contexts. Neoliberalism, David Harvey (2005, p. 2) argues, is foremost a 'theory of political economic practices that proposes that human well-being can be best advanced by liberating individual entrepreneurial freedoms and skills within an institutional framework characterised by strong private property rights, free markets, and free trade.' Bloom (2017) argues that under conditions of neoliberalism, new organization of capitalist relations and ethics for production have increasingly become total in their *external* and *internal* reach.

The advent of neoliberalism, particularly across the advanced liberal countries of the West, can be traced back to the late 1970s–1980s (although its conceptual roots can be traced to the early 1930–1940s), within a context of inflationary stagnation that challenged the logic of liberalism (Flew, 2010; Foucault, 2008; Harvey, 2005; Lemke, 2001). The limits reached to capitalist accumulation under the influence of liberalism in countries such as America, based on what is recognized as the Fordist model of production, characterized by the assembly line, division of labour, semi-automation and the disciplined inclusion of labour through specific patterns of organization of the work day (Holloway, 2005; Schoenberger, 1988), accelerated the critique of the state. The liberal state was seen as restraining markets and individuals from reaching their full potential. Under these conditions, there was a push to 'roll back' the (welfare) state not just in America but across several advanced liberal countries of the West and substitute this with markets for provisioning of public goods and services to enhance economic efficiency and international competitiveness (Bloom, 2017; Larner, 2000). Though reduced, the state's role was conceived as that of an *enabler*, responsible for laying the institutional conditions for markets to operate, by deregulating social sectors, removing restrictions on capital, increasing privatization in delivery of services and linking consumers with markets (Craig & Porter, 2003; Harvey, 2007; Olssen, 2007).

The simultaneous emergence of new digital technologies during this period further paved way for economic reform. Digital technologies allowed for the globalization of production, which seemed to offer a solution to the problems of 'stagflation' witnessed by the Anglo-American countries. Technological solutions were useful not just to address the limitations of the Fordist production system in which economic competition depended on the constant upgrading of machinery and tools of production, requiring considerable time and resources, through the more efficient solutions of reprogramming (Schoenberger, 1988). It also allowed for 'flexible accumulation' through the globalization of production lines and the sourcing of cheaper labour in the Global South, reflecting what is generally known as economic globalization. Along with this, the untapped markets within these countries also provided opportunities for the expansion of capital. Digital technologies further enabled more accurate decision-making within the global marketplace, by making more data or information available, giving rise to the 'information society' (Harvey, 2007) and the 'knowledge economy' (Gibb & Walker, 2011), in which knowledge or information have become the key factors of production.

The importance given to skilling in the present needs to be seen in relation to the social impact of these changes brought about under the combined influences of neoliberalism, economic globalization and the rise of the knowledge economy and information society. As Harvey (2005, p. 3) argues, neoliberalism has produced new 'divisions of labour, social relations, welfare provisions, technological mixes, ways of life and thought, reproductive activities, attachments to the land and habits of the heart.' Across several Third World countries, neoliberal economic policies, enforced through structural adjustment policies, have increased inequalities and enhanced economic distress (Craig & Porter, 2003; Harvey, 2007). The repercussions of neoliberal policies are now sought to be addressed through 'skilling' (Craig & Porter, 2003). Economic globalization has further entailed the flexible organization of labour, and the emergence of a knowledge economy has entailed the need for constant upgradation of knowledge and learning among employees. Skill development is seen as important to adapt populations, particularly working age groups, to all of these changes.

Thus skilling, within governmental rationalities, is imbued with several ends: they are seen as important to prevent social unrest among the poor and disadvantaged and those excluded from markets, by providing them with the means to become employable and compete within the market (Craig & Porter, 2003; Gibb & Walker, 2011). Short-term, modular and flexible skilling programmes are seen as necessary in order to facilitate conditions under which employees can become responsible for their own mobility, job security and outcomes, despite structural conditions of uncertainty and rapid technological and social change. Skilling programmes have contributed to the development of a learning society by offering avenues for lifelong learning which has become a social norm (Gibb & Walker, 2011). With the availability of a range of skilling programmes, expectations are placed on individuals to develop an awareness of their own human capital (Nikson et al., 2003) and to plan, find the resources and invest in training to deal with larger structural problems of cost cutting, low wages, job insecurities and employment by investing in themselves (Bhatia & Priya, 2018). Skilling programmes and discourse thus offer the critical infrastructure required to realize the neoliberal imaginary that seeks the entrepreneurial citizen and worker, that is, one who is an enterprise in himself/herself and one who can deploy his/her self 'as an infinitely flexible product re-shaped to meet market demands' (Gillies, 2011, p. 214). The neoliberal citizen and worker are expected to possess a set of individualized skills, internal control and the ability to market oneself in order to enhance one's employability (Kirpal & Brown, 2007). As several scholars note, the enhanced opportunities for skilling available in the current environment has allowed for the complete 'marketization' of the self (Gillies, 2011; Rose, 1999; Urciuoli, 2008) and a reshaping of one's consciousness as thinking, acting subjects of the market (Bloom, 2017).

In this context, it is not just technical skills that are required but other psychological traits and behavioural characteristics as well that are significant to the production process (Ainley & Corbett, 1995; Keep & Mayhew; 1999; Nikson et al., 2003). In the next section, I examine the range of personal attributes that are now sought to be shaped according to the neoliberal rationalities of government, euphemistically identified as 'skills', and discuss how these attributes become significant in the current context.

2.2. A Semiology of Skilling

While skills in an earlier context would have meant 'knowing to' (e.g., read, paint, cycle, fix a bulb) rather than knowing that or knowing how, the term skills currently encompasses not just abilities to do but also ways of being and behaving. Urciuoli (2010, p. 162) explains that in the present, 'every piece of knowledge one acquires can be interpreted and assessed as a skill, an aspect of oneself that can be considered productive by prospective employers.' As she further adds, 'Skills referents cover a range of disparate practices, knowledge, and ways of acting and being' (Urciuoli, 2008) and remain 'denotationally indeterminate', taking on meaning based on how and by whom it is applied (Urciuoli, 2008). This observation is significant to note, particularly when policy rhetoric marketing the liberatory powers of skilling only links it to the 'high skills', 'high income' California- or Bengaluru-styled information technology (IT) industry jobs that require the higher order cognitive skills of thinking, analysing, coding and manipulating information (see Brown et al., 2001; Gibb & Walker, 2011; Nikson et al., 2003;

Warhurst and Thompson, 1998). In reality, however, as Nikson et al. (2003) note, the largest number of jobs available are 'McJobs', not 'iMacJobs' at the lower ends of the urban, service economy, involving 'low skills', low wages and high degrees of routinization (Brown et al., 2001, Gibb & Walker, 2011; Jackson & Jordan, 1999; Nikson et al., 2003).[5] Skills within this context still remain important and necessary but entail altogether different kinds of training. That is, the skills deemed important within these contexts are the 'soft skills' of interpersonal communication and personal management, rather than 'hard skills' consisting of technical or vocational knowledges required to do a specific job well (Jackson & Jordan, 1999; Nikson et al., 2003; Urciuoli, 2008).

Reflecting on the proliferation of skilling discourses and the very different skills required for different jobs, Urciuoli (2008) presents a taxonomy of skilling, identifying the several kinds that have become necessary for workers within the current economy. Examining several skills training websites and programmes, Urciuoli (2008) notes that the expectations for workers range from having basic skills (such as listening, learning and thinking) to complex problem-solving skills, resource management skills and social skills (all of which she identifies as 'soft skills') to systems skills, which she argues are indeterminately soft or hard, and finally technical skills, which are definitively hard skills. Expectations with respect to these specific skills also vary based on job roles, with workers at the higher ends of the economy, those required to have 'high skills', most definitively requiring both the 'soft' and 'hard skills', while the large majority at the lower end expected mostly to have 'soft skills' in order to be 'flexible' and fit in according to organization requirements (Kirpal & Brown, 2007; Nikson et al., 2003).

While 'soft skills' of communication and interpersonal relations are necessary to smoothen the work process and train employees to

---

[5] This is also true for the Indian context, with the Confederation of Indian Industries' projections showing the eight sectors of retail, construction, transport and logistics, tourism and hospitality, handlooms and handicrafts, textiles and apparels, food processing, and automotive set to create over 100 million jobs by 2025 (The Economic Times, 7 March 2019).

put the organization's needs before their own (Jackson & Jordan, 1999), another set of skills that Nikson et al. (2003) have identified as fundamental to the economic process are 'aesthetic skills' or 'style' skills, involving the creation of service encounters that deliberately appeal to the sensibilities of customers in visual or aural ways, and the adoption of practices to 'look good' and 'sound right'. Such skills are specifically seen to be relevant in industries such as the hospitality and retail sectors, as well as in care work jobs in the medical and social work sectors, which draw upon the very self of the worker as the 'unique selling point' (USP) of the product and the value addition that the brand offers, entailing a commodification of the self. As Urciuoli (2008) argues, such demands placed on the individual to draw upon oneself in marketing the commodity blur the lines between oneself and one's work, 'making one rethink and transform one's self to best fit one's job'. Others such as Jackson and Jordan (1999) and Kripal and Brown (2007) argue that the large spectrum of skills (particularly soft skills) deemed necessary in the current economy 'break down strong worker identities' and 'deskill' workers by removing their collective powers of bargaining based on specific technical knowledges and skills.

These deep forms of psychological reconstruction of selves expected within the workplace, reducing the distance between the product and service, and the producer, I argue, require longer investments beyond the short term employment-oriented skilling programmes offered in relation to the specific work at hand, during the period of early adulthood. The reorientation of the worker requires the reorientation of cultures of the self (Foucault, 1983), drawing it away from its traditional moorings within family, local ecologies and cultures of the community and its norms, ethics and practices, to the realm of markets and economy, guided by new forms of expertise and modern knowledges that have established new norms for relating to the self. Pedagogic discourses and machineries of psychology and education are central to this, as I will discuss in the next section, through their markings of what constitutes the 'the successful worker', 'the skilled employee', 'the educated citizen', 'the failed student', 'the resilient subject', the 'risky youth' and the 'normal adult'.

2.3. Skills-based Education and the Psychological Reconstruction of the Neoliberal Citizen

In the previous sections, I identified the specific kinds of persons desired within the current global and economic context, that is, one who is enterprising and hardworking in producing themselves to fit in with the requirements of the neoliberal economy, while overcoming personal–structural disadvantages by taking on more responsibilities for one's personal outcomes. The production of this entrepreneurial subject of neoliberalism entails the reconstruction of the subject in all forms, that is, as citizen of the state; worker within the economy; consumer within the marketplace; as the educated subject of schooling; and even as responsible parents and adults within families and communities.

Central to this restructuring of the individual have been the knowledges of psychology and education that are closely aligned and function together as 'technologies of government'—the former by producing the scientific knowledge to bear upon the subject, and the latter providing the pedagogic space within which the knowledge of psychology is applied in producing the 'educated' subject. As Ilcan and Lacey (2011) have argued, psychological knowledges are centrally tied to practices of 'global governmentalities' or the development of 'governing efforts and representational practices' that set the understanding of social, economic and political problems and their solutions at a global scale, contributing to an increasing governmentalization of life. Discourses of psychology have been central to the reframing of problems of governance as problems of the self (Popkewitz, 1991), thus individualizing structural risks under neoliberal conditions. Political and economic issues, under neoliberalism, have been converted into manageable educational problems through psychology, requiring new strategies of teaching and testing (Popkewitz, 1991). Moral and political concerns have further been decontextualized and reformulated as pedagogic practices of 'helping' individuals achieve greater efficiency, while success and failure have been attributed to their own motivations and self-discipline by the pedagogic machinery of psychology and education. Thus, education and the knowledge of the individual produced by psychology have been key disciplinary technologies in shaping the neoliberal individual, and skill development programmes function as an extension of this technology of government.

Tracing the changes in understanding of the subject produced through psychology and education, concomitantly with the rise of neoliberalism since the 1960s across advanced liberal countries, critical psychologists Wendy Holloway and Lynn Fendler draw attention to the changes seen in the pedagogies of work and education. While psychological theory on the management of workers and *managerialism* prior to the 1960s focused on increasing productivity through the rationalization of movements and management of the individual worker, in line with the requirements of the Fordist models of production, Holloway (2005) argues that post-1960s, the limitations of these modes of production required new models of management. Growing instances of worker sabotage as a result of inhuman working conditions of capitalism led to new forms of management offering supposedly benevolent compensatory acts of nurturing workers' personal development through training. Coinciding with the rise of humanistic psychology, and particularly with Maslow's self-actualization theory, pedagogic supervision of workers involved engaging them in practices of managing the self, through counselling, peer and self-assessments.

These trends were also visible in the changes brought to education. With value placed on education as a nation's best economic policy,[6] changes to education in accordance with changes made to economic policies since the 1980s have been visible across the Anglo-American world. Drawing attention to the generalization of the values of 'fluidity' and 'flexibility', from economic to other domains such as business, politics and the individual domain of the self as well, Fendler (1998) has pointed to how education has become a site for the cultivation of these new values. Fendler argues that education, as a 'technology of government', also activates the practices of 'technologies of self', cul-

---

[6] The statement was made by the former Prime Minister of the UK, Tony Blair, who stated 'education is the best economic policy we have' (DfEE 1998, 1; as cited in Gillies, 2011, p. 211).

tivating the 'response-ready' and 'response-able' subject desired within the new economic context. Tracing the changes within educational technologies since the 19th century, she points to the shift in focus from concerns of preparing individuals for moral citizenship, to the interest in the cultivation of cognitive–intellectual abilities and social responsibility; followed by the Taylorist models of process-oriented learning suited to the Fordist assembly line system of production; and finally to the pedagogic concerns with the 'whole child' bringing the innermost aspects of individuals' lives, that is, their desires, fears, attitudes and aspirations under the pedagogic gaze, in order to enable the psychologically 'flexible' subject, in the present. In commenting on the preparation of the flexible and fluid worker–citizen, others such as Ailwood (2004, p. 29) have argued that 'Neoliberal and advanced liberal thought of adulthood requires new childhoods; childhoods that will produce lifelong learners, self-maximizers—the autonomous and rational worker/citizens required in neo-liberal and advanced liberal societies within knowledge-based economies', thereby pointing to the central role that education plays in this.

Kaščák and Pupala (2011) have also similarly drawn attention to how neoliberalism as the new mode of governance has co-opted progressive and liberal pedagogies of child-centred learning by fusing it with the rationalities of human capital theory in producing the self-regulating, entrepreneurial subject. Drawing on work by Nadesan (2002) and Ailwood (2004), they argue that the ethic of self-governance through freedom has captured all levels of development, even right down to early childhood, wherein new child theory emerging around the mid-20th century has called for an 'invisible pedagogy' through which parents and caretakers can steer children towards fulfilling their own expanding needs through carefully structured play and learning environments. While notions of lifelong learning are overtly associated with adult populations, in preparation for work, they argue that within the generalized entrepreneurial culture of neoliberalism, it is important to recognize how all systems from schooling onwards have been reorganized to cultivate the enterprising, autonomous subject, shaping his/her own successes in terms of his/her own existence within this culture (Kaščák & Pupala, 2011).

Thus, the whole child approach described by Fendler has complemented the 'whole school approach' described by several other scholars, with schools and teachers now responsible for deploying the pedagogic machinery of the school towards practices of social engineering in producing risk-managing, adaptable individuals (Coe & Natasi, 2006; Coppock, 2011; Down, 2009). As Coe and Natasi (2006) have noted, in the 1970's the teaching of socio-emotional skills of problem-solving and self-esteem emerged against concerns regarding the 'breakdown of a caring community of adults' and the increasing deterioration of mental health and growing concerns around adolescent risks such as teenage pregnancies, drug abuse, juvenile crimes and so on (Coe & Natasi, 2006; Coppock, 2011; Finn et al., 2010). Amidst the increased media-fuelled panic around youth, a functionalist understanding of society was adopted in which social competence was intimately connected to social adaptation, adjustment and instrumentality (Coe & Natasi, 2006). Psycho-educational interventions for problem-solving and self-esteem were seen as the 'social vaccine' (Cruikshank, 1996) that would teach individuals to live responsibly, inoculated from problems ranging from teenage pregnancy and substance abuse to welfare dependency and educational failure. Pedagogies for social competence were expected to deliver a 'technology of subjectivity that could solve social problems from crime and poverty to gender inequality by waging a social revolution, not against capitalism, racism and inequality, but against the order of the self and the way we govern ourselves' (Cruikshank, 1996, p. 231).

The teaching of social skills and competence within schools was to be modelled along the lines of the academic curriculum itself, with a sequential curriculum based on 'evidence based' best practices and a list of learning outcomes against which children's social health was to be measured (Coe & Natasi, 2006; Coppock, 2011). Thus, the whole school approach has entailed what Michaels (1991) has described as the 'dismantling or breaking down of narrative performances and the artistry—in favour of alternative forms of meaning-making deemed more scientific, rigorous, reliable, intelligent, and important'. The ever-increasing obsession with children's mental health, despite research that has indicated that a large majority of youth enjoy good health (Coppock, 2011; Finn et al, 2010) has led to the emergence of universal mental health and social skills programmes inside and outside schools. More significantly, such programmes seek to align individual children's aspirations with their role as future adults (Coppock, 2011; Down, 2009; Morrow & Mayall, 2009). While Coppock argues that psycho-educational programmes invite the individual child to self-actualize within the constraints of what he/she is expected to become as an adult, Morrow and Mayall (2009) point out that children are valued in terms of future human capital 'becomings'. Down (2009) further argues that through 'at risk' discourses attached to students that finds them wanting in the right forms of capital, attitudes and behaviours for the new workplace, schools are urged to do more, to develop the enterprising individual, who is flexible, risk-taking, self-managing and independent, shows confidence and resilience, required for the functioning of the 'properly enterprising form of free market economy'.

The interest in linking children's social and emotional health in the present to their economic participation and to nation's economic outcomes in the future is also evident from recent policy documents such as the European Commission's, which notes,

> The European economy will require skilled labour in the future decades, yet many children still leave education without complete secondary education qualifications. The attainment of general skills, educational qualifications and gainful productive employment thereafter are facilitated by good mental health (Jane-Llopis & Braddock, 2008, p. 9; as cited in Coppock, 2011, p. 394).

Accordingly, a range of programmes such as Social and Emotional Aspects of Learning (SEAL) in the UK, Social and Emotional Learning (SEL) in the USA, Mind Matters in Australia and the International Families and Schools Together have been deployed by governments across the world. In addition, programmes targeting mental health of students has also been popularized and introduced across different contexts by supranational agencies such as the WHO as part of its 'school mental health' (SMH) campaigns. In the next section, I will discuss in further detail one psycho-educational programme called LSE, advocated by the WHO that has found relevance even in the Indian context and show how it aligns with neoliberal agendas of constructing the entrepreneurial citizen.

2.4. Skills-based Education and the Psychological Reconstruction of the Neoliberal Citizen

In the Indian context, system-wide psychological interventions to regulate youth through education and schooling are still relatively rare, although the growing presence of number of state and non-state actors 'seeking to create heightened aspiration and expectations, promoting the ideology of self-making, providing self-help and self-development tools, as well purveying the evidence of success of self-propelled individuals as motivational instruments' has been noted (Gooptu, 2013, p. 8; as cited in Bhatia & Priya, 2018). A growing range of experts offering personality development, skills development and mental health solutions as 'technologies of self' have been engaged in creating new neoliberal discourses of 'Indianness' that is now reflected within Indian fiction, cinema and the new workplaces within Special Economic Zones (SEZs), IT companies and management schools (Bhatia & Priya, 2018; Vasavi, 2008). Alongside this, the small number of empowerment programmes to socialize marginalized youth to confront their personal disadvantages through the development of a critical understanding of their own social histories and to develop confidence by gaining the tacit cultural capital required for success within the new economy have also been growing (see Ashwini et al., 2017; Babu, 2020; Manasa et al., 2018; Nampoothiri, 2013; Vasavi, n.d.).

While several experimental psycho-educational models targeting learners' subjectivities have emerged in the last two decades, national-level programmes targeting young people's socio-emotional and mental health and personality (like SEAL and SEL) are yet to become entrenched into the state education system. One such programme that the state has tried to adopt as part of school education is LSE. LSE emerged as part of the United Nations Population Fund Activities (UNPFA) Adolescence Education Programme (AEP). But by 2007 it was withdrawn across several states due to public protests over teaching of 'sex education' to young students in schools (Bahuguna, 2007). On a smaller scale, LSE has been introduced within schools as part of SMH programmes in government schools (see Srikala & Kishore, 2010) and through the Central Board of Secondary Education (CBSE). In addition, several independent professionals—psychologists, educators, national and international corporate and non-governmental organizations (NGOs) advocate, sponsor and/or conduct LSPs within and outside schools, colleges and other educational institutions, forming what Mundy and Murphy (2001) call transnational advocacy networks.

Although there is a diversity of programmes available under the banner of 'life skills' ranging from skills for spoken English, computer literacy and financial management to 'soft skills' and personality development, the overwhelming interest lies in harnessing India's youth population, that constitutes its demographic dividend for the economy and in cultivating employability skills among them (Talreja et al., 2018). Though programmes targeting youth to improve school performance and learning outcomes as well as to prevent 'risky adolescent behaviours' are available (Talreja et al., 2018), goals of education development and health are also narrowly linked to concerns of future productivity and costs for the nation, rather than intrinsically valued for themselves.[7] The emphasis within these programmes remains tied to the economic goals of cultivating the adaptable and flexible citizen, evident from the definition of LSE given by the WHO itself.[8]

The WHO (1993, p. 1) defines LSE as 'the psychosocial abilities for positive and adaptive behaviours that enable individuals to deal effectively with the demands and challenges of everyday life.' The WHO lists out a set of 10 skills (Table 2.1) that cover all domains of the individual self—intrapersonal, interpersonal and cognitive.

---

[7] It must be noted that there are also certain exceptions to this general observation with some smaller, local programmes that are using LSE to bring about social change, particularly related to gender norms.

[8] Although LSE has been defined and categorized in several different ways by different agencies, I draw on WHO's definition and classification throughout this book, as it is one of the earliest and globally influential articulation and classification of life skills. For different LSE classifications, see Talreja et al. (2018).

Table 2.1 The 10 Life Skills by WHO

Skill	Description	Classification
Decision-making	Capacity to assess different options and effects of actions taken in relation to health, and to deal constructively with these decisions about our lives.	Cognitive skills
Problem-solving	Dealing constructively with problems in life, without which problems of physical strains arise.	Cognitive skills
Creative thinking	Contributes, both, to decision-making and problem-solving by enabling one to explore various alternatives and their consequences, even in the absence of a problem. Thus, it is seen as important to remain adaptable and flexible.	Cognitive skills
Critical thinking	Ability to analyse information and experiences in an objective manner such that it helps one recognize the influences on attitudes and behaviours, such as media influences and peer pressure that affect health behaviours.	Cognitive skills
Effective communication	Ability to express oneself and one's desires clearly, in culturally appropriate ways, when asked to engage in particular actions, and to ask for advice.	Interpersonal/social skills
Interpersonal relationship skills	Ability to maintain positive relationships, such as friendships and with family members, is seen as important for social support. It is also seen as the ability to end relationships constructively.	Interpersonal/social skills
Self-awareness	Recognition of oneself, character, strengths and weaknesses, desires and dislikes. It is seen as important for effective communication, interpersonal relationships and empathy, and to recognize when we are under stress.	Self-management/coping skills

(Table 2.1 Continued)

(Table 2.1 Continued)

Skill	Description	Classification
Empathy	The ability to imagine what life is like for the other person, accepting others who may be very different from us, such as ethnically different people, those suffering from AIDS or mental illness and to be caring and tolerant towards them.	Interpersonal/social skills
Coping with emotions	Recognizing emotions in oneself and others and its effects on behaviour and knowing to respond appropriately to emotions.	Self-management/coping skills
Coping with stress	Recognizing the sources of stressors in life, recognizing how it affects us and how to control it through strategies such as taking action to reduce the stressor or learning relaxation techniques.	Self-management/coping skills

Source: Adapted from WHO (1993), Pan American Health Organization (PAHO, 2000) and WHO (n.d.).

Significant to note about the WHO's definition is the construction of *everyday challenges* as a problem of *individual adaptation* that can be addressed through the right set of skills. The importance of LSE to a range of everyday contexts and life itself is discussed across different texts and documents on LSE including academic psychological literature and journals papers. For example, in a journal article on 'Enhancing Youth Development Through Sport', Danish, Forneris, Hodge and Heke (2004, p. 40) state that life skills are 'those skills that enable individuals to *succeed* in the different environments in which they live such as school, home and in their neighborhoods' (italics mine). As is evident from their account, life skills are conceptualized as skills that not only help fit individuals into various environments but more importantly as the relevant tools that will help them 'succeed' within these different environments. Other literature on life skills has further elaborated on how life skills contribute to making individuals successful, relating it not just to social, communal and academic goals in childhood but also to becoming '...skilled adults ... able to form relationships in their social contexts necessary in widening their social spectrum and intimacy' (Mofrad, 2013, p. 232). Thus, within academic–psychological literature, life skills have been positioned as skills to enable individuals succeed in the most intimate recesses of personal and family life as well.

Further, the LSE discourse also presents at least two distinct developmental ends of the state to which it can be applied. For example, the WHO has identified LSE as vital to indirectly combat a whole range of secondary social problems such as poverty, truancy and violence. The WHO (2009, p. 3) notes that

> Factors such as poor social competence, low academic achievement, impulsiveness, truancy and poverty increase individuals' risk of violence.... Thus, developing children's life skills ... improving their participation and performance in school and increasing their prospects for employment can help protect them from violence, both in childhood and later in life.

In these discussions, LSE is presented not just as solutions to personal behavioural problems but to larger structural issues of poverty and unemployment from which these conditions emerge, thus, 'responsibilizing' (i.e., making responsible) individuals for managing under difficult and unjust social circumstances. In fact, as can be observed from the account given before, personal qualities, such as impulsiveness, are placed alongside socially determined circumstances such as poverty, and all of these different conditions are levelled as similar kinds of 'everyday challenges' emerging from individual deficits that can be addressed through a universal set of skills. Thus, their value is seen to emerge from their potential at developing both self-regulating individuals who can be less disruptive to the state's development goals and self-responsible citizens who can bear the onus of achieving these developmental goals.

Further, while LSE is considered as integral to all daily aspects of living, paradoxically, it is these very skills that have been identified within literature as absent in an alarming majority of children and youth, thus positioning a large population 'at risk'. Reports by WHO, as that of other national and international agencies favouring these forms of skills training, state that:

> All young people today face significant stresses in their lives. Some changes are part of normal growing up, e.g., growth and hormonal changes, as well as the changes in relationships that young people experience with parents and society. Other stresses are more individual, involving pressures to advance in school and to earn a living, peer pressure, family moves, school changes, parental fighting and divorce, or pressures to engage in substance use. Sexual and physical mistreatment, AIDS, natural catastrophes and severe or chronic physical illnesses and hospitalizations may also cause significant stresses. Young people negotiate these stresses with varying degrees of resilience and mastery. (WHO, 1993, p. 1)

Positioning all young people as under some or the other form of risk, in this manner, developmental psychology, applied via policy discourses of international agencies such as the WHO, has established whole developmental periods of childhood and adolescence as under 'risk', when, in reality, a majority of young people have been known and reported to enjoy good health. Against this context, LSE has been conceived not just as a positive addition or buffer against risks, but its absence is equated with inappropriate development. Within psychological literature, it is argued that 'deficits in these life skills appear to play a critical role in the etiology of adolescent problem behaviors including drug abuse because poorly competent youth are highly vulnerable to the social, environmental, and intrapsychic forces that promote and maintain problem behaviors' (Botvin & Griffin, 2002, p. 42). In these accounts, life skills are established not just as a matter of learning or training but as an organic condition or variable of children's development. Childhood or children considered to be on the path of normal development has/have now come to be linked with the presence of the said skills. Positive development and socialization are associated with the development of certain specific behavioural and psychosocial changes, and 'risks' to be prevented have all been described in psychological terms, as all problems of development have been related to individual behaviours.

Skills in this context considered important are psychosocial ones, and despite the all-encompassing term chosen of 'life skills' (or skills related to all of life), the term in fact encompasses a narrow set of skills. In fact, within psychological literature, 'life skills' are clearly separated from other 'hard skills' or what are considered to be 'isolated behaviours' such as cooking or managing money (Hodge et al., 2012), or other skills needed for livelihood (WHO, 1999). The focus instead is more on a set of 'soft skills' to do with self-regulation and personal management. Presenting this difference, the United Nations Inter-Agency Working Group on LSE for all has also noted that

> One area of agreement from the exercise was that there are different types of skills–(i) psychosocial skills and (ii) manual or hands on skills. Psychosocial skills were recognised as already being defined as life skills *by some groups* (italics in original). While the group struggled with terminology [sic] to describe the concept, 'manual or hands on skills' were described as those skills related to 'making things or objects' or doing something, especially with the hands e.g. first aid bandaging skills, switching on a computer, or putting on a condom. It was agreed that these should not be considered 'life skills'.... (United Nations Educational, Scientific and Cultural Organization [UNESCO], 2004, p. 5)

Thus, life skills are mainly specified as the psychosocial characteristics (including the values, attitudes and knowledges) that underlie behaviour across all life situations, while contrasted with other skills that are non-psychological in nature (UNESCO, 2004). Since they are seen as characteristics that underlie *all* behaviour, they are, thus, also considered important for normal individual development and lifelong learning. Thus, 'risks' of inappropriate development to be prevented are also psychological ones, and problems of development are related wholly to individual behaviours.

While psychosocial in nature, what differentiates LSE from other psychological techniques and concepts, such as socio-emotional learning, emotional intelligence, resilience and positive psychology, is the emphasis on *skills* (Hodge et al., 2012), interactive pedagogy (Cuijpers, 2002) and the conceptualization of the tacit, spontaneous and immaterial aspects of everyday lives as a set of observable, repeatable, and *practice-able* abilities to be acquired through formal learning (Lau, 2012). Most LSPs are structured as a set of about 15 sessions or class periods (of about 45 minutes duration each), beginning during early adolescence (i.e., 11–12-year olds) and repeated over 2–3 years (Botvin & Kantor, 2000).[9] LSPs seek to engage learners in experiential moments of learning through which they may gain insight over their own behaviours and bring about self-directed changes (PAHO, 2000). Even through fieldwork what remained a visible feature of the LSPs was an atmosphere of warmth, fun and games through which a pedagogic concern with the 'self' was introduced. Skills such as self-awareness, critical thinking, decision-making, effective communication—all of which required self-introspection and reflective cultivation—were presented through games, songs, art, theatre-based activities, group discussions and debates by a group of young facilitators, not more than 10 or 12 years older than the children themselves.

[9] There are different models of LSPs: Stand-alone (as a subject on its own); Integrated (e.g., into a subject area such as social sciences); Extracurricular (mostly conducted by external agencies) or Blended (using a combination of the earlier listed approaches) (UNICEF, 2005).

2.4.1. The Self-Help and Skills Revolution within Psychology

The emergence of LSE and the shift towards skills-based pedagogic techniques, replacing earlier forms of individual-based, psychotherapeutic techniques modelled on the medical model of treatment, needs to be understood in relation to the social history of skills-based education and regulation described earlier. Interactive and pedagogic techniques within the disciplinary knowledges of psychology and its therapeutic practice emerged as a response to widespread critique of the uneconomical, psychotherapeutic model (Murray, 2012), which was found to be inadequate to address the social outcomes of advanced liberalism (i.e., mainly the social discontent and disruption caused as a response to changes in economic life). Within this context, there was a call from within for the discipline to become more relevant by the likes of the then President of the American Psychological Association, George Albee, who argued,

> The terrible suffering that exists in … society among the disenfranchised, the poor, the havenots, can only be remedied by direct confrontation with the establishment, by the socialisation of our care-delivery systems, by … using social models which can only be developed as creative people find out about the real problems…. The times are right for revolution! (Albee, 1969; as cited in Murray, 2012)

As described by those from the profession, the discipline of psychology underwent a 'self-reflexive revolution' (Hodge et al., 2012; Larson, 1984; Murray, 2012). New models to 'give psychology away' (Larson, 1984) and democratize it, by offering individuals psychological knowledge to self-regulate and attain greater control over one's life and behaviours, were established. Efforts were made to shift away from behavioural models, epitomized by B. F. Skinner's iconic statement, '… what do you say to the design of personalities? … Give me the specifications, and I'll give you the man!' (as cited in Lau, 2012, p. 89), that represented the final authority and conceit of the psychological profession. In its place, new models for a socially relevant psychology were put forth, marked by the publication of two seminal texts—Fishbein and Ajzen's (1975) *Belief, Attitude, Intention and Behaviour: An Introduction to Theory and Research* and Albert Bandura's (1977) *Social Learning Theory*. Acknowledging the need for individuals' participation in the process of change, these theories of learning and behavioural change posited new links between social problems and certain processes interior to the individual and beyond the access of the psychologist, such as motives, intentions and beliefs. Rather than reducing individuals to a set of conditioned responses and doing away with any understanding of human agency, these new models of socio-cognitive learning, essentially, sought to bring the precarious effects of human agency under control, by factoring in the 'whole' individual/child into the learning situation (Fendler, 1998).

Drawing on these new theories of behaviour change that factored in the agent's own 'rationality' and 'affections' into the process of learning and change, the new approaches to psychological health placed an emphasis on the active role of the individual in bringing about his/her own behavioural change. Attempting to bring these internal aspects into a predictive and calculable model of human behaviour, through which the problems of the times could be addressed, individuals were sought to be actively engaged in the management of their own problems. Thus, what this entailed was a new approach to psychological practice in which the previously applied psychological techniques of regulation came to be replaced by a language of self-management and skills. Urging individuals to take control of this psychological knowledge about the self and its management, this was presented as a set of 'psychological/self-help skills'. Individuals were also constructed through these new discourses as desiring of this shift towards greater responsibility for the self. Thus, in the first anthology on skills training approaches to psychological practice, psychologist Dale Larson (1984) argued,

> People's views of themselves and what they can achieve are changing. Many are actively seeking solutions to the demoralization (Frank, 1974) and alienation that characterize our times. We are witnessing what Rogers (1977) calls a 'quiet revolution' in which people are more and more, taking control of their psychological

and physical destinies. We are people who have grown weary of professional mystification and whether it is the art of medical care or psychological healing, Americans have an almost insatiable desire to 'do it themselves'—to learn skills they can use to enhance the quality of their lives and solve their own problems. (p. 2)

What is to be noted about this self-reflexive turn within psychology is that while, on the one hand, it was a means to address the criticisms of power/knowledge levied against it, on the other hand, these developments were linked to the desire within the discipline for greater control over the problems of social behaviour. With behaviour and its underlying motives conceived as 'skills' in which one could be trained, this offered the possibility for shaping individuals' behaviours in ways that would prevent their engagement with risks. Thus, interventions using the skills approach were also seen as preventive approaches through which the incidence of development of social problems and 'risks' itself could be reduced (Larson, 1984) by having individuals work upon themselves. (In essence, however, skills programme presented a euphemism for the governmental work of shaping desirable attitudes, values and behaviours.)

Various social skills training programmes have thus come to be recognized as the gold standard for the prevention of social problems (Gorman, 2003). LSE has developed from these very changes within psychological therapy and practice, drawing on the influential social learning approaches of Bandura and Jessor. Within this new context in which skills came to be seen as 'the competencies ... necessary for effective living (Egan & Cowan, 1979, p.8)' (Larson, 1984, p. 4), LSE has also come to be established as one of the most important forms of knowledge and training for life. Further, as Fendler (1998) has observed, as 'objects of science' that have helped demystify the vague and unknown aspects of 'the inner self' and bring it under the gaze of 'educational management' and control, they have contributed to bringing the self, more firmly, under political control.

The reconceptualization of (what are essentially similar to earlier behaviourally oriented, 'corrective') psychological interventions through the language of 'skills' has allowed psychological discourses and practices to gain a new attractiveness and normalcy (Coppock, 2011). This acceptance, as Coppock (2011) notes, has come from its ability to remain behaviourally oriented and remedial, yet without falling into the previous traps of categorizing normality. Instead, psychological interventions and therapeutics have been normalized (Coppock, 2011), allowing psycho-educational programmes such as LSE to become a part of the public discourse and imagination as solutions to various developmental problems. Made acceptable in this manner, programmes such as LSE have, in fact, become the tools through which standards for 'normality', 'success' and 'failure' have come to be established.

This discursive shift in the mode of psychological regulation can be gleaned through a historical examination of LSP and how they have been constructed and applied to sociopolitical problems of the times. For example, even with the first LSE programme developed by psychologist Winthrop Adkins to help unemployed youth find, get and keep jobs (Adkins, 1984), this subtle shift is observable. What can be observed from Adkins' (1984, p. 45) definition of LSE as the '… "fifth curriculum" (Adkins, 1974), …for helping people at every level of the educational system and at every stage of life [to] learn to cope with the predictable problems of living', is the absence of pathologization and an understanding of problems as a natural feature of every stage, requiring learning (not isolation or confinement). Observable here is the change in political interest around the categories of youth and the unemployed, which no longer rests on defining the 'unemployed' as a pathological category by listing out its aetiology or symptoms. The focus, as Rose (2004) argues, is not on establishing a 'know-how' of the individual, unemployed self. Rather, the aim here is to establish their roles and duties as members of society, within normal social life. In its aim of making individuals '…self-reliant, self-directing, employable citizens' (Adkins, 1984, p. 45), programmes such as this have also thus come to set the criteria for 'employability' itself. That is, through its programme pedagogy that provides suggestions for how to cope with these 'routine', 'developmental' tasks (i.e., related to the process of natural human growth) of managing oneself at work, by gaining skills to 'make decisions and choices, resolve conflicts, gain self-understanding, explore environmental opportunities and constraints, communicate effectively with others, and take personal responsibility for their actions' (Adkins, 1984, p. 44), the understanding of the 'employable citizen' (or the 'unemployed') itself is discursively set. Here, what is visible is the shift in attention from the conditions of employment to what it means, personally, to be 'employable'.

In a similar vein, applied to other social–developmental problems of governance, other LSP have also established an understanding of what it means to be 'healthy', 'educated', 'successful' and so on. For example, when observed in relation to formal education, LSE has been presented as that required to 'reform traditional education systems, which appear to be out of step with the realities of modern social and economic life' (WHO, 1999, p. 2). In reconceptualizing education in this manner, a new understanding of the 'educated subject' has also been established—as one who is prepared for and can comply with these demands of modern socio-economic life. Absent from these conceptions of education and 'educated citizens', then, are non-economic valuations of education as an intrinsic good, or of individual or social striving for knowledge, identity, power and well-being.

Having first appeared in the context of these new conditions, programmes such as LSE thus appear to be techniques for the cultural reconstruction of society along these lines of neoliberal governmentality. Neoliberalism, as pointed out by many scholars (e.g., Larner, 2000; Peters, 2001), goes beyond the level of economic policy or political philosophy and becomes the rationality for government itself. However, as noted before, the specific materialization of neoliberal ideologies and techniques of government widely vary and remain contested and appropriated in different contexts (see Kipnis, 2008 for more on this). Before describing the effects of LSPs then, it is first important to understand the context within which it has been introduced in India, within government elementary schools, in order to contextually understand their effects. I do this by providing a context to the government schools in India and, more specifically, the school sites in which my research was conducted in the next chapter.

CHAPTER 3

Cultures of Schooling in India

3.1. Schooling India: The School as a Site of Multiple Targets and Reforms

In the opening remarks of her essay on the 'Culture and Life of the Government Elementary Schools' in India, social anthropologist A. R. Vasavi (2015, p. 36) states, 'The school, going to school and ideas of mass elementary education have come of age.' The school, within popular imagination, is now seen as a symbol of development and progress and has come to be associated with varied aspirations of the nation, of individual citizens, and particularly families and communities seeking to overcome their marginalization. Catering to about 113 million school-going children (approximately 65% of all school-going children) (National Institute of Educational Planning and Administration, NIEPA 2016) and accounting for 74.5 per cent of schools in India (Kingdon, 2017), the government elementary school (GES) in particular bears the burden of public expectations that seek 'delivery' of its masses—that is, children belonging to the most historically and socially disadvantaged communities for whom the GES has become the last hope (Batra, 2013; Chavan, 2009; De et al., 2002–2003; Dyer, 2009; Kamat et al., 2016; Mooij, 2008; Vasavi, 2015; Velaskar, 2010).

Having grown into a site of 'welfare governmentality'[1] that must guarantee minimum levels of nutrition, clothing and other forms of provisioning to its subjects, and address social problems ranging from child labour and child marriages to inter-generational poverty and exclusion, the GES is urged to transform the life worlds of those it caters to, to overcome poverty and disadvantage (Vasavi, 2015).

However, a more careful, sociological examination of the GES is necessary to see how it is a 'layered', 'porous' and 'unstable' institution, carrying the marks of the number of historical agendas through which it has been wrought (Vasavi, 2015). Emerging from its colonial-Christian pastoral roots into a technology of the colonial administration, the government school in the present serves in many ways still as an instrument of the state (Kumar, 2017; Vasavi, 2015). While in colonial times, the school was the site upon which a new modernity was sought to be writ and transferred to the natives, in the present it remains a site of postcolonial nation-building, citizenship and, above all, a site for fulfilling the ambitions of a newly globalizing nation through the production of the global worker-citizen (Vasavi, 2015). Modern education, which progressed by delinking individuals' identities from traditional and parochial influences of the family and community,[2] maintains this divide in postcolonial times through its everyday rituals and routines of assemblies and drills, celebration of festivals and the authority of the textbooks and teachers, instilling a culturally inflected and gendered experience of nationalism, democracy and modernity that is far removed from the social and cultural contexts

---

[1] Vasavi (2015) draws on Sanyal (2008) to explain 'welfare governmentality' as the state's efforts at providing incentives such as free mid-day meals, textbooks, bicycles, etc., to its masses in order to stem the revolt against its other structures and mechanisms through which it forwards a neoliberal agenda of accumulation through dispossession.

[2] Note: While modern education required a fundamental split between the home and the school, Krishna Kumar (2017) has noted how this has not been true for girls, or women, who are seen as the 'carriers of culture'. Thus, he notes how, since colonial times, there has been a studied indifference and vagueness with respect to educational goals related to girls, who are marked by continuities of expectation between home and school.

and experiences of the child (Benei, 2008; K. Kumar, 1985; N. Kumar, 2001; Seth, 2007a; Vasavi, 2015). As Vasavi (2015) notes, with its historical structures dragged into contemporary times, the GES also continues to remain a vehicle for the reproduction of caste, class and gendered differences, owing to the differentiated and stratified schooling apparatus that has exponentially grown in the post-Independence decades (Kingdon, 2017), as a result of upper and dominant caste and middle-class political lobbying and capture of the state (Fernandes, 2006; Velaskar, 2010).

Thus, far from achieving the ideals of equity and social justice, through redressal of historical inequalities, the GES presents an ambivalence and several contradictions that have rendered it into a site of intense scrutiny, further destabilizing its institutional mechanisms (Vasavi, 2015). The GES has become a target of a number of international developmental agendas and market forces, from Education for All (EFA), to the Millennium Development Goals and Sustainable Development Goals (SDGs) that seek to bring about reforms in order to ensure the goals of development through the universalization of elementary education, improved administration and efficiency. The narrow targets and goals established by various international actors and agencies have diluted the state's own goals around equitable access and opportunities (Sadagopal, 2006), and understanding of 'quality', which has come to be delinked from questions of access and opportunities (Kumar, 2010; Velaskar, 2010; Vasavi, 2015). Caught between these contradictions, the GES has been re-imagined as a site that must afford wider access with 'Minimum Levels of Learning', while prescriptive demands and assessments by international development agencies such as the World Bank, which position education as 'human capital formation', call for greater privastization of education to gain more value from such investments (Vasavi, forthcoming).

Post-liberalization and the acceptance of the World Bank's structural adjustment programme, Indian education policy has come further to be dictated by external interests (Colclough & De, 2010). Not only have these influences reordered state goals of education but have increasingly pushed agendas of privatization, changing public perceptions around what constitutes quality and valid forms of education

(Vasavi, 2019). The growth of a tiered market in education, with over nine types of schooling (Vasavi, 2019) that cater to varied purchasing powers of its clientele, has further shaped ideas around education through a process of 'hegemonic aspirations' (Fernandes & Heller, 2006), that is, the shaping of desires and creation of markets in line with the consumptive practices of the dominant classes (Sriprakash et al., 2020).

Thus, largely vacated by the middle classes and the elite, and even the working poor who opt for English medium private schools that are the 'couriers/carriers of symbolic and social capital', and that are distanced from the state's regulatory mechanisms and driven by an internal competition among themselves (Vasavi, forthcoming), the GES is popularly perceived (by the public, media and even the educational bureaucracy) as in its death throes (Kumar, 2008; Sarangapani, 2010; Vasavi, 2015), even as a number of 'educational performitivity tools' are being applied to it (Vasavi, 2015).[3] The state's endorsement of the private sector and markets in shaping the educational landscape of the country (Vasavi, 2019) has further allowed for the import of technologies of New Public Management (NPM) within state educational institutions which promote competition and the outsourcing of services to the most cost-effective providers in order to improve the performance of the sector (Subramanian, 2018; Vasavi, 2015). A range of 'edu-entrepreneurs' consisting of corporates, philanthropic organizations, and individual citizens and civil society groups seek to intervene to improve the quality and performance of the GES (Vasavi, 2015), while also defining what constitutes as 'education' and management (Subramanian, 2018). A ready market of 'edu-services' providing

---

[3] While making note of this general dismal state of public elementary education, I am aware of the discussions on regional and locational (i.e., urban–rural) differences in the performances of government schools (e.g., see ASER, 2019; Kremer et al., 2005; PROBE, 1999). Specifically, I am aware of the achievements made by the Karnataka state government in expanding facilities, putting in place a system for quality assessment (i.e., the Karnataka School Quality Assessment Organization; see Mukhopadhyay & Sriprakash, 2011; Varghese, 2010), targeted reforms to identify out-of-school children and provide remedial education (Mukhopadhyay & Sriprakash, 2013), with contradictory outcomes however.

solutions ranging from 'tuitions' and 'coaching' for different levels and types of examinations, content and technology providers, providing curricular and extra-curricular material, assessment and other services, complementing the 'edu-entrepreneurs' have grown in shaping the directions of public and private education. New technologies of child-centred and progressive pedagogies have been introduced, which now share space with continuing forms of authoritarian and didactic teaching–learning practice (as will be discussed in the next section) within the GES, bringing little change to the context and quality of education or offering the forms of symbolic capital offered by private schools. The persistence of a culture of mediocrity within government schools despite these reforms has further become an excuse to legitimize the large number of school mergers and closures, explained as an outcome of students exiting the government schooling system and preferring private schools on account of quality. This has exacerbated the educational precarity of the most marginalized who are dependent on it. In the next section, I discuss the educational experiences offered within the classroom for those who remain within the system, with little other choice.

3.2. Classrooms, Pedagogy and Learning within Government Schools

A survey of the literature on schooling and learning in India will immediately demonstrate how schools have far from evolved into the democratic spaces of learning and social transformation imagined by critical thinkers such as John Dewey, M. K. Gandhi and Paulo Freire. Neither do they function as the 'totalitarian and coercive' (Sarangapani, 2003a), Foucauldian institutions regulating subjectivities and encouraging students to develop new internal relations to the self, in order to align individuals' self-governing abilities with the ends of government itself. Rather, the literature on contemporary schooling is replete with descriptions of schools alternatively as sites of inactivity and rote learning centred on the textbook (Kumar, 1988; Nambissan, 2000; Sarangapani, 2003b; Vasavi, 2015). In an evocative description of the classroom, Vasavi (2015, p. 44) describes the everyday processes of schooling as follows:

Long periods of inactivity are sometimes broken by teaching transactions in which drill-like methods are employed to dictate notes, read the lesson or provide instructions to copy from the board, which are the typical teaching transactions. Most classes are then marked by varying audio levels from high decibel noise levels broken by periodic silencing by the teacher to hushed silence in which terror-stricken children passively write/copy or listen to the teacher. Rare are the classes in which learning takes place and in which explanation, understanding, and engaged learning are key.

Class schedules and teacher allocated classes are more on paper than in practice. Teachers take classes at times and of durations suitable to them. Children lug all the books to and fro between home and school, and the class time-table is rarely followed. With lesson plans an idea that is yet to take root, classes predominantly consist of reading from the text, some explanation made on the board, and 'practice' (*abhyas*) sessions for a range of subjects. Where transactions take place at all, they are mostly routinised copying of words, sentences, questions, and answers either from the board or the textbook or as dictated by the teacher.

A 'domesticating orientation' (Anitha, 2000) prevails within the classroom in which the authority of the teacher, a 'meek dictator' with little autonomy in terms of curricular and pedagogic control (Kumar, 1991), remains unquestioned; the teachers' authority, drawn from his/her social status vis-à-vis students' (rather than through a demonstration of ability or knowledge), and camouflaged through discourses of merit, allows for corporal disciplining and discrimination targeting the social identities and perceived 'impurity' of students (Nambissan, 2000; Velaskar, 1998). The textbook, which remains the central pedagogic device applied within the classroom, further contributes to this domestication through the implicit ideologies it circulates. Valorised within textbooks are the knowledges and lives of the dominant groups, authority of the state and the family, and the importance of this authority within Indian social relationships and responsibilities and duties of the citizen (Advani, 2004; Chavan, 2013; George, 2004; Jain, 2004; Kakar, 1971; Kumar, 1991, 2004; Nawani, 2010) that students must learn in order to become 'educated'. Vasavi (2015, p. 45) argues that 'at the end of these transactions and under the imprint of such relationships the average GES pupil is typically rendered excessively docile, often incapable of independent thinking, and marked for life as a subservient subject.'

Despite the introduction of the constructivist National Curriculum Framework (NCF) of 2005 (National Council for Education Research and Training, NCERT, 2005), which has laid down guidelines for a child-centred pedagogy and re-designing of textbooks to link school knowledge to children's everyday contexts and experiences outside school, little has changed in terms of children's educational experiences. The introduction of child-centred and activity-based pedagogies 'has been positioned as a technical method rather than a set of pervasive social relationships between the teacher, the child, and school knowledge' (Sriprakash, 2012, p. 3). Based on findings from her study of an activity-based learning approach—Nali Kali in Karnataka, Sriprakash (2010) notes that the "invisible pedagogy' of learner freedom' that characterizes child-centred activity-based pedagogies 'is embedded in a strong regulative structure' (p. 634), managed by the social knowledge of the teacher. Thus, the activity through which the learner must construct his/her own knowledge and develop control over the learning process is delinked from the process of learning and becomes just a routine. (Observations of the LSPs show similar pedagogic processes and practices, corroborating these findings made by Sriprakash).

K. Kumar (2004) has similarly argued that skills to actively participate in the classroom, to learn, to solve problems, etc., are not on the agenda despite guidelines by the NCF and other progressive local frameworks of education. The reason for the absence of this shift towards progressive pedagogies has been identified by other scholars as a result of the lack of shift in epistemological frameworks that underlie these new forms of teaching–learning practices (Jeffrey, 2005; Sriprakash, 2012), without which activity-based and child-centred learning is seen as 'wayward' and chaotic, leading to the disruption of 'proper' hierarchies (Jeffrey, 2005). N. Kumar (2001) notes, these progressive pedagogies fail to be understood by 'provincial' teachers (who lack adequate training and orientation), students and schools that are imbued with a sense of the child as inherently chaotic and requiring external disciplining.

Such disconnects between the social knowledge and lived experiences of teachers and children, and pedagogic control located elsewhere (Sarangapani, 2011; Sriprakash, 2010), in fact, require a longer historical reading. Seth (2007b) links this to the nature of knowledge within the modern school, first introduced through the colonial apparatus of schooling, which presupposes a different relationship between the 'knower' and the 'known' or the 'subject' and the 'object' to be known. He argues that these new epistemologies of modern knowledge posited and presumed a certain subjectivity, irrespective of the intentions with which it was introduced, and required,

> Not just absorption of 'facts' and theorems, the replacement of one set of ideas with another set, but also a deportment, a stylistics, a whole series of 'adjustments' in how human subjects inhabit the world (a great many of which are informal rather than formal, unstated rather than thematized). (Seth, 2007b, p. 674)

Colonial education, as others such as Nita Kumar have also noted, placed expectations on the subject to break away from local ways of life, epistemologies, cosmologies and ethics and rendered these questions marginal to education, unlike native enterprises of education (Talwalker, 2001), which were multiple, served different purposes (i.e., material, spiritual and so on) based on individuals' social locations and were not clearly ordered into a singular, formal education system (Seth, 2007b).

Thus, despite the colonial government's desire for introducing a 'taste for literature and science' among the natives, in the hopes of 'hastening the regeneration of the country', over and beyond calculated rationalities of governance and preparing loyal servants for the colonial administrative services, the uptake of English education by the colonial subjects remained 'instrumental' (Seth, 2007a). Colonial subjects' relations to the new knowledge was characterized by an 'anxiety of cram' in order to pass examinations to obtain government jobs. The new knowledge was however viewed with a scepticism and lack of curiosity and was only seen as a means to an end. Thus, Seth (2007b, p. 675) explains, 'It was a failure of education because mastery of the task had been achieved by means that sidestepped the transformation of the subject and the subject/knowledge relation' (Seth, 2007b)—a feature that continues to plague educational outcomes in India even today (K. Kumar, 1988, 2004; N. Kumar, 2000; 2001).

As Vasavi (2015) and Sarangapani (2003a) remind us, the failure of modern schooling in viewing educational practice as a 'dimension of social practice' (Freire, 1999, p. 83) has meant that schools have failed to become 'total institutions' capable of initiating an order and discipline of the mind and body of the child, establishing new relations with knowledge that are significantly different from those produced within homes and local communities in making of the 'modern subject'. Thus, Nita Kumar (2007) notes, modern schooling in India has instead produced a set of 'winners'—that is, children from upper-caste and class homes with a longer history of schooling who have been more successful in imbibing these modern ideals— and 'losers' belonging to lower-caste and class homes, for whom the separation of the home and the school is not complete yet. Further, N. Kumar (2007, p. 46) adds:

> Provincial schools have not succeeded as little theatres of the nation to play out, or little workshops to create, the spokesmen, the elite and the intelligentsia (Srivastava 1998). Their discipline has been sufficient to cause pain at the micro level of everyday life for the children. But the discipline has been insufficient to produce the inwardly directed citizen subject of the modern nation state...for children and for the historian of children, a source of a doubled pain resides in their subjecting children to an inadequate disciplining and not even giving them a share in the spoils of modernity and citizenship.

Against this context, a whole new range of educational players, including corporates, philanthropic organizations and civil society members have emerged, claiming to enable a larger set of persons for the global workforce, while framing the current scenario of poor educational outcomes in the language of quality and performance issues of the GES (Vasavi, 2015). Alongside this, piecemeal efforts by the state in orienting the school curriculum towards developing the self-regulating subject and entrepreneurial worker is also visible, be it through LSE programmes, the 'happiness curriculum (Scroll. in, 2018), 'the entrepreneurial mindset curriculum' (IANS, 2019), or even the Rashtriya Madhyamik Siksha Abhiyaan–National Skill Qualification Framework Vocationalization of Secondary and Higher Secondary Education scheme (Maithreyi, 2021)—all of which seek to cultivate more than academic knowledge and target self-regulating capacities. The National Education Policy (NEP) 2020 is the latest of these measures that have been taken towards cultivating the individualized, self-managing learner. It is within this context of the school that I undertook my study on LSE, as I will show through a description of my field context in the following section.

3.3. The Government and Aided Schools in Bengaluru

3.3.1. An Understanding of LSE within the Field Context

In 2012, when I entered the field—a set of government and aided schools in Bengaluru, to gain a preliminary understanding of LSE, I was greeted by an 'absence' of LSE on field. By 'absence' I do not just mean the non-presence of actual LSPs but the absence of an understanding of LSE as I had understood it. Mentioned first in NCF 2000 to prepare adolescents to fight challenges related to drug addition, violence, teenage pregnancy and HIV/AIDS, as well as to gain knowledge of consumer rights, legal and civic literacy, the importance of LSE was reiterated in NCF 2005 in relation to the 'concerns of growing up' and to gain practical work experiences (NCERT, 2000; 2005). The recognition of LSE as an important tool in addressing adolescents represented a key shift in the state's discourse and practice in relation to adolescents who, as Boradia (2009) points out, were seen until then as a problem in relation to concerns of delinquency and population control. The introduction of LSE to deal with adolescent problems by the Tenth Five-Year Plan (2002–2007) signalled the state's reconceptualization of adolescents as capable of independent self-direction (Boradia, 2009). Schemes to support non-governmental agencies for adolescent development through LSE, counselling and career guidance were thus set up by the late 2000s. Specifically, an AEP, in collaboration with the National Aids Control Organisation, coordinated by the NCERT, was developed to impart 'life skills among adolescents to enable them to respond to real life situations effectively', particularly in relation to adolescent reproductive health and sexuality, in the context of the 'the overwhelming reality of HIV/AIDS pandemic' (Boradia, 2009, p. 9). It was planned to introduce the AEP in three of the national school systems—CBSE, Navodaya Vidyalaya Samiti (NVS) and Kendriya Vidyalaya (KV), as a co-curricular subject (UNPFA-India, n.d.). The plan was to use a cascade training approach by which master trainers would train nodal teachers in each school, so that by the end of 2010 at least two nodal teachers from 3,500 CBSE schools, all the 919 KV schools and all the 583 NVS schools would have received orientation on adolescence education issues (UNPFA-India, n.d.).

In Karnataka, LSE was similarly planned to be implemented by the Department of State Educational Research and Training (DSERT) as well as by the National Institute of Mental Health and Neurosciences (NIMHANS), in collaboration with the Department of Public Instruction, in public schools in Karnataka. NIMHANS developed a health promotion LSE programme based on a 'train the trainer' cascade model, which was implemented in four districts of Karnataka, covering 261 government secondary schools (Srikala & Kishore, 2010). The model used the strategy of training 31 'master trainers' who were then in charge of training nodal teachers from identified government secondary schools (Srikala & Kishore, 2010), thus enabling the spread of LSE across the state. Awareness workshops were also conducted for block education officers.

However, by 2007, LSE had to be withdrawn from state schools due to huge public protests by parents and teachers over the teaching of 'sex education', as state-directed programmes on LSE largely revolved around concerns such as adolescent sexuality and reproductive health. In the absence of a physical programme that I could observe, attempts to gain an understanding from teachers regarding the programme only led to further confusion, as teachers referred to circulars and orders directing them to implement new pedagogic practices within the classroom, when asked about LSE. For example, Neerja, a social science teacher at a government girl's high school in north Bengaluru, explained it to me as follows: 'The department gives us some training. From this year, how to conduct the new syllabus, how to teach in a new way. We have to bring changes in children...children who don't concentrate, those children will improve in examination.'[4] Another teacher, Gayathri, from a Government Girls High School (GGHS) in north Bengaluru, explained that teachers tried to meet the expectations of providing students with 'life skills' by drawing on resources beyond the textbook, for example, in this case, Gayathri asked her students to read and learn more about menstruation from newspapers and come and discuss it later with her.

The lack of clarity among teachers regarding what LSE entails is perhaps understandable, considering the emphasis that has been placed on introducing it within an otherwise content-heavy and didactic schooling system, with little reference to underlying epistemologies and pedagogies that must accompany the programmes within scheme and programme documents. With LSE simply seen as an additional set of 'skills' to be given to students, in addition to the knowledges and values inculcated by the traditional education system, rather than as ways to remake oneself, even the sub-assistant director of public instruction (SADPI) for adolescent education and life skills, from the DSERT, offered an explanation of LSE as follows:

> They (i.e., children in government schools) need everything. Adolescents need health, hygienic [sic], values, discipline, then life skills. We have included all this. [Showing the life skills manual] This also – yoga, physical education, this is about food, proteins, related to health and hygienic [sic]....then kitchen garden, school garden. We focus on all this.... Whatever the case, think critically. Think creative and critical thinking [sic]. Similarly decision making...Children must know what decisions to take.[5]

---

[4] Personal communication, 4 February 2013.
[5] Personal communication, 12 December 2012.

Why they (children in government schools) require this (life skills) is, if there are suicide cases also, this will work...when the results come, what will happen to them? They'll try to commit suicide. For other things as well...[6]

The SADPI further pointed to other areas of learning that she also considered as part of LSE, such as menstrual hygiene and other behaviours such as distance to be maintained between boys and girls and how to behave appropriately in different social contexts. 'Life skills' was seen as *information* related to these various topics, rather than the *skills* to do something (e.g., take a decision), per se. This in fact became very clear from her emphasis on life skills as knowing *what* decisions were to be made, instead of *how* decisions were to be made. Specific skills (such as decision-making and critical thinking) were linked to particular ways of behaving (e.g., *Yaara jothe hēge irabēku*, that is 'knowing how one must behave with whom' [ibid]), thus, showing how LSE was understood as conventional forms of social and moral disciplining. This observation was supported by the descriptions of the earlier programmes given by the SADPI, that she argued had no activities and only gave children information on relevant issues such as health, hygiene and discipline. This then also explained teachers' such as Gayathri's understanding of LSE and how they had put it to practice within their schools.

Thus, what appeared to be the primary understanding of LSE here, within local government schools and among officials, was the idea of socially, morally, intellectually reforming the child or disciplining them according to social–patriarchal expectations for behaviour. Rather than referring to the practices of self-regulation or responsibilization, seen within Anglo-American accounts, approaches to the programme fundamentally diverged in the Indian context along the lines of how they conceived of young people. (This is an important distinction that will be discussed in more detail later.) In fact, as these accounts show, with the dominant understanding of LSE seen as information to 'guide' children in appropriate behaviours and the

---

[6] Personal communication, 23 August 2013.

right path, the new cultural expectations around self-regulation set by the pedagogic project of LSE, in relation to certain culturally sensitive topics such as adolescent reproductive and sexual health, themselves caused dissonances within the public sphere, bringing the state LSE and adolescent education programmes to a halt across several states, including Gujarat, Madhya Pradesh, Maharashtra, Rajasthan, Kerala, Chhattisgarh, Goa and Karnataka. With the culturally appropriate view to 'prevention' being one of 'protecting' children from exposure to such information and experiences, rather than teaching them to self-regulate their behaviours, the SADPI explained how the LSE programme came to a halt in 2007. Pointing to the opposition to the LSE programme, she stated:

> Biology teachers themselves hesitate to do these topics when it comes in the syllabus—like the reproductive system. Our values and culture are like that. Nowadays everything is very advanced… and because of mass media there is a chance of children getting spoilt. By giving this education, they will know of the parts…what is there…it's natural. Every human being has these parts. Gender-wise also they will know there are different parts. Otherwise it will be like we are hiding some secret from them. That shouldn't be done. But there will be opposition against this also. They say we are teaching sex education. Someone has written a letter (opposing this)…we are discussing that only currently. It's not sex education …. this is about the changes in adolescents' bodies.[7]

Overall, initial interactions with teachers and educational department officials drew my attention to the very different meanings that were attached to LSE on the field. Having understood the concept of these skilling programmes very differently and having encountered them 'everywhere' (within my own social 'field'),[8] it was only the encounter with the government and aided schools catering to individuals from a different social group compared to my own that helped me recognize the specific circuits within which these discourses travelled.

---

[7] Personal communication, 22 August 2012.

[8] 'Field', here, is used to represent my own social context and people, practices, environment, institutions and codes that I was familiar with.

It brought me to recognize how these Western psychological discourses of the self as an autonomous, self-maximizing being was still largely absent from the lives and experiences of a large majority of lower-caste and class families and children, within government schools. LSE in this context was still considered important, based on a deficit framing of the poor child within the institutional context of the school. Teachers and state officials argued for the need for LSE to 'put good sense into children' (in Kannada, *OLLe buddhi hēLikoDuvudakke*). Teachers referred to the 'culture of poverty' that children came from and expected that LSP would compensate for the deficit of knowledge around 'good behaviours' seen as unavailable within their own contexts.

3.3.2. The Targets of Life-Skills Interventions

Most schools in my study (as is the case with most government and aided schools in India) were made up of those who Nita Kumar (2007) has called the 'provincial other', that is, those far removed from the discourses of 'modernity' and the circuits of the global knowledge economy that the elite, 'new middle class' (Fernandes, 2006), urban India occupies, even when located at the heart of India's Silicon Valley—Bengaluru. With a preference for private schools (which constitute almost three times the numbers of government schools in Bengaluru), even among the working poor (Navya, 2018),[9] the children I encountered in these schools were those who mostly belonged to most disadvantaged communities, such as that of Scheduled Castes, Scheduled Tribes, and Other Backward Classes, for whom government schools have become the last hope and refuge. Children belonged to migrant families that had traditionally been occupied in agriculture or artisanal work (e.g., communities such as that of Vanniyars, Yadavas, Kurubas, Kumbaras, Labbais and also Gowndars, Mudaliars, Vokkaligas). There were also a small portion of Muslims and Christians in some of these schools.

---

[9] In 2016–2017, there were 1,403 government schools and 3,426 private schools in Urban Bengaluru (Navya, 2018).

Hailing originally from rural Karnataka and Tamil Nadu (e.g., Mandya, Raichur, Belgaum, Gulbarga, Kanakpura, Tirpatur), many of their families had moved to the city in search of better job opportunities. However, as Velaskar (2010) notes, within these urban contexts, it is these groups that have to deal with the greatest number of insecurities linked to food, housing, jobs and education. With parents who were employed in the informal sector (as garment-factory workers, drivers, masons, construction workers, welders, coolies, domestic help, watchmen, plumbers, electricians, carpenters or plumbers) and an educational status of Secondary School Leaving Certificate (SSLC) or below, they were often perceived by the teachers as 'backward' and illiterate. Thus, they were also seen as incapable of providing adequate and appropriate sociocultural training and care for the child. Teachers thus blamed this 'culture of poverty' that the children came from (often highlighting its negative features such as alcoholism, broken families and illness) as responsible for the academic failure and other 'deficits' in the child. Further, they pointed to a lack of parental time and investment in children's education and socialization as also one of the prime reasons for school failure among these children. In fact, some even pointed out that unlike private middle-class schools, to which their own children went, they even took care of children's homework and exam preparation at school itself, since these would not be addressed at home. (As an indicator of this, I often saw teachers in these government schools asking children to copy answers over and over again into their notebooks as practice or to copy and answer question papers more than once. During exam time, children, in some schools such as a government high school in south Bengaluru, were also seated in long rows on the playing field and were made to rote learn their lessons.)

Thus, blaming the children's background and culture as contributing to 'deficits', teachers, by and large, appeared to reproduce the stereotypes and practices of social discrimination prevalent within the larger social set-up within the site of the school. This included labelling of many children within these schools as 'coarse', 'dull', 'rowdy' and 'unmanageable', primarily lacking 'discipline'. In fact, these stereotypes about children's behaviours also took on gendered forms, with boys, mostly, considered to be 'rowdy' and girls seen to be given to the dangers of sexual attraction, elopement and exploitation within the school, as well as within its neighbourhood. Thus, teachers constantly spoke to girls about the dangers of attraction, warned girls particularly about auto drivers, stating many girls had eloped with them, only to land in trouble later.

3.3.3. Disciplining Interventions Observed within School

Children were, therefore, primarily seen as requiring 'discipline' to overcome these behaviours and all means were seen as legitimate to achieve this. This was also gendered in many ways, with instructions on how to behave within and outside the school (e.g., being demure, walking with one's head bent down, going home straight after school, without hanging about on the streets) targeted at girls and the use of corporal punishment with boys. Corporal forms of discipline thus were a constant feature of the education process. That corporal punishment was considered a legitimate means towards this process of disciplining was evident from the fact that the use of this authority to correct children's behaviours was even awarded to 'teachers' agents', that is, senior, male students,[10] who were recruited by teachers to maintain class discipline, reduce noise levels in class and ensure completion of desired tasks at some schools such as a government school in south Bengaluru that I visited weekly as part of my fieldwork. In fact, during one of my visits to the school, I was also able to overhear some teachers rue the fact that they would no longer be able to recruit a particular ninth standard student to maintain order, since he had hit another child badly on the chest and injured him the previous day. This had led to the child's parents threatening to complain to a local gang that was politically connected, and the situation had become complicated. During another visit to the same school, I had witnessed the ninth standard boy entering an eighth standard classroom and pulling children up by the collar in the presence of the life skills facilitator

---

[10] This was usually the 'alpha male' within the student body, who was generally feared by most of the student body and who wielded considerable power over the other students.

and myself, demanding that they pay up towards the Gauri-Ganēsha festival that the senior boys were organizing. Some girls from this class had also reported that this boy had used an iron rod to hit those who had not paid up, on an earlier occasion. However, there appeared to be an informal acceptance of this kind of authority wielded by the student, with neither students nor teachers objecting to his behaviour.

Further, other forms of disciplining included segregating children seen as 'dull' and 'unmanageable' into separate classrooms (that even the life skills facilitators were dissuaded from visiting) as well as legitimizing practices of servility (such as having children serve food and wash teachers' used plates and cups, sweep the staffroom, run errands for them, vacate seats for them on the bus and so on). These latter practices were again divided along gender lines with tasks such as washing of vessels and plates falling to the girls, while running errands and sweeping tasks were given to the boys. Teachers understood these tasks as preparing children for their future roles (e.g., domestic roles, in the case of girls), and these expectations were also internalized by the students themselves, who saw all of these tasks as their sacred duties. (This was expressed through the term '*GurugaLige gaurava koDuvudu*', meaning to 'respect and honour the teacher.' In fact, my refusal to be a part of this tradition, by allowing students to wash my plate or serve me food at school, became a significant hurdle for me in building rapport with them and assimilating within the school, since students saw my practices and beliefs as foreign and upper class and were, therefore, cautious in approaching me).

In this manner, all the different non-academic practices applied within the schools (from corporal punishment to assignment of tasks such as cleaning plates) were all seen as educative experiences for the child, in order to develop the appropriate personal, social and cultural behaviours and attitudes in them. In fact, a wide range of external programmes that I was able to observe within the schools that intervened into its schedule and disrupted classes, all appeared to be seen as beneficial for intellectually, morally and culturally improving the child. These ranged from health awareness, environmental awareness (which included a special programme during Gauri-Ganēsha on using eco-friendly idols made of mud and a campaign to ban plastic from the school's premise, on Teachers' Day, undertaken by the corporator, at the south Bengaluru school), civic awareness, citizenship education, LSE, moral and value education and remedial learning programmes.[11]

Interestingly, these external programmes were often recruited to achieve the schools' own notions of discipline and cultural improvement—a point that was also reiterated by the life skills organizations I worked with (a point I will further elaborate in the next chapter). Similarly, children also understood these programmes as a continuation of school learning and culture and oriented to even fun-filled, activity-based programmes for self-reflection and development, such as LSE, as programmes that taught them to be obedient, to respect teachers and how to lead life. (This will also be discussed in more detail in the subsequent chapters.)

Thus, from these observations made within schools, what emerged was a picture of the school as a space for culturally disciplining the child, by preparing him/her to comply with established norms, roles and expectations of society. Rather than being spaces within which students could develop into autonomous, self-managing individuals, schools appeared as spaces of regulation, based on socially sanctioned norms for children's development. Within this authoritarian cultural context of the school, the introduction of progressive, child-centred pedagogies (including LSE), that envisaged a particular kind of agency and self-direction on the part of students, remained largely alien and externally imposed, both, on students and teachers.

3.3.4. 'Disciplining' of the LSE Programmes within School

In fact, 'disciplined' by the school culture, the LSPs observed within the schools fell short of wholly adopting a progressive pedagogic practice. Programmes were disciplined in three ways: spatio-temporally through the pervasive authoritarian culture and practices of schooling in dealing with children; through limits imposed on learning and knowledge; and

---

[11] In fact, on some days, I was able to even observe two different organizations conducting the same programmes (i.e., LSE) within the same school and classes.

through specific expectations for results set on the programmes. All of this determined how programmes unfolded within the school context and how students responded to this, as I will describe below.

3.3.4.1. The Spatio-temporality of Schooling

Spatio-temporally, as well as ideologically, the school imposed itself on the programmes, regulating the manner in which learning occurred. With the exception of a few programmes, since most were conducted within the space of the regular classroom, they were also subjected to the spatial arrangements and timetables of schools. This, in turn, had implications for how the programme could be conducted. LSE pedagogy, spatially and temporally, requires a broader conceptualization of space and time for carrying out experiential learning. Psychologically, it requires a non-authoritarian, safe atmosphere for introspection and self-directed behavioural change (as will be further described in Chapter 5). However, the spatial and temporal structuring of the Indian classroom and school disallowed for these practices of non-hierarchical, participative formats of learning. Marked by a culture of formal, authoritarian relations between teachers and students, and practices of 'giving' and 'receiving' (knowledge), the transformation of these physical–cultural spaces into spaces for participation and dialogue remained absent, since children continued to view life skills classrooms as a continuation of schooling (even when these programmes were conducted by external agents) and oriented themselves to passively follow instructions given within the programmes. Even when activities in the life skills classroom demanded creativity or improvisation, children demanded that they be given the 'right answers' to activities. Facilitators and I were seen as teachers with the authority to prescribe what was 'right' and 'wrong' and as authority to be respected and followed.

Some of these ideas were reinforced by the facilitators themselves[12] and through the spatial structuring of the pedagogic process

---

[12] Facilitators exerted this authority by having children address them as 'miss', in order to be able to have control over the classroom.

adopted within the classroom. While pedagogies of participation and facilitation were usually meant to adopt a circular seating arrangement, in order to facilitate discussions and face-to-face contact among all participants, the LSE programme continued to use the frontal seating structure of schools. Even though the circular format was important to ensure that no one individual was at the head of the group, in a central position of authority, so as to encourage participation and co-construction of knowledge, the LSPs retained the position of the facilitator as the head of the class. Part of the reason for this was the high number of students (anywhere between 60 and 90) within each class, with the exception of the programme offered by IP.[13] IP catered to a smaller batch of students in each class, since its classes were conducted after-school hours and participation in the programme was voluntary. This restricted the numbers in each batch to between 20 and 25, since parents were often reluctant to allow children to stay back after school in the absence of the regular school teachers or because of lack of transport, which was seen as an issue particularly for girls.

Other organizations conducted their classes as part of the school day—either by incorporating their classes within the timetable (as in the case of VYB) or by fixing a particular time during the school day to take classes (as in the case of MFCL).[14] Thus, they were required to cater to the entire strength of the class. Owing to these large numbers that made classroom control difficult and the shortage of space for accommodating these large groups in a circle, frontal learning was adopted even within the life skills classroom, with the facilitator standing at the head of the classroom (near the teachers' table, in front of the black board) facing the children. Students were seated as in the case of regular classrooms, in a file of rows facing the teacher to make 'surveillance' of individual students possible. The frontal learning format that privileges the teacher as the point of authority within

---

[13] One of the NGOs covered in the study, which is described in more detail in the next chapter.

[14] Names of organizations providing LSE, which are also discussed in further detail in the next chapter.

the classroom, to whom all children must 'report', answer or attend to (Hargreaves, 1988; Smyth, 2006), thus, did not manage to break the hierarchical nature of learning at school and construct an atmosphere of non-hierarchical learning, in which the facilitators partner, rather than supervise, the learner.

Further, due to this large group size (including in the case of IP's programme), an intimate and safe space also could not be built within the session, and neither did it allow for participation by all children. With respect to the first problem (i.e., the lack of a 'safe space'), pre-existing group dynamics and interpersonal relations among members of the student body affected the processes of building a 'safe space'. In building a 'safe space' and in developing relations of trust, the facilitator had to rework these existing dynamics and relationships. With large groups, this became particularly difficult, since the facilitator had to have a knowledge of, and remain aware of, how these various interpersonal dynamics came into play in sessions, during tasks such as performing oneself, expressing one's creativity or revealing one's innermost self during reflection.

Further, within these large groups, it also became difficult to pay attention to individual students, their feelings, relationships and doubts. Therefore, it also became difficult to engage the entire group in the process of activity and reflection. Often a large portion of the class was left unengaged and students would be involved in their own activities (such as exchanging or copying notes, completing homework or classwork, talking or playing among themselves). With the facilitator unable to pay close attention to every participant, their responses, feelings, gestures, expressions and behaviours, the process of facilitation itself was not able to dynamically reflect the thoughts, values or beliefs brought into play during the course of the sessions, and this, therefore, limited the extent to which children's understanding of themselves, as autonomous and self-regulating individuals, could be reworked and shaped.

An additional problem resulting from this large group size was linked to the temporal requirements of the programme, which was mismatched with the temporal structure of the schools. Since most programmes were planned to be held during the school day and were scheduled as a 'period' (which were, mostly, of 40–50 minutes duration), sessions also had to be accordingly planned. With the programme structure requiring adequate time for all students to participate and reflect upon themselves, the large group size and limited classroom time did not allow for this. Thus, not all students of a class would get an opportunity to undertake the activity and learn or apply the skill experientially. Only activities that involved stories or activities that could be administered in groups, such as writing or art activities, were possible with all students. Thus, organizations such as VYB and MFCL (that catered to large class strengths) limited the use of activities such as theatre improvisations, games, role play and other activities that could not be administered on groups.

Even when group activities, such as stories or writing tasks, were used, only a few children had an opportunity to share their thoughts, ideas and experiences. Typically, this took the form of the teaching–learning conducted in a regular classroom, with a few students raising their hands to share their 'answers' and the facilitator offering these students an opportunity to answer, following which s/he summarized the key points. Thus, the sessions never took on the format of a group discussion or brain storming, where participants could co-construct knowledge among themselves. This left a majority of the children unengaged in the process.

Thus, what could be seen from the modification of programme practices to suit the school structure was not only how school timetables determined the format of the classrooms, but also how (by extension) they conditioned children's understanding of their selves. That is, they reinforced self-perceptions cultivated within the regular classroom of children as lacking knowledge and authority to engage as equal participants in knowledge production; as those who must speak only when spoken to; and as those who must have their 'answers' validated by more knowledgeable adults.

In fact, schools even seemed to impose these ways of being on the facilitators themselves, setting limits on their behaviours and their techniques of bringing about behavioural change. These forms of regulation of facilitators' conduct and behaviour were seen in simple daily routines to which facilitators were required to comply, such as reporting to the school (rather than the organization that the facilitators worked in), marking their attendance with the school, applying for leave with the school, participating in other duties such as teaching, invigilation, organization of extra-curricular activities by the school, following the dress code given by the school and so on. Explaining how schools regulated their conduct and practices, Nayanika, a facilitator from VYB, explained how schools initially had not understood their methods and imposed their norms of working upon them. Questioning their efforts at personal counselling and building rapport with the children, she pointed out that teachers would reprimand her (a female facilitator) for talking or spending time with the adolescent boys and for sharing physical proximity with them. Another facilitator, Kaveri, from IP also provided an example of the headmaster (HM) of her school expressing his anger against the life skills facilitators, since he perceived their techniques of participative learning and the absence of standards of 'discipline' and punitive action to be responsible for the increase in 'bold' and 'rash' behaviours in children. Giving the example of a tenth standard student, who had locked some junior students in the toilet, she explained that the HM thought this to be a result of the freedom given by IP's LSE programme. Thus, schools expected facilitators to maintain authority over students and formal distance from them.

Suspicions around facilitators' behaviours and the curricular and pedagogic practices of the programmes shared by the regular teachers and HMs of the schools often led to teachers and the heads of the institution threatening to supervise these sessions. For example, during one such instance, at a Tamil minority aided school in east Bengaluru, class monitors of an eighth standard class informed the facilitator that the HM was going to observe the session and had asked to be called when the class started, since he had received complaints that children made noise in the LSE class and that they did not listen to the facilitators. Though the HM eventually did not attend the session, the monitors were asked to bring the children who made noise to him. While the facilitator Kaveri, from IP, and I tried to intervene and explain to the children that this was not necessary and that it would take away from the 'safe space', the monitors were insistent on taking the children who did not stay 'silent' to the headmaster.

Thus, programmes deployed within the context of the school were conditioned by the regulations of the school itself, and this had implications on the outcomes of the programmes with respect to cultivating specific forms of subjectivities in students.

3.3.5. Overlooking Structural Inequalities within Schools and LSE Programmes

Further, the targets of learning of such programmes, such as the ability to independently and critically think, were in conflict with the behavioural targets that were of interest to schools, namely, marks, attendance, pass percentages and other overt behaviours that signified respect and obedience (e.g., wishing the teacher, speaking to the teacher deferentially). With schools placing expectations on external agencies, such as life skills organizations, to cultivate these behaviours, what was largely ignored, both by schools and the programmes, were critical questions around the relationship between schooling and the larger context of the children's lives.

For example, for a large number of children, in the schools I visited, schooling had to be balanced with work as car washers, newspaper boys, cooks, flower sellers, etc., in order to support the family's meagre income. In other cases (most often, in the case of girls), it had to be balanced with domestic chores such as cooking, washing, cleaning or looking after young ones, since parents often worked long hours in physically challenging jobs that left them with little energy when they returned home. In other instances, prolonged illness or alcoholism of parents had forced some of the girls to attend to these household chores of cooking, cleaning and looking after their younger siblings. In such cases, girls were expected to take on regular domestic duties. This, often, affected children's performance and motivation to attend school.

In other instances, poverty, which loomed large over their lives, also led to instances wherein education was at the verge of being discontinued (particularly, in the case of girls). I had a chance to witness this on a couple of occasions on field. For example, during one field visit, an eighth standard girl, Ramya, from the aided minority school in east Bengaluru, who had returned to school after a prolonged period of absence, tearfully explained to me the condition at her home. With her brother and she having fallen ill, a large portion of the family income had to be utilized for medical expenses. Following this, the family had found itself in a tight situation, with not enough resources to even purchase bus tickets to send the children to school. Under these circumstances, her mother, she had explained, resented the expenses on schooling, considering it a luxury, when they did not even have money to celebrate the Pongal festival.[15] Therefore, she had told Ramya's father to at least remove Ramya from school. It was the foresight of her father who, Ramya reported, had borrowed some money from neighbours to bring the children to school, that had saved Ramya from losing out on education.[16]

In other instances, the relation between schooling and poverty manifested itself in other ways. For example, as several children explained to the life skills trainers and counsellors, who sought to help them perform better academically at the government school in south Bengaluru, undertaking academic work at home was constrained by their living conditions. Many of the children lived in single room houses in crowded, low-income colonies or slums in Bengaluru (such as Venkatapura, Belandur, Iblur, Tannery Road, Jeevanahalli, Ambedkar Nagar, Dodigunta, Chennakeshwara Beedhi, Tin factory, Jogpalya, Lido, Kagadaspura, Indiranagar, K. R. Puram). The single-room dwellings necessitated that activities such as sleeping and

---

[15] Pongal is the harvest festival celebrated by the agricultural class in south India, particularly, in Tamil Nadu, at the beginning of January (in the Tamil month of Thai). Since 2008, this has also gained a political character, with the Dravida Munnetra Kazhagam also recognizing it as the Tamil New Year (which was otherwise celebrated in the month of April, or the Tamil month of Chithirai). DMK, a political party in the state which has won credence as an anti-Brahmin party, has sought to make this change as a counter to the hegemony of Brahminical rule and as a celebration of the victory of the farming class and other marginalized groups.
[16] Personal communication, 15 January 2013.

studying were coordinated with the activities of other family members, due to constraints of space and other resources. Thus, many children reported being unable to study after eight- or nine 'o' clock at night because lights in the house would be switched off early. Their parents, who would come home tired from a long day of work and would have to leave early the next day, would insist on this, so that they could go to bed early and get a few hours of sleep. In other cases, children spoke about the distraction and noise from the television set (with cable connection that was, remarkably, one of the few amenities possessed by all children, even those with the lowest family incomes) coming from the closely packed accommodations in the neighbourhood or even from their own houses. Thus, in many cases, children reported having to use parked vehicles near the house, such as autos, scooters, bikes and other abandoned sites and structures, if one had to escape this noise and study undisturbed.

This extension of the house onto the streets and into the neighbourhood was also noticeable in other ways, during house visits, which revealed the poverty of space and resources that these children and their families had to deal with, on an everyday basis. The shortage of living space meant that the street itself was transformed into one's personal living space, and it lent itself to a number of daily routines, including cooking, cleaning grains, washing and drying clothes, giving children a bath and even to leisure activities such as play (for children) and for gambling,[17] meetings and discussions (for adults).

These structural conditions of living created real barriers for children's participation in education but were routinely 'misrecognised' (Bourdieu, 1990) as problems of individual behaviour and motivation. In addition to constraints of space and time, another barrier to 'studying', faced by children, was the alternative values that took precedence in families, such as the celebration of festivals, *ooru habbas* (village festivals), *jaatres* (fair) and so on. Due to frequent occasions such as these, prolonged absence was a common phenomenon, since

---

[17] Games of dice or cards could be seen being played on the roads near some accommodations.

children would be taken back to their native places and villages for these celebrations. Similarly, following big festivals, such as Gauri-Ganēsha, or Dasara for which the school and the state provide holidays, it was noticed that the class strength dropped to nearly half, since families would extend their stay or holiday.

While these alternate cultural values that led to absences were considered significant factors affecting children's performance, the structural challenges mentioned before, as well as the various 'absences' associated with school, were never seen as contributing to these conditions of failure. For example, teacher shortage was a common phenomenon across several schools. Teacher shortages as affecting school quality in urban Bengaluru has also been noted by several scholars and activists, such as Niranjan Aradhya, who has noted that there were over 28,000 vacancies for government elementary school teachers in Bengaluru in 2016–2017. In many cases, he has noted that there are only one or two teachers in the school, with no HM, thus, forcing teachers to take on a lot of administrative duties (Navya, 2018).

In fact, during visits to some schools, such as a government high school in a southern suburb of Bengaluru, the headmistress discussed this situation in government schools, stating that the education department had not appointed any teachers in the last few years. Yet, she pointed out that they were forced to go on local drives in order to enrol more/all children from the community by the local politicians every year, who sought to gain a good image with the public through this. She added that this amounted to spoiling the future of the child, since they did not have adequate teaching staff to cater to this volume of children.[18] Faced with such shortages, schools resorted to using external persons, such as the facilitators from the life skills organizations, as additional hands and expected them to help out with both regular classroom teaching as well as with other duties such as preparing classrooms for examinations (by writing out the roll numbers on each bench), invigilation and paper correction. Further, they also opened

---

[18] Personal communication, 11 February 2012.

up the space to trainee teacher-students, from nearby colleges, who formed a constant second cadre within the school.[19]

In addition to the shortage of teachers, 'absences', in terms of teacher accountability and adequate usage of school time, were also noted.[20] That these too need to be taken into account when considering student performance, however, was never given attention. There were several instances on field when classes were disrupted due to school or teacher-related factors; for example, there were instances when teaching activities were disrupted due to the space that schools provided to various external actors—from middle-class citizens to local MLAs and corporators, trainee D.Ed. teachers, NGOs and corporate organizations—to carry out their own experiments in education. These various actors, who had their own ideas and agendas, were allowed to easily enter and exit the school space and carry out their activities during the regular working hours of school. This often led to the suspension of regular classes.

In some extreme cases, classroom time was disturbed due to a lack of accountability among teachers, who suspended classes on occasions such as a colleague's house-warming ceremony. (An instance of this was observed at a government school in south Bangalore wherein the entire staff of teachers went to attend the ceremony, even when the HM explicitly forbade them. This resulted in the entire afternoon session being suspended, since teachers who left at lunchtime had not returned post-lunch). In another instance, a teacher at a government middle school in north Bengaluru was seen using class time to practise

---

[19] These trainee-teachers who were pursuing their Diploma in Education (D.Ed.) sought to teach in these schools in order to fulfil the practical requirements of the degree.

[20] While the issues of teacher accountability in India is highly debated (e.g., see Azim Premji Foundation, 2017; Batra, 2014; Duflo et al., 2012; Kremer et al., 2005), I make note of these instances here to point to how public discourses on government school and student performances narrowly locate student outcomes within individual performance rather than considering the multiple factors that affect schooling outcomes, ranging from infrastructural and HR shortages, issues of governance, accountability and transparency, and individual student backgrounds and performance.

riding a bike. Thus, such instances represented a lack of accountability on the part of schools and teachers. This was, however, never discussed in the context of factors that affected students' performances.

Further, the quality of teaching also never came under review, especially in cases where trainee D.Ed. teachers, with little experience and familiarity with the students, were used, as seen at the government high school in south Bengaluru.[21] In fact, in this context, what was also noted was that these teacher-students, who belonged to the eastern states of Orissa and West Bengal, were not even familiar with the local language, Kannada, that the students were most comfortable with. This is significant because, within these schools, a knowledge of Kannada was important and central to teaching even within English-medium sections of the school, since children did not have adequate exposure or training in other languages such as English or Hindi. This, therefore, raises questions about the efficacy of teaching carried out in these schools, which also affects students' performance.

In addition to these internal factors related to the school, other political factors, external to the school, also contributed to the loss of learning time and quality, such as a series of bus strikes and bandhs, between August and September 2012, due to which classes were nearly suspended for a month. All this made school a 'porous' site, within which programmes such as LSE seemed to be filling up the cracks (i.e., both academically as well as in relation to the social–moral disciplining), by taking on the character of the school itself. This was a significant finding about the programmes, since the organizations themselves appeared to have different ideas about the programmes, and it was only through this close comparison of the organizations with the schools that I was able to identify how LSPs became sites for 'disciplining' the child in many different ways.

---

[21] For a more detailed discussion of quality of pre-service teacher training and privatization of teacher preparation programmes, see the '*Vision of Teacher Education in India: Quality and Regulatory Perspective. Report of the High-Powered Commission on Teacher Education Constituted by the Hon'ble Supreme Court of India*' (MHRD, 2012).

In the next chapter, I present a more detailed account of each of the organizations followed in the study and their programmes. This is important to explain some of the findings presented later in the study. Mainly, I present the middle-class cultures of the organizations, which stood in sharp contrast to that of the government schools. The cultural analysis of the LSE organizations presented in the next chapter lays the context by showcasing the contrasting set of values (in comparison with school culture) and the expectations this laid on students, in the course of the programmes. This is important to explain the cultural disconnects between programme intentions and outcomes, and the regulative effects of programmes and production of subjectivities within local context.

CHAPTER 4

Schooling, Skilling and a Range of Actors Redefining 'Educated Youth'

Diary Entry: February 17, 2012; 5:30–7:00 am, Eidgah Maidan, Bengaluru.

In the cold, dark morning, with the sun yet to rise, around 20 boys from the nearby BOSCO shelter home are quietly warming up as they wait for their coach to arrive. The boys seem highly organised and self-motivated, as they wait to start the day's game. Soon two young men arrive on a bike. As I sit and watch from a distance, they split the group into two. The senior coach, John, takes the older group of 13–14 years old, and starts a game of football. He doubles as referee and coach as the game gets into motion, simultaneously calling out the rules, and instructions for how to defend or pass. At the side-lines, a younger coach handles a group of 11–12 years old. After passing and handling exercises with the ball, he organises them into a circle and plays a game called 'Lion and Deer'—a game in which children must strategise in order to prevent the child playing the 'lion', from catching the child playing the 'deer'. By 7:00 am the sun is finally up, and the group breaks up for the day; but not before the coaches quickly facilitate a discussion around the important 'skills' of teamwork, strategy, and support that the children had learnt from playing the games. Though the session seemed to be more about football and football skills, the coaches assure me that they had a discussion about these vital 'life skills' with the children. Then the group heads off to a nearby 'darshini',[1] for breakfast sponsored by IP, the NGO to which the coaches belong.

Even as the state-run LSP remained suspended from schools during the period of my study, and deliberations over a new LSE curriculum was still underway within the DSERT, a number of non-state agencies providing LSE were active within state and aided schools in Bengaluru. While LSPs were available in state and elite, private schools during this period, a remarkable number of programmes specifically targeted the poor child.[2] These programmes deployed by a variety of private or corporate and non-governmental agencies targeted poor and disadvantaged children in state and aided schools, often without permissions from, and knowledge of the department, with arrangements made at the local level with individual vice-principals or HMs, who sanctioned these programmes within their respective schools. This is in fact reflective of the general pattern of spread of corporate and philanthropic initiatives in government schools in the city, ranging from provisions of funds to infrastructure and even science or computer labs, without coordination or streamlining by the department of public instruction with the result that quality and performance of government schools within the city highly vary (Navya, 2018).

Considering the controversy that the teaching of LSE in schools had created, the availability of these multiple, external LSE providers within state and aided schools, without vetting of the programmes by state officials, appeared to be somewhat surprising, also hinting at the state's lack of concern over the messages circulated via the programmes. While in some cases, the LSE providers had attempted to deflect attention away from the earlier controversy over the teaching of life

---

[1] Local eatery.
[2] Five of the seven organizations covered as part of my ethnographic fieldwork too catered exclusively to children in government and aided schools.

skills by renaming their programmes (e.g., from '*Jeevana Kaushalya*', meaning 'life skills', as it was referred to in Karnataka, to '*Jeevana Amulya*', literally meaning 'precious life'), for the most part, external LSE providers continued to offer life skills training with little modifications to their design or content.

The lack of public objection and implicit acceptance of the programmes within schools, even by the education department, became clearer in subsequent discussions with the DSERT and the LSE organizations themselves. On the one hand, the programmes within the schools raised little suspicion as they had a starkly different orientation compared to the state's AEP and LSE, as they were directed away from questions of adolescent sexual and reproductive health, as will be apparent from the discussions that follow. In addition, the easy acceptance of the programmes into schools also appeared to be a result of how programmes positioned themselves and were perceived by the education department and the schools as well, as forwarding their own goals. For example, explaining her implicit approval of the programmes (despite no permissions sought from or intimation given to the department by the LSE providers), the SADPI (in charge of LSE at the DSERT) explained that the programmes required no permissions as long as they did not require state funds, as it was useful to have these interventions since 'they (i.e., children in government schools) need everything.'[3] LSE within schools were seen as an aid for the many different kinds of learning and responsibilities placed on state schools—from assuring learning outcomes to addressing matters such as personal hygiene, social decorum and regulation, and emotional aspects of children's development. Interestingly, in the SADPI's accounts, these goals were also to be achieved by providing children information on 'how to behave' or 'be' rather than through the development of skills through which they could independently reason about their own behaviours and bring about changes in themselves.

Like the SADPI, teachers within schools also explained the importance of the programmes to 'put good sense into children' (in Kannada, *OLLe buddhi hēLikoDuvudu*), again implying the importance

---

[3] Personal communication, 12 December 2012.

of teaching and telling children how to be and behave (rather than developing skills), and further elaborated upon this by noting how programmes were expected to improve results, attendance and behaviours of children. School staff and representatives of the education department justified the role of the external trainers within school by referencing children's backgrounds and the perceived 'culture of poverty' that they came from. Teachers such as Hemalatha (a Hindi teacher in a GES in south Bengaluru) argued:

> Life skills is important for all children, but government school children need it more. Here, at government schools children are beaten by parents badly and they need it to correct behaviour and for support. They need someone to listen to them and advise them.[4]

Hemalatha further pointed out that 'with book knowledge one could manage life but living is different', and stated that the LSP provided by the NGO working in her school 'brought them (i.e., the students in her school) to a level...and had an impact on dull students who were often absent and who had problems at home or were naughty'.

As evident from Hemalatha's accounts, LSE was expected to address a number of child-related behaviours, but more importantly, LSE was seen as necessary not just to compensate for children's home backgrounds but to help children manage and improve in school despite it. School and education department personnel transferred their own responsibilities of ensuring students' well-being and outcomes to the LSE providers, expecting the programmes to compensate for the failure of schools and the education system as a whole in addressing the specific needs of children from marginalized backgrounds within education. Despite the poor quality of schools, lack of contextualization and absence of efforts to foster meaningful learning, LSE were expected to be the cement that would seal up the cracks within the system, through which marginalized students were expected to fall. Thus, LSPs were expected to achieve a number of targets—from improving learning outcomes and attendance to improving behaviour, while also providing counselling and emotional

[4] Personal communication, 6 August 2012.

support, to bring about drastic changes in the individual student and in turn improve outcomes of the school.

Similar accounts were put forth by managerial staff of the LSE organizations interviewed, who explained that permissions to enter and work within these schools were obtained by guaranteeing improvements in school outcomes. Managers such as Pavan Ragunath of VYB (one of the NGOs covered as part of my study) explained, 'Schools are interested in our programmes only if we can assure them improved results.' He further added that VYB therefore entered schools by promising them better attendance and pass percentages, though their own philosophy of LSE had been different. While programmes thereby assured schools the outcomes they desired, organizations had starkly different targets and pedagogies for their programmes that were in contrast with the concerns and rote cultures of schooling.[5]

An observation of the curricular structures of programmes showed that the pedagogic approach was designed to introduce an atmosphere of warmth, fun and games, through which a pedagogic concern with the 'self' could be introduced (as seen from the diary entry given before). Skills such as self-awareness, critical thinking, decision-making, effective communication—all of which required self-introspection and reflective cultivation—were to be presented to students through games, songs, art, theatre-based activities, group discussion and debates, by a group of young facilitators, not more than 10 or 12 years older than the children themselves. Though the facilitators used this space to draw children's attention towards 'how to be' (e.g., 'responsible', 'enterprising', 'disciplined', as will be explained later), middle-class organizers of these programmes like Devesh Arya (the founder and CEO of IP) explained their work as 'social entrepreneurship'.[6] The aim, they argued, was

---

[5] Though this was largely true of most programmes, some did adopt didactic formats similar to school, while all programmes were 'disciplined' by the school culture in some ways.

[6] While I'm aware of the complexity of defining the 'middle class' in India and recognize the heterogeneity of this group, the terms 'middle class' and 'non-middle class' is used through the book to simply make a contrast between groups of actors with very different social histories, backgrounds and social and cultural capital. I loosely adopt the terms middle class and non-middle class to distinguish between

to 'give back' to society by teaching children from disadvantaged communities skills that had made them personally successful. Skills related to communication, creativity and enterprise were identified by Arya and others such as Aamir Raza (Managing Director of an educational services provider, MFCL, also offering LSE) as the skills that had made *them* successful. Others like Garima Acharya (the Chief Operating Officer of IP) and Pavan Raghunath (of VYB) argued that these skills were already available to 'us' (i.e., the middle class). Arya, Raza and others viewed their social interventions within government and aided schools as the critical knowledge that would enable children belonging to low-incomes communities 'escape their cycles of poverty'. Pointing to the 'unsupportive' homes and the culture of alcoholism, single parenting and poverty that children in government schools came from, Raghunath argued that these LSPs would 'empower them' and help them 'taste success' and build confidence. In this manner, the middle-class (and largely upper-caste) managerial staff of these organizations offered an 'ideology of merit' (Upadhya, 2007, 2011) in explaining the goals for their programmes, that is, a strong belief that children from these disadvantaged circumstances could individually determine their own outcomes in life through hard work and talent, while overlooking their own caste and class privileges that had contributed to their successful life outcomes.

Simultaneously, poverty and the home cultures of children in these schools were also seen as pre-disposing conditions for 'risk behaviours' such as delinquency and crime. Identifying LSE as the 'social vaccination' that could inoculate students from these risks, programme organizers such as Rajesh Sridhar (Director of VYB's Inspire programme) discursively positioned these risks to be similar to other epidemiological risks. Others such as Joel Mathias (of IP) pointed to the various ways in which they were addressing social problems, including that of poverty, delinquency, violence and gender disparities, and pointed

---

what I refer to as middle class 'managers' or 'producers'—a group of young, urban, corporate professionals-turned-social workers with access to English language and its attendant culture; and the children and facilitators, without a similar exposure to elite forms of schooling and its attendant progressive cultures, pedagogies and exposure to English language and practices of self-making.

to the contributions they were making to the nation's development and progress. Similar to discussions on LSE seen within secondary literature, discussions on the field placed LSE as a solution to all developmentally undesirable conditions, while discursively placing onus on individuals to work upon themselves to overcome their structural conditions of disadvantage.

In spite of such strong articulations of the social contributions and service made by these organizations within society, the chapter presents a detailed description of some of the organizations in order to establish how they functioned as 'social enterprises'. I describe them as 'social enterprises' based on observations of the priorities within the organizations, which largely focused on building the organization as a 'brand'; 'scaling' programmes; and findings ways to 'productize' life skills training. Wedding the concepts of social service, with their personal spirit of entrepreneurism, heads of organizations presented their work as 'social entrepreneurism' and sought to create niche positions for themselves within the growing market of educational and self-development programmes targeting youth, while also differentiating themselves from commercial enterprises and self-identifying as 'socially responsible citizen-entrepreneurs'. The managers of these programmes sought to present themselves as 'role models' for others, from both the labouring class (who were urged to adopt the skills they had to offer, to escape their circumstances and become successful like the middle class) and the middle classes (who they sought to involve in their activities through the promotion of 'volunteerism' as a desirable form of personal conduct).

Though similar in these many ways, the organizations covered as part of the study were also significantly different from each other in their approach, organizational structures and methods. While seven LSPs were observed in various depth, in this chapter, I describe three programmes and organizations conducting them—VYB, IP and MFCL—covered most in detail. Describing the structures and everyday routines of the organizations, I show how they sought to impact not just individual students but more broadly normalize a 'youthful culture' which has been identified with practices of lifelong learning and working upon the self to remain young, dynamic and relevant through the life course, and through the course of structural changes within the economy and economic cycle (Ruddick, 2003). This was reflected in statements made by key members of organizations, such as Arya from IP, as can be seen further:

> Whatever you study, in five to seven years is going to go waste—the technical skills. But what we can take ahead is our ability to be adaptable and flexible. This is a life skill. Twelve to 14 million people graduate from our country but don't get jobs. If the ultimate aim of education was to help you lead a high quality of life, and one part of quality of life was a job, then education is failing us somewhere. One part of that was skills for a job. Only a small part become engineers, but others become auto drivers, call centre executives, etc.... [there's a] mismatch between skills and the job... [Our vision] is to empower every child in this country with life skills. 'Life skills' sits at the foundation of our values. Our values is [sic] that every child deserves a quality of life, quality education, and that every child is unique and special.[7]

Statements such as these, by Arya and others, not only showed how these programmes sought to normalize new meanings and cultures of lifelong learning, self-work and adaptability as the main functions of schooling and the education system, but it also showed how ideas for, and meanings associated with, education were drawn from the managers' own middle-class upbringing. In the circulation of these discourses through material and immaterial practices such as LSPs and discourses about education, Arya and other LSE organizers were also shaping public discourses regarding how educated citizens must behave—through self-governance and appropriate forms of participation in social, economic and civic life.

Much has been written about the middle classes in India and their politics of representation and capture of public discourses through which state structures and public institutions in India have been shaped (see Baviskar & Ray, 2011; Fernandes, 2006; Gooptu, 2001). Analytical accounts of India's middle classes have shown how, through their resources of language and education, the middle classes

---

[7] Personal communication, 15 May 2012.

have claimed authority over and knowledge of common interests and goods, and the ways in which a common civic order and goals can be reached. Such civic order and values (also shaped through philanthropic, charitable and educational activities of the middle classes, for example, through the deployment of programmes such as LSE), however, rest on socially segregated conceptions that view the poor as a threat to social order (Fernandes, 2006). Observations of the LSPs not only revealed how the middle classes were shaping ideas around education through their backward and forward linkages with schools, teachers, students and parents, on the one hand, and policy makers, aid organizations, businesses and other NGOs, on the other hand. What was also visible through a closer examination of the programmes was how these educational interventions of LSE served to foster middle class visions of development and neutralize the perceived threat to them, by incorporating the poor, by working upon them to remake and recast their identities, and de-historicizing and de-politicizing their social locations of caste, gender and poverty. Thus, in describing the organizations in detail, I aim not just to show how meanings associated with education are being refigured through new state–non-state partnerships but also highlight the middle class politicking through which expectations for youth and youth identities are being recast.

4.1. Life Skills Organizations as Middle-Class Cultural Spaces

In the following section, I provide a detailed description of three LSE organizations and their programmes, namely IP, VYB and MFCL.

4.1.1. Imagine Possibilities (IP)

IP is a young organization that began as a volunteer initiative in 1999, and that was formally registered as a 'professional charitable trust' in 2003. What started off as a group of young, 'new middle class' professionals (Fernandes, 2006), from different fields,[8] coming together over

---

[8] These include marketing, management, software engineering, chartered accountancy, business and entrepreneurship, photography, advertisement and contemporary dance.

the weekends to spend time with underprivileged children from shelter homes in Bengaluru has grown into an organization working with over 5,000 children, 24 partner NGOs and schools, 1,000 teachers and adult workers and 3,000 volunteers providing life skills training.

IP's goal (as stated on their website) is to 'empower young people from vulnerable backgrounds to escape their cycle of poverty, overcome adversity and flourish in a fast-changing world'. According to Garima Acharya, the COO of IP, this vision grew from their observation that young people from vulnerable backgrounds returned to the streets and were unable to get and keep jobs, when asked to leave shelter homes at the age of 17–18 years. Elaborating upon this observation, she explained that children from vulnerable communities are not prepared adequately to deal with the challenges of life. She argued that 'Even if they get a job, they don't know how to conduct themselves at a job or manage conflicts at work....' She further explained this stating that the critical missing element amongst these youth was life skills and added that 'You and me, daily, use life skills to manage conflicts. ...For children from difficult backgrounds, they address these challenges by substituting themselves with alcohol, crime, drugs or just being poor'.[9]

IP, she explained, had therefore developed as an organization wholly dedicated to building 'life skills' in children from difficult circumstances.[10] Significant to note from Acharya's rationale for their LSPs is the conflation made between 'difficult circumstances' (such as that of poverty and vulnerability) with personal behaviours and conduct, and the marking out of risk behaviours such as addiction and crime as exclusive to the poor. Poverty itself was constructed as a form of disorder or risk, similar to addiction, and life skills were positioned as the behavioural–psychological solution to address a wide range of deficits, including structural ones such as poverty.

IP's initial work had, however, not begun with life skills training.[11] Rather, having felt the positive effects of their weekend engagement on the behaviour of terminally-ill children at various shelter homes, the

[9] Personal communication, 29 July 2012.
[10] Personal communication, 29 July 2012.
[11] As stated by Devesh Arya (Personal communication, 28 May 2012).

organization had started as a means to provide vulnerable children with opportunities for positive engagement. This was provided through 11 different sports-based programmes, along with other activities, such as weekend outings and dance therapy. A critical part of the initial work had also included raising sponsorships and funds, through their own wide network and connections with corporate organizations (that was available to them as a result of several members of the team having served in various multinational companies previously).

It was only in 2004, when Devesh Arya (the CEO, and a former venture capitalist, who had given up his profession to enter the social sector fulltime) happened to chance upon a WHO curriculum for substance abuse, that the term LSE was adopted to their work. Arguing that the work they had already been undertaking was very similar to what the WHO recommended as LSE, Devesh explained that he decided to adopt the term to his programmes, as it would offer his work 'credibility' and the 'NGO language' that it lacked.[12]

IP's life skills classes were delivered using one of two main formats—through an arts-based delivery model or a sports-based model. Programmes were delivered free of cost, afterschool hours in 24 aided and charity-based schools in Bengaluru,[13] for children between 8–14 years. Weekly sessions of two-and-half hours each were conducted for a batch of 25–30 children (grouped age wise), who voluntarily joined one of the programmes (i.e., arts or sports) that took place within school premises. A total of 20 sessions (15 structured and 5 unstructured)[14] were conducted over the academic

---

[12] Personal communication, 28 May 2012.

[13] When asked about tie-ups with government schools, the COO, Acharya, informed me that they were not working with government schools because of the difficulties in getting permissions from the education department (Personal communication, 17 April 2012).

[14] Structured sessions are sessions for which lesson plans were given in the training manual given to the facilitators. Unstructured sessions were ones in which the facilitators were free to decide the course of the class. Typically, the unstructured sessions were supposed to be interspersed with the structured sessions. Particularly, facilitators were supposed to judge the mood of the class and use an unstructured session by orienting it towards the needs of the class.

year for each batch of students, focused around five core skills that have been identified by IP. (These skills were explained as the meta-level skills that made up the 10 life skills listed by WHO.) The five core skills included 'interacting with others', 'overcoming difficulties and solving problems', 'taking initiative', 'managing conflict' and 'understanding and following instructions'. Children were expected to attend the programme for a minimum of at least two years, since IP argued that this is the minimum time required for the programmes to have an impact. (This was also informed to the schools and had been negotiated with them in advance.)

In addition, IP ran three supplementary programmes that were offered in addition to life skills training in schools. The first was a Youth Centre for young people in the age group of 14–18 years, to equip them with foundational skills required for career development, and 'to help them make healthy career choices and transit successfully' (as mentioned on their website). The second component was a volunteer-engagement programme, to sensitize others from the middle class regarding the difficulties faced by marginalized communities, since IP believed that this awareness was a crucial ingredient for creating a non-discriminatory world. One part of this volunteering programme consisted of a mentoring component which used non-professionals or lay persons from the middle classes as volunteer-mentors to disadvantaged youth, to support and guide them on future decisions and handling everyday challenges. Mentors, who were mostly individuals with corporate and professional backgrounds, with little or no training in psychology (like the managerial group at IP itself), worked with youth through regular weekly contact sessions, during which young people shared their difficulties and challenges and sought mentors' feedback and inputs. The weekly sessions sometimes even entailed providing the youth from marginalized communities new experiences, such as a visit to the mall (which, IP argued, could be anxiety provoking for them and yet a desired dream).

Another component of the volunteer engagement programme was a corporate volunteer engagement model, through which IP sought to provide customized volunteering experiences to various corporate organizations seeking to fulfil their quota of 'corporate social responsibility' (CSR). With modifications in the Company's Act (2013) that not only made CSR compulsory for corporates but also pushed companies to manage their CSR quotas through direct employee volunteering (Deshpande, 2018; Ramanathan, 2015), several companies looked for opportunities to engage their employees. IP capitalized on this demand from the corporate sector and sought to create unique experiences through which they could engage volunteers from corporate organizations in their work.

A final component of IP's programme was a teacher training programme (TTP), through which they sought to develop empathy in teachers and expand their creativity in working with children from vulnerable backgrounds. This component of their programme was also a strategy to reach their goal of 240,000 children (indirectly) by 2015. As part of this expansion plan, regular schoolteachers were to be 'empowered' with life skills so that they could, in turn, train children and help IP reach its large target group. Since IP did not have the required manpower of facilitators to reach this target alone, this was sought to be reached indirectly through the TTP. The TTP was started in mid-2012.

This also made it necessary for IP to increase its base of 'lead facilitators' (i.e., adults trained in the pedagogic knowledge of how to facilitate life skills classes), who could train other adults (like schoolteachers) in working with children. Prior to 2012, IP had a small base of 'lead facilitators' (less than 10), mostly drawn from its middle class, senior managerial group and/or from other volunteers or consultants who were also largely from the middle class. However, with the need to address this larger number of children and with the rolling out of a new HR policy (which sought to regularize the contract of facilitators, occupy them with full-time work and award them incentive-based promotions) in mid-2012, the base of 'lead facilitators' was expanded to include some facilitators as well.[15] (The selected facilitators had to

---

[15] The facilitators—as noted earlier, a young group of individuals, not much older than the students—stood in many ways as a 'foil' to the middle class managers' sensibilities and culture, coming mostly from non-middle-class backgrounds or even from impoverished, working class homes or the street, as will be discussed later.

undergo a separate training for this which was different in orientation when compared to the training they had received as facilitators. This was because the focus here was not simply on affording them an experience of experiential learning practices or drawing their attention to how to make a session experiential. Rather, the focus was also on building the skills required to help other adults recognize the skills required for facilitation.)

The TTP was a cost-effective strategy conceived by IP in order to scale their programme. It provided an economical solution to replace the otherwise more expensive direct training programme (since that would require IP to employ a larger number of facilitators on its payroll and incur costs on training and monitoring them regularly).[16] In its place, IP had signed agreements with several different schools and NGOs that had voluntarily agreed to bear the costs of training their teachers, in return for the 'expertise' that was provided by IP. These costs were mainly those of hiring a training facility (which could be met within the school itself, if the school had space) and food (which, in the case of the training for the low-cost private schools, was brought from the teachers' and headmaster's homes). Thus, in contrast with IP's internal trainings for facilitators and volunteers, which were held in more elite, paid, community halls and training centres such as Ashirvad and Mobility India (in Bengaluru), TTPs for the private schools were organized in more modest spaces such as the Bruhat Bengaluru Mahanagara Palike Samudaya Bhavan[17] (with even toilet facilities not available in some of these spaces. During one such training, in fact, the school made provisions for the teachers and the training staff to use a local pay and use toilet located opposite the centre by providing us with coupons for this).

I describe these differences in detail, since I will come back to discuss this point on scale later (in Chapter 7), while discussing the importance of these training programmes for IP. I also undertake

---

[16] An individual facilitator's monthly salary was approximately ₹7,250 (as retrieved from IP's website, 3 February 2015).

[17] A government-run community hall that is lower in cost compared to the ones at which IP held its internal trainings.

this detailed description as a way to point to the kinds of spaces for which non-middle-class facilitators turned lead facilitators like Jaffar (who co-facilitated the training at the Samudaya Bhavan mentioned before) were trained for. (I contrast this with the mostly middle-class lead facilitators who conducted trainings internally for the facilitators, or for other middle-class volunteers, which again seemed to suggest a segregation of roles based on class. The middle-class members of IP would also not be seen at trainings for children in the government and other low-income aided schools, except when they came into school occasionally to monitor sessions.)

Programmes, especially the school LSE, were planned to be highly experiential in nature, consisted of activities such as games, stories, creative writing exercises, drawing, theatre-improvisation activities, group discussions and so on, and the activities were expected to be followed by a deep reflective discussion. Language was employed conspicuously in many of the activities as a critical tool to bring about behavioural and individual change (as will be discussed in more detail later), resembling practices of 'concerted cultivation' that Annette Lareau (2000, 2003) identifies as markers of parenting and socialization practices within middle-class homes. Describing practices of concerted cultivation, Lareau draws attention to the efforts that middle-class parents make to engage their children in various forms of organized activities and, particularly, use language to reason about their behaviours, in order to build social prowess and skill to navigate structured and institutional spaces, such as schools, workplaces, political bureaucracy, etc. In a similar manner, IP's programme sought to use a combination of activities and reason using language about one's behaviour that emerged during activities in order to build 'life skills' in children.

Each session had a main activity focused on one of the five core skills and supplementary games and routines, such as warm-up activities, a segment called 'check-in/check-out' at the beginning and end of each session to ascertain children's state of mind, and provisions for personal time and conversations with the facilitators in order to build an atmosphere of trust and warmth within the sessions, in order to facilitate self-work. The curriculum and structure of the programmes had been sourced from two international agencies working in the area of youth empowerment and contextualized to suit Indian schools. The collaborations had been initiated after IP had been unsuccessful in developing its own curriculum and had admittedly found it difficult to find other like-minded organizations within the Indian context to develop the curriculum, 'who would see life skills as already present within individuals, waiting to be discovered, rather than as something fixed', according to Acharya.[18]

Another significant feature of IP's model was the choice of facilitators employed to conduct the programmes within schools. Facilitators or life skills trainers were recruited from similar social backgrounds and communities as the children in the charitable and aided schools, since IP argued that individuals recruited from children's own communities would be better able to understand their language and needs. Accordingly, most facilitators of IP came from lower middle class or working-class backgrounds; some had also grown up in shelter homes or on the streets. A few of the trainers had also undergone IP's LSP as students (i.e., had been exposed to it at schools or shelter homes they were part of). Many were also local, small-time artists and sportspersons, who had joined IP to supplement their incomes. (IP, in turn, had hired these sportspersons and artists as they had initially offered programmes wholly focused on art and football, before the development of a formal life skills curriculum in 2012–2013).

Field observations showed that the facilitators were in fact the only members of the organization with a deep connection to the young people in the schools in which IP intervened and those who were able to understand their cultures and knew their local languages and dialects (e.g., Kannada, Tamil and Telugu). This was in stark contrast with most of the other (managerial) members of the organization, who were not even familiar with Kannada. Thus, owing to this significant difference between those who had conceived and envisaged these programmes, and the facilitators who came from local backgrounds, IP had not only conceived of a curriculum that they argued must be deliverable by anyone but had also invested heavily in training, in order

---

[18] Personal communication, 17 April 2012.

to affect changes first in the personal cultures and social behaviours of the facilitators, through whom it was expected to be transferred to the children. These changes were mainly ones that would induct them into the youthful cultures of the 'new middle classes' (Fernandes, 2006), comprising personal attributes and other knowledges of language, dress, mannerisms and consumptive practices, which also embody a certain way of being in the world. The behaviours and knowledges that IP focused on were also those that have become a visible part of India's new workspaces and corporate culture, that the managerial team of IP had themselves earlier been a part of.

Thus, rather than focusing on pedagogical knowledge of LSE, training was focused more to enable personal transformations in the facilitators and took many forms that included reflective exercises around the self as well as organization of everyday routines that offered an immersive culture of learning. Facilitators reflected on these new expectations placed upon them, not just to develop a set of professional skills but also to personally adapt to a new work and personal culture with mixture of awe, excitement and unease. Many explained how these changes expected them to adapt to the workplace with new habits of greeting and dress. For example, facilitators explained that after joining the organization, Arya, the CEO, had introduced them to everyday routines of high-fives and hugs, allowing them a sense of the 'flat' and casual nature of work relationships, as opposed to the formality and hierarchy that characterize traditional workspaces. Others described the casual, 'young' and 'hip' dress code adopted by members of the organization, consisting of branded T-shirts, jeans and skirts, rather than formal wear, as a novelty. Some spoke of their initial discomfort in adopting these clothes (being used to more traditional dresses consisting of salwar-kameez), but that had become necessary, as IP's dress code (or uniform) for team members during external events consisted of custom-made T-shirts and jeans. Thus, induction into a middle-class habitus was achieved through the consumptive practices of dress, interactions within the workplace, work culture and also through expectations to get familiar with technology and participate on platforms such as social media to promote the organization's work.

Though acclimatized to an organizational culture that appeared to be flat in so many ways, facilitators were also introduced to, and expected to, learn the subtle ways in which hierarchy was enforced within the organization. Hired as part-time, contractual staff, for the sole purpose of delivering the curriculum, facilitators lacked a say in curriculum and organizational planning, unlike other full-time, organizational staff from the middle classes. This arrangement changed somewhat towards the middle of my field work in 2012, when IP introduced a new HR policy. Regularizing the contract of the facilitators, IP decided to make them more accountable to the organization. The new policy also sought to bring in a more precise system of accounting of the hours put in by the facilitators by offering them benefits such as promotions and performance-based incentives in relation to the number of hours put in. Thus, facilitators were voluntarily allowed to take up additional portfolios, such as that of 'lead facilitator'[19] or 'programme facilitator',[20] which offered them an opportunity of mobility within the organization.

However, facilitators still enjoyed little say over matters such as curriculum, as was also visible from curriculum planning and feedback sessions observed towards the latter part of my fieldwork. At one such session attended,[21] I observed Gautam, a facilitator, providing feedback to Christiana Munro, the international curriculum development expert from the partner organization that was supplying the curriculum.

[19] Lead facilitators were those in charge of training other adults (such as schoolteachers) to conduct LSPs with children.
[20] This was the lowest level managerial position within the organization and mainly involved the supervision of other facilitators. The programme facilitator was in charge of ensuring facilitators' attendance, punctuality, completion of their duties such as collection of school data, data entry and preparation of reports. They also supervised the usage and return of resources given to facilitators to conduct sessions and were in charge of inventory management. They also attended meetings with the school management, receiving complaints and feedback from them. While a fair evaluation could not be made of these new arrangements by the end of my fieldwork in 2013, since sufficient time for facilitators to be promoted to higher management levels had not elapsed, what could be seen up to the point of my field work was that promotions were still limited to clerical jobs or roles of routinely monitoring other facilitators.
[21] The session was observed on 8 October 2012.

Reflecting on the newly introduced curriculum, Gautam explained to Munro that children do not connect the activities (which were heavily metaphorical in nature and relied on a familiarity with specific kinds of language use, as will be shown later) to everyday life. Munro responded to this by telling the facilitators to use stories from their own lives, in explaining to children how these skills can be applied. Gautam again tried to explain to her that such strategies resulted in children repeating the stories that were told to them, and that the only way to know if children had understood what was taught was by encouraging them to come up with their own stories. Despite expressing such difficulties with the format on the field, Christiana continued to brush these concerns aside, asking them to suit it to the children's needs, not paying heed to a significant issue that the facilitators were trying to point out to, regarding the starkly different cultural contexts of the school and children's home backgrounds and how this posed hurdles in achieving expected outcomes of the programmes. Thus, despite recruiting facilitators from similar contexts as those that the children belonged to, in order to aid managers in understanding children's contexts, facilitators' knowledge of these contexts hardly figured into the planning of the programme.

In other areas too, such as team meetings, explicit forms of hierarchy were absent, while implicit rules for participation governed exchanges between team members. For example, in the year that I followed the organization, team meetings, which were attended by all full-time staff (from the CEO to the admin assistant), were consecutively chaired by members holding lower positions within the organization. At these weekly events, all matters from board-level decisions to events on the field were openly discussed with all members, who could cross-question each other on these matters, including the CEO. Thus, on the surface IP appeared to be a 'flat' organization; yet, underlying this structure was a strongly inscribed, tacit hierarchy that set limits on individual members. For example, an opportunity to observe how this tacit hierarchy functioned became visible during a weekly team meeting that I attended.[22] At this meeting, Arya, the

---

[22] The observation was made on 13 April 2012.

CEO, had planned to show a sensitizing film to the team and had wanted to discuss its relevance following the screening. This was, however, not received with enthusiasm by the team, and one of the members, Riya Mathews (a programme anchor) even informed Arya of urgent work she needed to complete. Informing Arya that she had an appraisal of one of the facilitators scheduled, she added that she would be able to reschedule this for later only if the facilitator was able to wait. Stating this, she turned to the facilitator in question, John, to check about when he would be leaving. To this, Arya, immediately replied, 'Well, not before the appraisal is over,' and continued to screen the film. The incident was a telling example of how authority was subtly enforced, and how staff at different levels implicitly understood expectations placed by those higher up in the hierarchy.

Another opportunity to observe this enforcement of authority became available again following the screening of the film. Post the screening, Arya waited silently for the group to share their thoughts around the film, having made it clear initially itself that he expected the group to reflect on the message of the film. However, a long silence ensued with no one willing to share their thoughts. Taking this as a cue to break up the meeting, Joel Mathias, the head of programme delivery, stood up to leave, but no one else moved. Suddenly realizing this, Joel asked out loud, 'Isn't the meeting over?' Another team member responded stating 'No, Devesh (Arya) wants to debrief.' After some more silence, finally, Acharya, the COO, opened the discussion by sharing some of her thoughts, and this was followed by a few other members sharing their ideas. However, the exchange was a telling example of how hierarchy was tacitly established and followed within the organization.

Thus, the organization in many ways functioned less as a traditional NGO and more like a new-age corporate firm, with an everyday work culture characterized by a curious mix of strong accountability and casual informality. While work hours and targets sought to be strongly monitored and clocked, everyday interactions were marked by easy interpersonal relationships and a lack of formality and hierarchy at the surface level. Structured in these many ways as a formal, corporate organization, everyday work was marked by formal meetings (aided by google mail and calendars that were used to coordinate formal requests for such events, even though members sat in adjacent rooms or tables less than 10 feet apart). Further, goals of networking, visibility and scale became the most visible feature of everyday work. In fact, most of the discussion within the organization and during team meetings, mainly, revolved around these topics, rather than on the LSP itself.

For example, during one such team meeting attended on annual plans, goals and objectives, the focus remained on the importance of 'scaling' IP's programme.[23] Beginning with a discussion around the induction of a new board member, Rohan Ferreira, Acharya introduced his vision for the organization by stating that Ferreira's sights were set on expansion, since he believed that it was 'irresponsible not to scale'. During the same meeting, models to achieve 'rapid scale' were also discussed, which mainly revolved around designing short, two-day training programmes for partner NGOs and teachers, as a way to indirectly reach a larger number of children. The importance of branding IP's programmes and networking were also discussed as strategies through which the target of scale could be achieved. Thus, plans to develop a new corporate brand image that would establish the idea that 'life skills means IP', was also discussed during this meeting.

Other ways in which IP sought to 'scale' was by increasing visibility for the organization and its programmes by regularly participating in the various 'runs' and 'marathons' that have become popular in Bengaluru over the last decade. IP also urged its employees and volunteers to participate in these activities and encouraged them to bring as many additional participants as they could, in order to increase their visibility at these events. IP even provided employees with incentives for recruiting the largest number of volunteers for such events.

Another growth strategy was linked to sourcing funds by setting up a chapter of IP in the UK. In 2012, IP opened a chapter in the UK to be able to participate in various charity events and better network with charities and individuals in the UK, and obtain more funds to expand their programme. IP's funding thus came from national and

---

[23] The observation was made on 20 April 2012.

international sources, with the largest share of funds coming from grants and corporate foundations, followed by corporate CSR donations, individuals and events organized by IP.

4.1.2. Viveka Youth Brigade (VYB)

In stark contrast with the small, yet, growing character of IP, VYB was an old, established, not-for-profit development organization, with several years of grassroots experience. Started by a group of local medical doctors from Mysore, in 1984, to provide medical services to the poor, over the years it has grown into a large organization of over 450 employees, with more than 50 projects spread across the districts of Mysore, Hassan, Kodagu, Dakshin Karnataka and rural Bengaluru, and with several national and international collaborations. VYB is primarily engaged in providing health, educational and socio-economic empowerment-related programmes to rural and tribal communities.

LSE was one small component of one of the educational projects conducted by VYB. The project named Inspire had been initiated and managed by Rajesh Sridhar, a US-returned, senior-level marketing professional of a large American IT firm. A personal crisis and a period of soul searching during his corporate tenure had led Sridhar to explore several psycho-therapeutic options, such as neuro-linguistic programming (NLP) and Myers–Briggs Type Indicator personality inventory (in which he also subsequently obtained training). It was this training and experience that he applied to the development of LSE programme for underprivileged youth following his return to India.

Once in India, Rajesh made contact with VYB and associated himself with its work, wanting to contribute meaningfully to society. On expressing his desire to start a programme for the urban poor, Sridhar received support from VYB to start the Inspire project in Bengaluru (supported by funds from Dell Foundation). The project was designed to provide academic support to the urban poor along with LSE, as Sridhar believed that 'personality' was an important component of academic and career success. For my work, since my primary interest was in LSPs, I mainly followed the Inspire project, which had been an independent component, delinked from the other projects and teams of the organization, during the initial period of my field work. The aim of project was that of 'breaking the cycle of poverty for families by improving the quality of education at the school level and encouraging students to pursue job-oriented degrees by providing scholarships and innovative family saving programs' (as stated on its website). The project had four main components:

1. An academic tutoring programme that made use of audio-visual aids to support slow learners and revise topics already completed at school. Supporting this component of the programme, VYB's Bengaluru office had a huge team of content writers, proofreaders, video editors, etc., who were in charge of creating audio-visual modules based on the Karnataka state education board syllabus.
2. An additional, academic and personal mentoring programme for bright students, who scored above 60 per cent and whose monthly family income was below ₹20,000, who were tracked and were given help in accessing higher education.
3. A programme that sought to incentivize parents to save for their children's higher education, by setting up a recurring deposit towards which parents contributed ₹100 every month and to which VBY added a sum of ₹50 monthly. (This initiative was supported by McAfee.)
4. An LSE programme, based on WHO's model to develop confidence and self-esteem in children and train them to adapt positively to their context.

Based on this plan, Sridhar's initial attempt had been admittedly to provide 'soft skills' for children of the urban poor in all government schools and pre-university colleges in Bengaluru. However, schools had shown no interest in this but were mainly concerned with academics. Thus, the initial plan of the programme had to be modified, and the programme started by providing educational infrastructure and support for teaching–learning to schools.[24]

---

[24] As told to me by Pavan Raghunath, the former HR and life skills team manager at VYB (Personal communication, 8 February 2012).

Interestingly Sridhar and other managerial staff at VYB used the term 'soft skills' rather than 'life skills' to refer to the non-academic skills programme, reflecting not just their prior corporate experiences, but also the close associations and perceived continuities between life skills and soft skills within public discourse on skills training. But the use of the term 'soft skills' was also a point of contention with other staff within the organization and pointedly revealed the class divide between 'managers' and others, namely the field-level implementing staff of the programmes. Facilitators, who delivered the programmes within schools, belonged to more modest backgrounds and were trained in psychology, and strongly protested the use of this term, seeing it as a denial of their knowledges, training and role within the organization.

Like IP, VYB was also divided along class lines. As mentioned earlier, the Director—Sridhar was a middle-aged, upper-caste professional belonging to the 'new middle class'. Others, who similarly oversaw the management of the programme also belonged to more conservative sections of the middle class and had upper-caste backgrounds. Some had previously worked in the public sector or small private companies. The management here was also largely middle-aged, unlike at IP. Only the lowest rung of field workers (i.e., those who conducted the programmes in schools) and the technical team in charge of producing the audio-visual aids were in their mid-to-late 20s, and early 30s. This group was also predominantly female, from lower middle-class backgrounds, many even having come from smaller towns or rural districts of Karnataka, with education in government schools and second tier colleges. 'School managers', who oversaw the implementation of the programme at schools, reporting on attendance, schedule completion and conduct of the field staff, formed a cadre between the field staff and managers. They were mostly male, in their early or mid-30s, and also belonged to lower middle class, rural backgrounds and were, mostly, Kannada-medium educated. Thus, it appeared that field-based managerial posts and monitoring jobs at VYB too were reserved for male, lower middle-class employees, while those who delivered the curriculum in government schools created teaching videos and managed data about the projects, such as its statistics and impact (i.e., jobs which were mostly routinized) were largely young, lower middle-class women.

The life skills facilitators, who also belonged to the cadre of field staff, were among the highest qualified members of the organization (with a master's training in psychology), belonged to small towns; many had been educated in rural or government, Kannada-medium colleges and had a poor understanding of psychology, and occupied one of the lowest rungs in the organization. Despite being trained in a 'modern' discipline such as psychology,[25] their exposure was extremely limited and they had, in fact, no knowledge of LSE itself, before joining VYB.

Organizational culture was made up of strict formality, bureaucracy, authoritarian relations, hierarchical division of labour and top-down planning and management. Different sections of the organization (both vertical and horizontal) appeared to work in silos, with a complete lack of transparency or accountability across the organization as a whole. Accountability, largely, seemed to be maintained only in the form of one-way reporting to senior levels, about the goals and targets met. In fact, this complete absence of transparency and accountability became vividly apparent and created a major problem for the organization, towards the middle of my fieldwork, when Sridhar, the Project Director, suddenly took seriously ill. With Sridhar away, some members of other divisions of the larger organization were brought in to manage the project. At this point, financial embezzlement by some managerial-level staff of Inspire that had been going on for some time came to light. This discovery led to the Inspire project being more tightly integrated with the main organization for the first time since its inception, and its vision was sought to be aligned more along the lines of the main organization, based on its values of truth, non-violence, service and sacrifice. Thus, for the first time, even lower-level staff, such as facilitators and teachers of the remedial training programmes,

---

[25] I use the term 'modern' to describe the discipline of psychology not only due to its late origins as an academic discipline in the 19th century, but also to refer to the post-enlightenment principles of individual autonomy and rationality, upon which it is based.

were introduced to the main organization and its head and were also made to undergo an induction programme at the organization's headquarters in Mysore.

Further, a new manager was appointed and sent from the headquarters in Mysore to look after the project in Bengaluru, replacing some of the older staff. This new manager, Ranjit Kumar also sought to bring a change to the culture of work at Inspire, insisting on greater accountability, work commitment and goal orientation on the part of the teachers and life skills facilitators, and other lower-rung staff. (This new work ethic, with emphasis on self-responsibility to reach targets was, however, not well-appreciated by the facilitators and other staff, who had been used to the largely bureaucratic structure of Inspire.)

In terms of its programmatic structure, the Inspire project was conducted for high school students and used an in-school model, wherein teaching assistants (with Bachelor of Education degrees) and life skills facilitators were assigned full-time to a particular school and conducted their classes during the regular school day. That is, the life skills (and academic tutoring) classes, for each class of the school, was scheduled into the regular timetable of the school. Thus, the teaching assistants and life skills facilitators came to be seen as regular staff members of the school and were also expected by the school to participate in its various daily routines (from regular classroom teaching and examination invigilation to disciplining children, participating in events such as sports day and Teachers' Day, Saraswati puja and other such functions celebrated in school). Students, too, oriented to the VYB staff as they did to regular schoolteachers, paying equal respect and importance to their authority and knowledge. Similarly, the facilitators and teaching assistants from VYB, also took their roles as teachers within these schools seriously, involving themselves in the day-to-day affairs of the school, while simultaneously respecting and upholding the implicit hierarchy between them and the regular teachers, who held a higher status within the school, because of the nature of their appointments and years of experience.

The LSE programme was planned as a three-year intervention, to be carried out over the entire academic year, with a specific set of skills planned to be taught for each year. Thus, in the first year (eighth standard), children were taught skills of emotional management, self-awareness, empathy, concentration, reading and sequencing. Along with this, a unique component of the VYB LSP was the teaching of basic academic concepts in the first year (i.e., alphabets, numbers, strengthening basic mathematics operations, Kannada alphabets and so on). In the second year (ninth standard), children were introduced to cognitive skills such as critical and creative thinking, problem-solving, stress management, time management, study habits and handling failure. In the final year (tenth standard), the focus was on exam preparation, peer pressure, goal setting and decision-making, accepting the self and preparing for the transition to college. Thus planned, over 60 hours of training were assured to each child.[26] Sessions used stories and topics for group discussions around the aforementioned skill areas, and while games were used, they were mainly to develop skills of attention and concentration.

With LSE understood within the organization as an add-on programme to supplement the academic learning programme that VYB conducted, the development of the LSE programme and training for facilitators had been outsourced to a private psychological consultancy firm. Even during the period of my fieldwork, the LSE component of Inspire received little attention from the management and was mostly managed and organized by the facilitators themselves—many of whom were fresh graduates with an inadequate understanding of the subject and little experience with children. Thus, with this inadequate training, what became another prominent feature of the programme was the excessive 'psychologization' of students by these novice facilitators and the use of inappropriate psychological terminologies and techniques to address behaviour. To give just a few examples of this, terms such as 'ADHD' were used to describe entire classrooms.[27]

On other occasions, senior facilitators, such as Nayanika, could be heard explaining the post-intervention results they had received, on a test of critical thinking, to the team in the following manner: stating

---

[26] Pavan Raghunath (Personal communication, 8 February 2012).

[27] Attention deficit hyperactivity disorder, a clinically significant condition that has specific symptoms and treatment protocols.

that categories such as critical thinking must not show much improvement, she explained that too much improvement would mean that 'either you have manipulated the data, either you are God, or either you are psychotic.'[28] Such inappropriate usage of clinically-significant conditions (such as ADHD and psychoses) and inappropriate explanations for human behaviour clearly showed how the facilitators had little understanding of psychological development and LSE.

With this inadequate knowledge and understanding of children's psychological development, team meetings (called debriefs) were mainly spent discussing various psychological strategies to manage children at school, to ensure the academic goals desired by the organization. Thus, children would be discussed as 'cases', and psychological explanations and labels were provided for them. Discussions on types of interventions (e.g., cognitive behaviour therapy, mindfulness training and group counselling) to be undertaken to address these problems were conducted without an acknowledgement of the fact that each of these methods were long-term therapeutic solutions to be undertaken by trained professionals. With most other members of the organization unfamiliar with these psychological practices (including those in managerial roles), this form of 'psychologization' continued unchecked, throughout the period of my field work. Even those who were appointed to supervise the life skills team, such as Pavan Raghunath (with a Master's degree in Public Governance, and experience with communication management for NGOs), and Ranjit Kumar (an engineer by training), had no experience or knowledge of psychology or LSE. Thus, what was mainly seen missing with respect to the LSE programme deployed by this organization was adequate supervision and planning of this component, suggesting the little importance paid to it. As many of the facilitators pointed out to me, in personal interviews, they had been provided little training on joining the organization and had been directly inducted into school. They had also received little support in handling the challenges faced at school.

Nayanika, the senior facilitator, also informed me that she had come to understand her role late, only after she had started delivering

---

[28] Personal communication, 17 March 2012.

classes in school. She explained that she understood the organization's expectations of introducing 'behavioural reinforcement techniques' to bring changes in students' behaviours when she had personally started reading about LSE.[29] However, while it seemed that the organization gave little importance to the investments that had to be made into the programme, expectations from it were high. Thus, there was a great pressure placed by the organization on the life skills facilitators to meet multiple objectives of: reducing student drop-out rates by identifying the children 'at-risk', tracking them and increasing their attendance and motivation for school by providing them personal counselling; improving academic results by ensuring that basic concepts were well-developed in students; and taking on responsibility for ensuring tangible, measurable results for tacit qualities such as creativity and critical thinking. In fact, the quantification of these skills as measurable outcomes was a goal that the organization struggled with.[30] Yet, there was constant pressure on the facilitators to perform and prove themselves on these targets (since, they were seen as the specialists with psychological knowledge, who were failing in their commitments to the organization in bringing about behavioural change in students).

With training in psychology, facilitators were also expected to take on the emotional burdens of the students and handle serious problems such as suicide, domestic or sexual abuse, broken families or alcoholism that they encountered in the schools. However, as the facilitators constantly told me, they were both untrained and unprepared to handle these large challenges that were personally draining on them and for which they needed constant emotional support. Yet, this form of support and handholding was largely unavailable to them, both within the organization as well as in the form of professional counselling and mentoring services that they requested for, and that was only occasionally provided using external agencies.

In addition to these challenges, facilitators also faced other challenges at school that made it difficult for them to reach the targets set for them. For example, they had to constantly negotiate for

---

[29] Personal communication, 29 March 2012.
[30] Ranjit Kumar, Personal communication, 13 December 2012.

additional classes (since their assigned periods would often be taken to complete the regular academic syllabus, or for other activities, at school). Thus, completion of planned activities, such as the designated number of sessions and evaluations of other planned activities became difficult. This led to constant conflicts between the management and the facilitators at VYB, leading to a low morale and lack of esteem among the facilitators. Facilitators were constantly pulled up within the organization for not producing 'tangible' outcomes and not taking ownership of the programme.

This orientation towards a concrete measurable outcome (such as scores on paper and pencil tests) was also indicative of the instrumental approach through which LSE was managed within the organization. In fact, in order to provide these results, Nayanika, who also managed the team (in the absence of a full-time team manager), constantly urged her team to 'revise' the skills with the children, set up a competitive spirit in the class, which would encourage the children to provide more answers and to provide children with the right cues on the paper-and-pencil tests on life skills that were conducted. This instrumental understanding that dominated the LSE component was also seen with respect to other strategies used by the organization, such as ensuring 100 per cent retention of students 'at risk' for dropout. While facilitators were expected to make a note of children 'at risk' of dropping out at the beginning of the academic year and track these children and ensure their retention, they noted how the children that they had identified would often not be the ones who dropped out at the end of the year. This resulted in a situation wherein they were always able to present a result of 100 per cent retention of children at risk of dropping out. Instances such as these, and the others recounted before, provided examples of how VYB's LSE programme was poorly thought out and managed. Within the larger organization, the LSE component was also, therefore, understood as an unreliable and incalculable psychological intervention that could not be budgeted in economic terms. Thus, it received little visibility and resources within the larger organizational set-up. The focus at VYB, unlike at IP (where life skills were mainly seen as tools to develop self-regulating youth), largely remained on improving school outcomes and developing desirable attitudes towards schooling among the urban poor, including school completion. Explaining this, middle-class managers such as Raghunath explained:

> Whether we like it or not SSLC becomes important. Life is in a very different dimension if you do not cross this. Therefore, we want to push them to pass and give them that confidence. When we are pushing for academic needs, we understand that just tuitions is not enough...personality is important in making them successful.[31]

4.1.3. Media for Change Limited (MFCL)

Unlike the other two organizations, the last organization, MFCL, was not an NGO but a private limited firm providing different media solutions for education. MFCL offered educational programmes to both children in private, elite schools (for a fee) and provided free services to children in government schools. This was also, perhaps, a reason for the restricted access they offered me to their programmes, as much of their content was copyrighted and 'productized' (by which I mean sold as 'packages' to schools for a cost). Consequently, there were tight regulations of my presence at MFCL programmes and at their office.

This difference in access that was afforded to me at MFCL seemed apparent right from the beginning, with MFCL appearing to me as a 'closed' organization (unlike the other two organizations at which I had free access to the office space, staff and programmes). The 'closed' space of the organization was epitomized in the design of their office space itself, which was, again, stratified along the lines of occupational roles and class. Spread across three floors, the office space was designed in a manner to prevent easy accessibility to those in charge of content management and in decision-making roles. On my first visit to the office (which was strictly 'by appointment' only), I encountered a small front office, on the ground floor, blocked by a tinted glass door. This space (of about 15 feet) housed a reception desk that covered most of the area and blocked view of the space behind.

After being made to wait in this space for a considerable time (even after having arrived on time for my appointment), I was led through

---

[31] Personal communication, 23 February 2012.

a small passage that ran by the side of the front desk. Passing a set of small rooms, I was led to the back office, where my key informant, Sukumar G. (the manager of the LSE programme for government schools), sat. What I could gather from this visit was that the ground floor was mainly occupied by those who worked on the more routine, clerical tasks within the organization, such as dispatch, courier and front-desk services. In addition, the back rooms (almost hidden away) were occupied by the life skills team that conducted the free programmes in government schools (which did not appear to use proprietary content).[32]

On a following visit, again based on prior request and appointment with the Managing Director (MD), Aamir Raza, I was once again made to wait at the front office on the ground floor, for a considerable period of time. Finally, after my arrival was announced through the intercom to the MD, I was led up to the second floor on which his office was located. The floor had a distinctively different structure, when compared with the ground floor. The MD's office was located in a large glass-panelled room, which occupied most of the floor. In front of Raza's office was an open terrace that was used as a discussion-cum-waiting space. In between the MD's office and the terrace, there was a long hall that was occupied by a set of young, middle-class, content development personnel and managers, who worked on MFCL's private school programmes. What seemed most remarkable about the architectural layout of the floor was how it had been designed to allow the MD an opportunity to observe every entry and exit made and supervise every employee on the floor, who would be visible through the glass walls of his office.

Thus, this structure of the organizational space itself provided clues to the tight central control and confidentiality that formed the prime features of the organizational culture of MFCL. That the organization's space and activities were strictly regulated and kept

---

[32] I make this assumption, since unlike the programmes for elite, private schools, these programmes did not seem to be accompanied by any curricula, videos, workbooks, etc., that had been developed internally within the organization, like the other paid packages for private schools.

closed from outsiders became further evident through the course of my field work, particularly through the interactions with various team members. The lack of transparency within the organization further became apparent when I was regularly and explicitly dissuaded from getting to know more about the organization. For example, on one occasion, having heard from one of the facilitators (during a field visit) that MFCL was having an education conference—a free event—the next day, at the Indian Institute of Science campus (which was also the campus on which I was located during the course of this research), I had decided to drop by at the event, hoping to understand more about their activities and meet some more members. The facilitator, Vrinda, who had informed me about this event had also told me that I could come by. However, on arriving at the venue, I was immediately intercepted by Sukumar, the manager, who informed me that I could attend the event only if the MD gave me permission. He then went up to the MD to check if I could attend the event, and only on receiving a confirmation from him did he allow me to attend the programme.

On another occasion, following a field visit with Vrinda and her team, I had casually mentioned to Vrinda about accompanying them back to their office, to meet other members of the team. Vrinda immediately dissuaded me from coming, stating that they would all be busy. When I persisted, stating that I had an open invitation from one of the other members, Tanya Lewis (a manager with the research, training and content development team), who had asked me to drop by her office whenever I had time, Vrinda immediately called her manager, Sukumar, and informed him of my plans. I then received a call from Sukumar, who also dissuaded me from coming that day, and thus I had to drop the visit.

With little access provided to the programme and having to work hard at obtaining permission or information about the programme, the details gathered about the organization and its programmes are mainly based on three meetings with the manager, Sukumar—one meeting with the research, training and content development team manager (who was in charge of the programmes provided to the private schools) and two meetings with the MD, of which one took place along with his programme delivery team (consisting of Sukumar, another senior manager of training and the former assistant director). In addition, it includes observations made during three field visits with the life skills facilitators, wherein I got an opportunity to observe them deliver the life skills classes and also conduct interviews with some of them. (Of the three visits, one was to a private school at which MFCL was providing their paid service, and the other two were at government schools.) In addition, it also includes data from one other, unexpected encounter with the team at a government school that I had been routinely attending, to observe the LSE programme conducted by one of the other organizations. (Here again, I had an opportunity to observe the classes being conducted and have a discussion about the programmes with the facilitators.) Finally, it includes information got through one other event attended—the education conference mentioned before. Apart from this, access to their curriculum and other written documents was restricted. Some information could be gathered from their websites, but mostly, information about the programme given here is as it was reported by Sukumar, with whom I was able to have the most detailed interview. However, more details, follow-ups and clarifications that were required could not be obtained, as despite repeated phone calls and emails, he remained unreachable. Based on these interactions and observations, what could be gathered about MFCL's programmes was that it was divided into four verticals.

1. An event management programme for youth and children (mainly from elite, private schools) covering 85 cities and 20,000 schools in India, Pakistan, Sri Lanka and Nepal.
2. A film-based learning programme through which life skills, values and attitudes were taught. This was again targeted at elite, private schools, and this content and training was provided for a fee.
3. An English magazine aimed at principals and educationists focusing on educational issues, learning and school experiences. Contributors to the magazine included educational experts, principals and others successful in various walks of life. The magazine is circulated across 11,000 schools in India and has a readership of 150,000.

4. Project Leap, an LSE programme based on the WHO model that was started in 1999. There are two sets of programmes offered under this vertical—one that catered to private schools[33] and the other supported by various donors, such as Akshaya Patra, Manipal Foundation and Bangalore Electricity Supply Company Ltd, that catered to children from government schools.

Again, what could be observed about the organizational structure was how these different programmes were managed by individuals belonging to different classes. For example, the programmes that were offered to the private schools were managed by a group of young, 'new middle class' (Fernandes, 2006) individuals, with English medium education, global exposure and conspicuous consumptive practices. They were mostly involved in content development and research. On the other hand, those who managed the LSP for the government schools, such as Sukumar and Vrinda, belonged to the lower middle class, came from small towns and colleges and agricultural or petty trader households. These differences in class (and caste) positions and organizational roles also translated into tacit codes for interpersonal relationships and status within the organization. Thus, for example, those who managed the government school programmes showed 'fear' of transgressing organizational codes and would be afraid of taking even simple decisions, such as inviting me to the organization, independently. The members of the other team, such as Tanya Lewis, on the other hand, appeared to enjoy more freedom on these matters and, thus, invited me to the organization readily, and also shared a more casual relationship with the MD. However, having made connection with the organization through Sukumar and others who managed the LSP for government schools, I was unable to cash in on such opportunities, as Sukumar, Vrinda and others from the Project Leap team seemed to hold themselves accountable for my participation. Thus, despite invitations from Lewis, I was expected to follow Sukumar's lead on when I could undertake a visit to the organization.

---

[33] This component of Project Leap was mostly defunct, with this having been replaced by the film-based learning programme. Thus, for my research, I mainly focused on the LSE programme conducted within government schools.

MFCL's LSE programme for children in government schools was described on their website as 'Enabling children from weaker economic background to develop into responsible social beings with a sense of community and competence to respond to their personal, social and cultural needs.' In stark contrast, the description of the (previously operational) LSE programme for private schools was described as helping children deal positively with stress and emotions arising from our current 'fragmented value system, too antiquated to suit the needs of children in the Information Age'. A comparison of the rationales offered for the two programmes showed how the former had a remedial intent and saw the child as having certain deficits, while the latter was largely envisaged as a support system in the context of a dysfunctional environment, which was identified to be the cause of problems. Supporting this difference in the orientation of the programmes, Sukumar also pointed out that the problems among the two kinds of schools were different. He argued that while, in the private schools, the generation gap had led to the lack of transfer of values to students, in government schools, competency levels and confidence of children had to be improved. Further, he argued that LSE was required in this latter context to build a competitive spirit and improve students' motivation towards education.[34]

The government school LSE programme, which catered to 130,000 children across four states in India, was developed as part of MFCL's CSR plan. Started as a pilot programme in 2006 with 2,000 children from municipal corporation schools, the aim was to use LSE to improve the percentage of children scoring 90–93 per cent in these state-run schools. Arguing that children in government schools had 'talent' and 'capacity', Sukumar pointed out that they lacked confidence and a long-term vision about the future. Providing an example of this, he explained that the students in these schools would choose work over education, in order to buy a pair of jeans with the money earned, but they would not think about the future. Further, he argued that since their parents, too, had limited exposure, they too only prepared these students to set their sights low and follow along their lines. Thus,

---

[34] Personal communication, 6 March 2012.

to overcome these conditions, he argued that children within these schools required LSE and counselling 'to dream big'. Sukumar also pointed out that their LSP was focused on bringing about a process of three-stage change. Starting with developing self-esteem, it further sought to 'develop the inner world of the child' and, finally, his/her relations to the outer world. The programme was supposedly modelled along the lines of the WHO model, with training starting from the fifth standard and going on up to the tenth standard. Students between fifth to seventh standards formed the junior division and those between eighth to tenth standards formed the senior division.

In addition to the 10 life skills, the programme, according to Sukumar, also provided modules on topics such as 'know my rights' and 'communicating with parents'. Each class received 12 sessions, of which 10 focused on the WHO-listed skills and two were used for 'talent development'. 'Talent development' referred to classes on art or public speaking that gave children an opportunity to participate in these novel activities and gain confidence. (Sukumar explained that this was a unique component of the programme for government schools and was not included in the programmes given to private schools, since it was understood that children within these schools already had access to these opportunities.)

Some sessions were also organized to develop community awareness and leadership in children. Explaining that children within urban communities did not know about their neighbours and the neighbourhood, Sukumar explained that awareness campaigns and road shows were organized as part of the government school LSP to inculcate a sense of social responsibility and a sense of community (i.e., to promote a sense of 'my people, my country') in children. (This did not form a part of their private school programmes though.) As a part of this, children were helped to identify topics relevant to their communities—for example, topics such as cleanliness for the Muslim community of D. J. Halli[35] or smoking for children from Jogupalya who, Sukumar argued, were influenced by the IT companies nearby.

---

[35] This stereotype about a lack of cleanliness among the Muslim community was made by Sukumar.

As part of the leadership programme, children were encouraged to take up community initiatives, such as taking care of cleanliness in the neighbourhood. Leadership roles were also encouraged by having 'good' students help out 'dull' students with their work.

In addition to these various components of the programme, Sukumar also pointed out that counselling support was provided to children for issues related to marriage, love, alcoholic parents, support for education and so on. MFCL set up 'help centres' in schools (avoiding the term 'counselling' as, according to him, it had a negative connotation) to develop self-esteem and career awareness in students. Workshops for principals and teachers were also organized in order to give 'tips' and teach them about life skills.

Classes were conducted fortnightly. Unlike the other two organizations, these classes were neither pre-scheduled (through inclusion into the school timetable), nor conducted as regular, afterschool sessions. Instead, MFCL contacted the various schools that they worked with, once in 15 days, and would be given one class in between the school day. (This meant that sometimes, other regular classes would be disrupted, as was observed at one school in south Bengaluru, where I unexpectedly encountered the MFCL facilitators, while I was attending the programme by VYB.) According to Sukumar, sessions were planned after an initial survey of the school, since it was understood that the requirements might be different among the different populations of students. The assessment was based on inputs from students, teachers and 'experts', as well as by taking into account the education department's needs. Modules were prepared in-house and then shared with experts. The format used for training supposedly included group discussions, theatre, role play, brain storming, use of stories and real-life examples.

However, within the sessions that I had a chance to attend, these formats were rarely used. Programmes mainly took on a didactic approach. While MFCL was reluctant to share their curriculum, observations of classes across three schools, by three different facilitators, all seemed to show the programme to be focused explicitly around disciplining children in a fashion very similar to the government school. Much of the sessions observed were spent by the facilitators on pointing out children's unruly behaviours, reprimanding them, advising them, chiding them and correcting their behaviours, thus reproducing the disciplining practices of the schools themselves. Activities such as games, when used, appeared to be incidental to the main task of advising and reprimanding children for their conduct. Other activities such as stories were used to convey specific messages about duty and responsibility. Further, the classes appeared to begin and end with a drill, in which facilitators made children clap their hands to a particular count. (This component of the programme was taken very seriously by the facilitators, and children were strongly reprimanded for failing to remember this or for asynchronous performance.) Classes also ended with children being made to recite a list of self-affirmations about behaviour and duties that were associated with the 10 life skills (e.g., being polite, showing care and concern for others and accepting responsibility for oneself and one's goals), which was structured in the form of an oath.[36] Practices such as these were reminiscent of other kinds of disciplinarian training (such as that of a religious or military order) that worked upon individuals through shared routines, symbolic performances (such as oath-taking) and codes, in order to discipline them according to its ideology.

Training for life skills facilitators was supposedly provided using a cascade 'train the trainer' model. Life skills facilitators, who already had a master's degree in social work or psychology, were further provided need-based training and an annual three-day training at which they interacted with experts and master trainers. (While Sukumar gave me this information, from the facilitators I got to know that the annual training was mostly only conducted by the MD, Aamir Raza, who is reputed to be a powerful motivational speaker, along with another member of the advisory team of the organization.) The facilitators were also supposedly monitored and evaluated closely, based on the weekly reports and monthly reports they were expected to submit, through appraisals, observations within classrooms and through demonstration classes that they were asked to provide on certain new topics.

---

[36] The full list of self-affirmations about behaviour that children were made to recite is presented in the appendix.

Overall, the LSE programme for government schools seemed to be differently positioned when compared with the programmes offered to the private schools. One observation at a session at a private school in Bengaluru showed how these sessions were also focused on developing socially desirable behaviours (e.g., listening to one's parents, appreciating their contributions and sacrifices, learning to be disciplined from them). However, what seemed specific to the programmes for government schools was how these children and their communities were constructed as socially irresponsible. Topics selected for sessions as well as the classroom transactions constantly referred to a lack of discipline, culture, cleanliness and responsibility in them. Articulating these deficits, programmes then sought to train children to be 'disciplined' as desired by the middle class.

Having presented a detailed description of the programmes, particularly highlighting the rationales that underlie them, in the following chapters, I discuss the nature of classroom pedagogies and transactions. Specifically, I show how, despite being positioned as forms of 'empowerment', they functioned more as disciplinary technologies through which poor and disadvantaged youth in government, aided and charitable schools were shaped according to the neoliberal ethic of self-help. Though programme organizers articulated a vision of developing young people's capacities to critically exert their 'choice', the 'disciplining' aspects of the programme came out strongly through accounts of facilitators such as Nayanika Ramesh (of VYB's Inspire project), who noted that they had to use 'nasty', 'manipulative' NLP techniques to ensure that their programmes changed children to adjust to their circumstances since they could not change the child's social or economic environment.[37] Here, disciplining entailed not just self-introspective change, facilitated through the adoption of experiential pedagogies, but also an internalization of the failures and deficits through which poor and marginalized youth were framed within these schools, by middle class teachers and LSE providers.

Further, disciplining also entailed a subjection of the programmes themselves to the conventional ideologies and practices of schools that

---

[37] Personal communication, 29 March 2013.

overtly lay expectations on students in relation to academic outcomes, behaviour and civic responsibilities. Thus, programmatic goals and practices often appeared to be focused on facilitating conventional discipline in students (i.e., complying with the overt authority and expectations for marks and attendance set by schools), rather than cultivating habits for self-help or regulation. While this can be partly attributed to the co-location and co-option of the programmes within and by the schools, a critical factor for this was also the tacit nature of 'skills' (i.e., attitudes) that LSPs seek to develop, for which organizations struggled to find appropriate indicators to measure success. With funders demanding accountability, and tools to measure life skills (e.g., creative or critical thinking) not sufficient to meet the 'objective' and positivist standards of measurement adopted by evaluation programmes and 'scientific discourses' of evidence-based interventions, organizations were forced to fall back on conventional measures of attendance and pass percentages, that then became the prime targets to achieve.

CHAPTER 5

Life Skills Education as Pedagogies of 'Discipline'

In the previous chapters, I established the genealogy of LSE and described the structural and discursive contexts of their production, circulation, modification and adaptation within the Indian context. Together, the chapters described how life skills have been positioned as a specific set of skills to manage 'everyday' life and succeed despite structural risks and how the absence of life skills has been established as the pre-condition for 'risk'.

Further, the chapters drew attention to the ways in which the discourses of LSE have facilitated various discursive ends of 'government': such as in bringing larger populations of youth, that previously remained outside the 'gaze' of expertise (e.g., educational, clinical, developmental and social–entrepreneurial) under scrutiny, through the adoption of a preventive approach to youth development and the generalization of psycho-remedial interventions to *all*. Discourses of LSE have also served other ends of *government* through the establishment of new norms, cultures and relations to the self, drawn from the middle classes that have uncritically been positioned as the 'merit' for success. Concomitantly, based on this normative understanding of behaviours for success, training for poor and disadvantaged youth to view a whole range of developmental problems—from poverty, educational failure, violence, poor nutrition, hygiene and health—as rooted within individual behavioural and skills deficits has been legitimized. In this manner, LSPs and discourses have facilitated the 'responsiblization' of the marginalized while shifting attention away from class inequalities and structural advantages enjoyed by the middle classes and responsible for their successes, within an intensifying context of neoliberalism.

The current chapter extends this discussion further, by drawing on concrete instances of LSE practice observed within classrooms. Specifically, it draws attention to how regulation and 'disciplining' of personal conduct is enabled by examining the pedagogic formats of LSPs. By 'disciplining', I refer to the ways in which targets of the programme (i.e., students in schools as well as the facilitators, belonging to non-elite backgrounds) were taught to understand and relate to themselves in line with the expectations of various authorities (i.e., schools, teachers, employers, etc.). Attending to the pedagogies of LSE, it elaborates upon the multiple pedagogic components of the LSE format that together facilitate the development of these new relations to the self. It demonstrates how modern pedagogies of progressive education in fact closely resemble the older technologies of pastoral care in producing the desired subject. Historically analysing the relationship of care that is central to both these educational technologies, I aim to show how individuals become subjected to authorities, in the process of subjecting to oneself, within pedagogic encounters of care. Further, I also discuss the underlying dialectical tensions through which the subject of reform is produced within these educational encounters, by paying attention to the contradictory ends of cultivating self-directed individuals with the capacity for independent reason and action; who is, however, also aligned in this process with the ends of governmental reason, through modern, liberal and progressive pedagogies of activity-based and experiential learning of LSE. That is, the chapter attends to the contradictions within liberal formats of pedagogic action and projects of education, such as LSE, that lay claim to the Enlightenment's autonomous subject of reason, and the fundamental objectives of these pedagogic projects that are focused on cultivating the capacities of self-regulation and self-maximization, to fit the conceptions of the subject within (neo)liberalism. In this process, the chapter captures the educational conundrum emerging from the tension between a humanist imaginary of the subject of education as one with the individual abilities for democratic legitimation (humanist liberalism) and, on the other hand, as the individuals with the capacities to foster capitalist accumulation (market liberalism) (Peters & Marshall, 1993). I return to this discussion later, after presenting a more detailed account of the pedagogy of LSE.

5.1. The Structure of the 'Pedagogy of Discipline'

In elaborating further on the 'disciplining' aspects of LSE, I start by drawing attention to how life skills have been described by the Interagency Working Group on Life Skills in Education for All, as 'not just a set of skills', but an 'approach'

> ...for the acquisition of knowledge, and the development of values, attitudes and skills to develop capacities to take control of [one's] own life, to continue learning, to participate fully in society, and to work, through equitable access to appropriate learning and life skills-based education related to specific learning areas. (UNESCO, 2004, p. 5)

Significant to note here is the emphasis laid on 'life skills' as not just a set of hard, technical skills but also attitudes and values, importantly to 'take control' of one's own life. Such a positioning of LSE by influential developmental agencies of the UN make it evident that right from the start LSE has not only been conceived as a pedagogic device to work upon the internal aspects of young people's lives, such as their attitudes and emotions, but also hints at the neoliberal ethic of self-regulation that it seeks to enable among youth. I further show how the pedagogic practices of LSE enable these objectives by unpacking the structure of programmes.

Based on Bandura's (1977) Social Learning Theory and Jessor's Problem Behaviour Theory (Jessor, 2016), the pedagogic structures of LSE emphasize opportunities for experiential learning that are seen as critical to bring about attitudinal and value changes, through an introspection of the self. Underlying these assumptions is a liberal conception of the individual as a rational, self-efficacious subject, capable of learning through observation, imitation and reason. The teaching–learning model (as observed on field, but which were mostly drawn from principles and directions provided by international agencies such as WHO) was conceived as

'having an experience' → reflecting on → changing
the experience behaviour

Central to this learning format is also a 'relationship of care' (Foucault, 1982), both to oneself as well as between the facilitators and children, through which new relationships to the self could be established, in order to bring about behavioural change. The 'relations of care' embedded within the pedagogic format of LSPs were also what differentiated it from other forms of self-disciplining, such as moral or value education. New relationships to the self were established through three main pedagogic practices, namely, by designing opportunities and creating 'safe spaces' for participation and visibilization of the internal aspects of the self; use of language as pedagogy, to establish specific relationships with the self; and through the session structure itself, which specifically affected the body, rhythm and mood. While the programmes observed on field adopted these practices to varying degrees and effects, a close examination of the theory, curricular material and classroom practices showed that this was the general structure of most programmes. Further, I describe each of the elements of the LSE pedagogy and the structure of the classes to demonstrate how the format was critical to regulating youth and cultivating new norms for understanding and relating to the self.

5.1.1. Participation and the Practices of 'Care', Confession and 'Visibilization'

One of the first observations made about the LSPs was the importance paid to establishing 'relationships of care', through which internal aspects of students' selves could be opened up, examined and individual behaviours corrected. To explain the concept of 'relations of care', I draw on Foucault's (1982) conceptualiztion of the novel forms of power through which modern (Western European) states undertook their projects of government. Arguing that this was fundamentally different in its modus operandi from political power, Foucault (1982) showed how this form of governance drew its tools from the techniques of 'pastoral care' used by the church in governing its subjects and keeping its congregation together. That is, highlighting the techniques of personal care and concern for the well-being of individual subjects, ensuring their salvation through pedagogic techniques of confession and self-disciplining to purge their sins, Foucault (1982) states that the church was able to 'visibilize' the innermost aspects of people's lives and thereby gain greater control over them. Pointing to similar practices adopted by modern states through the establishment of institutions such as prisons, juvenile homes, the apparatus of law and, most importantly, compulsory schooling, Foucault (1977; 1980) and other Foucauldian scholars such as Nikolas Rose (1999) and Ian Hunter (1996) have pointed to how control and regulation have taken the form of a 'pedagogy of care' that promotes self-inspection, visibilization and correction.

An important distinction that Foucault made, however, in elaborating upon these 'pedagogies of care' was in noting how these functioned as modes of subjectivation, as opposed to the practices of 'taking care of oneself', practised in antiquity that subjected individuals to him/herself. Through a detailed analysis of classical texts in his work on *The Hermeneutics of the Subject*, Foucault (2005) argued that, in ancient times, the two principles of 'knowing oneself' (*gnothi seauton*) and 'care for oneself' (*epimeleia seauton*) were inextricably linked in the Greek and Roman cultures. Foucault points out that in the first and second centuries AD, caring for oneself, retreating internally was in service of arriving at a greater knowledge of the self, to be fundamentally transformed, achieving an ethical self, which was the site of production of subjectivity. With later Christianity and particularly since the Cartesian moment, Foucault has explained how the precept of 'care for the self' was delinked from the emphasis on cultivating knowledge of the self, thus replacing the 'subject of right action' of antiquity with the 'subject of true knowledge' of the modern West (Gros, 2005). This disconnect in the practices of the self is important to note. The delinking of the two functions of care and knowledge in the modern interpretation of the subject, as I will show, has also interpellated frameworks of psychology and, particularly LSE, despite overt claims regarding LSE as empowering techniques that allow the subject to 'care for him/herself'. The delinking of care of the self from knowledge of the self is also what enables the 'disciplining' effects of the programmes, through which subjects are guided to undertake behavioural changes to meet certain ends, without an accompanying self-transformation.

I argue that though, structurally, pedagogic formats of programmes such as LSE appear as modern developmental techniques in the context of the 21st century, they in fact resemble practices of Christian pastoral care. Advocated by states, international developmental agencies, NGOs and corporate organizations, LSE appear to offer a similar kind of protection for 'risks', such as poverty, by recasting 'salvation' as a practice of gaining training and development of life skills. Below, I describe some of these key elements through which life skills classes are structured in similar ways as Christian confessional practices, allowing for internal aspects of the self to be revealed and corrected.

'Safe space': Fundamental to the pedagogy of LSE was the opening up of individuals, in order to make visible the internal aspects of their self that had to be corrected, in order to align them in line with the expectation of authorities. Encouragement to individuals to open up further required the creation of a 'safe space' similar to a confessional. The idea of a 'safe space' entailed not just physical safety but a psychological space wherein participants would not feel threatened and could, therefore, express their thoughts, beliefs and values without the fear of being judged.

In creating this safe space some organizations, such as IP, invested greatly in practices such as having the facilitator engage in personal conversations with participants, spend additional time outside the classroom in discussing their lives and building a rapport, work actively at establishing a non-authoritarian environment within the classroom and build community trust (i.e., trust within the group in which reflection was to take place) through shared goals and agreements for participation. In establishing a closed community of trust, IP even spent the first session of their programme in collectively thinking of the agreements for participation and putting these up on charts or white boards that were displayed throughout the sessions. The agreements included commitments from participants to 'participate fully', to overcome inhibition, 'to not laugh or put down others, or oneself', to put one's phone away and agree to not use it through the session and so on. (Some of these commitments were even voluntarily initiated by the participants themselves with a little encouragement from the facilitator.) Facilitators would often draw attention to these agreements, if during sessions they found participants to be reluctant to participate or not showing interest.

Experiencing skills: In addition to the creation of this space, a second distinct pedagogic marker of the programmes was the creation of a space for participation, for individuals to gain active experience. Experience was central to gain insights into one's behaviour and thoughts 'in-the-moment', and to gain knowledge of how to apply a 'skill' (e.g., decision-making) or behaviour (e.g., being empathetic). Thus, the programmes were meant to engage each individual in the process of applying the skill/demonstrating the behaviour through the medium of an activity (e.g., a game involving decision-making, artwork which could provide opportunities to feel certain emotions).

Reflection. The final step within the programmes, following participation in activity, was to have a deep, introspective discussion about what the activity led the participants to realize. This discussion was to be guided by the facilitator in a manner that would allow participants to explore different aspects of their self. As will be further discussed below, these latter two elements of participation and reflection were the key technologies of 'pastoral care' and 'confession', in that they served to render individuals 'visible' and, thus, make it possible to apply techniques of correction to them.

LSPs and the pedagogy of 'visibilization': Experiential learning practices made 'visible' behaviours, movements, gestures and expressions, as well as internal processes of thoughts, feelings, beliefs and values. As an illustration, below, I present an account of a life skills class observed for eighth standard students of an aided Tamil medium school in east Bengaluru.[1]

During this session, children played a game called 'Where's my monkey?' that was facilitated by Bharath (a facilitator from IP). In the activity, one member of the group (the 'denner') placed a bottle (the 'monkey') behind his/her back (while he/she faced the wall). The task for the remaining members of the group was to start quietly approaching the individual from a point marked as the 'start line', retrieve the bottle without the knowledge of the 'denner' and return safely to the start line. If any child was caught by the 'denner' during this process, then he/she would have to take the position of the 'denner'.

While children made many attempts to retrieve the bottle without getting caught, on repeated trials they were unsuccessful at this. During reflection, Bharath asked the children to think of why they had been 'unsuccessful'. Questioning the strategies used by them, he managed to draw attention to their behaviours of rushing forward, making noise, lacking a plan to retrieve the bottle, lacking teamwork and so on as reasons for this 'failure'. Thus, behaviours revealed during performance became valuable sources of information about the self with which Bharath was then able to guide children's behaviours towards important ends, such as learning to control one's excitement, learning to speak softly, learning to work in a team and so on.

Visible, physical aspects of behaviour was just one level at which programmes operated on individuals. On other occasions, activities designed were even able to make visible internal thoughts, emotions and beliefs. For example, during another class observed at the same school,[2] children were engaged in an activity called 'Portraiture', in which they were asked to lie down (face up) on a large sheet of chart paper, with their arms and legs spread out, so that another child could trace them out on the sheet. Following this, each child (whose

---

[1] The class observed was conducted on 15 January 2012, by IP.
[2] The class observed was conducted on 18 December 2012, by IP.

portraiture had been made on the sheet) had to write about themselves on it. While right from the beginning, it was observed that many girls in the class were uncomfortable performing this activity (since they felt 'exposed' lying on the sheet with their arms and legs spread out, in front of the boys in the class), these strong emotions linked to issues of body image, social conventions and gender norms, and the self came out most strongly in Radhika's case. Observing the portraiture made by her friend of her, Radhika felt that the picture was making fun of her and started crying. In this manner, her internal feelings and beliefs linked to her sense of identity were revealed during the course of the activity.

What was significant about these sessions was how, once visibilized, facilitators then modified the behaviours to suit normative expectations of schooling or the larger patriarchal society, as I will show with the next illustration. During this session,[3] an activity called 'Teasing Tableau' was conducted by Bharath, in which children discussed and enacted different instances of eve-teasing. During reflection, children were asked how they would face such challenges of eve-teasing. After listening to the various responses given by the children (e.g., 'scold them', 'tell my mother', 'ignore them', 'appeal to them to treat us as their own sisters and mothers'), Bharath presented these various options to the class in order to have them evaluate the responses in terms of their appropriateness. In the case of the response of scolding eve-teasers, only one girl, Deepika, originally from north Karnataka, argued in favour of this. Stating that girls too have feelings and would feel angry, she asked why they shouldn't get angry if teased. While not explicitly rejecting this response, Bharath picked up this response and put it to other children for suggestions, asking them if this was appropriate. Questioning this response multiple times, encouraging and vigorously nodding his head in response to those who stated that this was wrong as it would worsen the situation, Bharath seemed to indirectly establish the response as inappropriate. While allowing the conversation to focus on its negative effects, he never steered the discussion towards the sense of frustration felt by Deepika on having

[3] Observed on 27 November 2012.

to face these instances, or towards solutions that could make her feel more empowered in such situations. Rather, through the discussion, he seemed to establish the responses that are normatively considered appropriate for girls, such as walking away or avoiding these situations of confrontation. Thus, in having made her thoughts and emotions visible, he was able to draw attention to how this linked to behaviour and the consequences of it, thereby creating an opportunity within the classroom to question, challenge, interrogate and correct even the innermost aspects of the students' selves in accordance with dominant expectations for it.

This last instance is a telling example of both how programmes sought to discipline students externally, without any underlying transformation in beliefs or attitudes, as well as how the programmes, rather than encouraging students to be empowered to care for oneself, expected their individual reason and action to be aligned with dominant social reason and expectations for young people, particularly occupying marginal positions in society. As Deepika's illustration shows, the programmes aimed to give students a new way of understanding and relating to themselves that were often not aligned with their self-interests and, instead, produced an 'objective' knowledge of the self that was seen as sufficient data to invoke behavioural change. As I will discuss further, the aim appeared to be of having students identify and acknowledge the external goals set by authorities for their behaviours, repeat these and reproduce these on tests, assessments or classroom examination of learning. But before describing this further, I first turn to two other elements of the pedagogic process—role of language and structure of activities to modulate mood, rhythm and body.

5.1.2. Role of Language within the Programmes

In addition to these practices of 'visibilization', programme design included language in specific ways, so as to have effects on behaviour. Foucault (2005), and other Foucauldian scholars, such as Thomas Popkewitz (1998), have pointed to the role of language in being more than just a medium of communication and representation, and have sought to show how the norms of language construction play a constitutive role in the creation of identities. Similarly pointing to the constitutive effects of language, I try to show how language use within the curriculum was meant to have certain performative effects on the subjects on field.

While LSE is supposedly value-neutral in its approach, unlike value or moral education, that consist of specific propositional knowledge of 'good', 'bad', 'right' and 'wrong', it was through metaphoric and metonymic usage of language that such normative understanding of behaviour was established. I discuss this further, drawing attention to three specific ways in which language was used within the programmes.

Language use and the enablement of ideas about the self: This was more evident in the curriculum and practices of IP, compared to the other two organizations. IP used language in more strategic and pedagogically impactful ways than the other organizations. Unlike the other organizations, IP's curriculum not only had a more defined structure but also made use of linguistic devices, such as metaphors and other verbal and non-verbal cues in deeply psychological ways to draw attention to the self. (As will be discussed later, this also led to certain problems, since cultural differences in the use and understanding of language proved to be one of the main hurdles for the translation of these programmes into practice.)

For example, there were several metaphorical devices, such as 'safe space' and personifications, such as 'voice of doubt', 'creative spirit', etc., that were used in the course of the programmes, in order to reconstitute inner emotional, affective and cognitive states and behaviours that could not be easily verbalized or visibilized. Taking 'safe space' as a case in point, it can be seen how the effort within the programme was to assure more than physical safety and develop psychological conditions of safety through the affective labour of facilitators conducting the programmes within the classrooms. In communicating to the facilitators the idea of how to structure the classroom to allow for maximum self-visibilization and confession by students, the metaphorical language of 'safe space' was used to indicate the need to create a classroom wherein children would be comfortable, active, vocal and unafraid of authority. A sense of the hard-to-explain psychological characteristics of such a classroom was sought to be given to the facilitators through an image—qualifying the image of 'space' with the word safe, what was attempted was to evoke visceral memories of a place in which one felt at home and comfortable. The transfiguration of the idea of space as a psychological state of care and protection was thus achieved through the discursive use of language. Through an extended discussion during training, on facilitators' own sense of psychological and emotional comfort experienced during training, attention was drawn to a broader idea of 'space' as an extended relation between the bodies and the environment, and the concept of 'safety' as a layered process, ranging from physical comfort to psychological and mental comfort. Using the metaphor of the safe space, facilitators' attention was turned towards their own personal resources of caring, understanding, supporting, being trustworthy and so on, through which such a space could be produced.

While establishing 'safe space' as an aspect of the facilitator's work, produced through his/her affective labour, other aspects of the facilitators' selves were also brought under scrutiny through the use of language. Capturing the facilitator's performance as a relationship with his/her 'creative spirit', IP sought to increase and improve facilitators' performances through exercises that engaged them with their 'creative spirit'. Thus, embodying abstract aspects of performance (such as creativity, enterprise, productivity) as an animate being, inside of one's self and to be taken care of, facilitators were encouraged to have a conversation with, request support from, discuss misgivings and receive reassurance from the 'creative spirit'. The creative spirit was embodied as a small voice within themselves. Through such personifications of creativity, a culture of 'self-work' was established through which facilitators could be made constantly responsible for their performances, upon which the success of the programmes rested. During training, facilitators were made to close their eyes, enter a zone of introspection and practice speaking with this 'voice' or the 'creative spirit', in order to derive guidance and support from it—a practice they were expected to fall back upon through the course of the academic year.

Further, doubts regarding performance, creative blocks and inhibitions to performance were also symbolized as a 'tiny nagging voice at the back of the head' (the language of which closely resembled the ideas of a 'nagging doubt' or 'nagging pain', both of which are best to get rid of). Further, the use of the word 'tiny' itself seemed to give an appearance of something that could be done away with easily. Supporting this image of non-creativity or non-performance as 'pain', the group was encouraged to collectively 'pull out' this 'tiny nagging voice', by physically reaching out to the back of their necks and throwing it away, during training. Converting aspects of the self that may have otherwise remained unacknowledged or unadmitted into a level of concrete action, through these metonymic devices that allowed it to be first verbalized and then performed, IP attempted to powerfully impact facilitators' beliefs in their own self and abilities.

Language use, encouraging participation: In addition to the use of language to condition behaviour, language was also used as a medium to ensure specific kinds of involvement to bring behavioural change. For example, as explained earlier, the introductory session of IP's training programme for children and adults (such as teachers, facilitators and volunteers) was called 'Goals and Agreements'. The title of the session, along with the activity that was undertaken during the session was mainly designed to enforce a sense of commitment on participants to engage fully and in an uninhibited manner, so that individual behaviours and intentions could be revealed during the course of the activities. Thus, the session was structured as a 45-minute process of jointly evolving guidelines on how to participate (by facilitators and participants). Through a discussion around the need to build a supportive community, by ensuring not to put oneself or others down, on having fun and letting go of inhibitions, the aim was to build an atmosphere in which individuals would open up. In presenting these preconditions or requirements for participation in the programmes as a set of 'goals and agreements', the primary effect sought to be achieved through the session seemed to be one of establishing an air of formality of contract in relation to participation and create a sense of obligation on the individual to honour the contract by remaining open and willing to behavioural change.

Further, adding a performative end to this heavy discussion, in order to strengthen the obligation to the goals further, IP had also instituted a practice called Sealing the Deal, in which participants were required to stand in a circle, with one hand extended out in front of them and the other hand raised over their head. Upon having finalized and accepted the goals and agreements for the sessions, they were asked to, jointly, bring down the raised hand in a clap to 'seal the deal'. This terminology and performance, used at the beginning of a life skills course, to set the atmosphere and expectations from participants through the course of the programme, had a specific role to play. As mentioned in the trainer's manual, it was meant to steer the group away from the need for external 'punishments, and towards ways of working together, supporting each other, and taking responsibility for themselves and each other',[4] for bringing about behaviour change. Further, reinforcing this point about replacing external disciplining strategies with self-discipline in children, Christiana Munro, the international curriculum expert for IP, who had designed the curriculum, noted that the session on 'Goals and Agreements' was essential; since in its absence, the programmes would 'just bleed into school'.[5]

Language use and behavioural reinforcement: In addition to using language in setting the conditions for performance during the sessions, IP also used language as a form of reinforcement to bring about behavioural change. Using a format called TLC praise (tell it; label it; celebrate it), facilitators were asked to cultivate appropriate behaviours in children using the following steps: first, by identifying the behaviour to be praised and *stating or telling* it (e.g., X came early to class today and set the table along with the facilitator); second, by giving this behaviour a *name* or '*labelling*

---

[4] As given in IP's arts-based curriculum and trainer's manual (2012, p. 13).
[5] As stated by Christiana during a curriculum feedback session with the facilitators, on 18 October 2012.

it' (e.g., so this makes X 'helpful'); and third, by using a distinct format of appreciation to *celebrate it* (i.e., to make it special and to think of something different from mundane options such as clapping. This could be giving the child a hug or making a 'whooping' sound indicating praise, etc.).

What was significant about this practice of reinforcement was the emphasis laid on clearly stating or verbalizing the behaviour and labelling it. Thus, the label made the particular quality/characteristic of the child a visible feature by which he/she would be recognized by others and would recognize himself/herself. This practice, then, 'subjected' individuals to specific identities, to which s/he was obligated to live up to.

Language as activities: Finally, language-based activities were also an important feature of IP's curriculum, through which behaviour change could be ensured. To give an example of how language was used as part of activities to condition behaviour, I give the example of a warm-up game called 'Yes and…', played at the beginning of a session on teamwork. In this warm-up activity, participants had to build a story, with each participant adding a line at a time to build the story. After each person had made his/her statement, the next member of the group added his/her line after having affirmed the statement made by the person before (e.g., Participant 1: 'Today it rained so heavily that I could not go to school.' Participant 2: 'Yes and I played football.').

As per the trainer's manual notes, the point of the activity was to encourage group work through acceptance of others' idea, even when one did not agree with it. This point was also validated by Christiana, during the aforementioned curriculum feedback session. The point of the activity appeared to be to train children in the standards of politeness and social decorum that can be observed within bourgeoisie spaces (e.g., being amiable, even when not in agreement; refer Ainley & Corbett, 1994).

That these strategic patterns of language use in these activities could have certain material effects on individual's selves and beliefs, if understood, became amply evident through instances when facilitators and children were unable to access the cultural registers of meaning involved in such practices. While the use of 'Yes and...', in the activity, was to function as a conjunction or as merely an acknowledgement of the other's position (indicating socially approved conventions for turn-taking and polite conversation, even under conditions of disagreement), a translation of this game into Kannada created significant problems for children and facilitators. While one may acknowledge the other's position without accepting it as a truth claim with the use of 'Yes and...' in English, the facilitators' conversion of the term in Kannada to *Houdu matte...* created dissonances; since, as they noted, this translation did not work and seemed odd to the context. To explain why this was so, I present the following illustrative example in Kannada:

Participant 1: *Ivattu jōraagi maLe bandiruva kaaraNa naanu shaalege hōgakke aagalilla.* (Today, because it rained heavily, I could not go to school.)

Participant 2: *Houdu, matte, naanu ivattu football aadide.* (Yes and I played football today.)

The real problem was that *Houdu matte...* had very different implications when compared with 'Yes and...', since the use of the term *houdu* implies a verification, rather than mere acknowledgement, in Kannada. A suitable translation that may have caused less cognitive dissonance for the facilitators, would have been the use of *seri* ('OK'), which would have implied an acknowledgement of the speaker's statement, while still providing scope for disagreement, or for introducing a new independent clause or statement that need not have to follow from the former. However, the facilitators' inappropriate translation of the term was indicative of the lack of access to the middle-class cultural codes of polite conversation that was sought to be taught through the activity and the lack of resonance this had with experiences in their own life worlds.

Further, the fact that these subtle changes in translation could have very different effects on speakers and listeners is also telling of the effects of linguistic structures and rules of language (not just the semantics of it) on behaviour, as noted by Foucault (2005) and

Popkewitz (1998). This, therefore, also caused a sense of dissonance for the facilitators, who were unable to understand the goal of the activity and translated it using inadequate syntactic structures in Kannada.

5.1.3. Modulation of Body Rhythm, Mood and Behaviour

Having discussed the role of language as a key pedagogic device in LSPs (rather than as just a medium of communication), a final pedagogic device within LSPs that served to shape the self was the planning of session structures in definite ways, so as to regulate body rhythms, moods and behaviours. Specific tasks, such as 'check-in', 'check-out', 'warm-up' and 'closing', that were included in IP's curriculum had the function of regulating participants' mood and tempo. This became apparent in the discussions observed between facilitators and master trainers such as Christiana, who explained the role of these sub-tasks included in the session plan. For example, when Arvind, a facilitator, told Christiana at the curriculum feedback session that he did not know what to expect as answers (and, therefore, did not understand what was to be learnt) from 'check-out' questions, Christiana responded by stating, 'That is not what check-out is for. Children should learn messages during reflection and warm-up.' In response to his question about what a 'check-out' question does, she stated that it was for children to take back whatever they personally felt like taking, but added (referring to the particular session that was being discussed), 'In this case, because they have been so wild in activity,[6] the check-out lets them leave quietly. We don't want them to go to teachers and parents wild. It lets them become quiet.' Thus, Christiana explained to the group that the role of the check-in and check-out activity was to condition group dynamics and the energy level of the group.

---

[6] The activity that Christiana was referring to was a painting exercise called 'Water Colour Monsters' that children generally enjoyed very much. In this, children created abstract shapes using water colours and tried to imagine pictures of monsters in it. This activity was done with fourth and fifth standard students.

As was explained in IP's facilitators' handbooks and during training and feedback sessions, each component of the lesson plan had a specific role to play. While 'check-in' and 'check-out' were conducted in order to gauge the mood of the classroom or close the session on a particular note respectively,[7] components such as 'Goals and Agreements' (that were to be discussed at the beginning of every class) were used to shift children's orientation within the classroom towards practices of participative learning and self-introspection, drawing their attention and motivation to be committed to a process of self-directed change (which was in contrast with the school culture of learning). The 'warm-up' activity that followed this (involving a short game or activity) was meant to build up energy, interest and enthusiasm for the main activity, which was then followed up by a closing activity that would, once again, calm down the excitement generated during the course of the activity. As Christiana made it clear ('We don't want them to go to teachers and parents wild'), despite being participative and activity-based programmes that held different conceptions of learning, the programme nevertheless sought to align behaviours and moods with what would be considered appropriate at school and home (i.e., being disciplined, quiet, calm, less active or fidgety and so on).

Similarly, other organizations such as VYB also sought to regulate behaviour by prescribing the mood states or feelings students were to be left in at the end of each session. For example, for the session on self-awareness, the curricular document stated that the aim was to 'leave the group in a state of thought or contemplation and also feeling happy about the rolls [sic] we play in our lives.'[8] The module on creativity instructed facilitators to 'leave the student in a state of high energy with a sense of achievement that they can also have so

---

[7] Check-in and check-out were short activities conducted at the beginning and closing of every session, consisting of simple questions about personal preferences, current mood states or specific experiences that were to be answered with a single word or short phrase.

[8] From VYB's curriculum document titled 'SS_ Content _Final Version_Class VIII, C08_S04_Awareness of Self' (2010, p. 1).

many ideas.'[9] Thus, by associating feelings such as happiness with an awareness of one's roles, the pedagogic structures of the programme also sought to associate the expected changes in ways of being and behaving, with specific mood states and emotions, thus targeting changes at a bodily level.

As can be seen from the preceding discussion, 'disciplining' through LSE was layered, targeting overt and covert aspects of the self and through the use of multiple pedagogic techniques and practices that were tacit and explicit. Targets of the programmes—students at the government and aided schools, as well as the facilitators—were subjected individually, and at multiple levels, through engagement of thoughts, feelings, emotions and beliefs to behaviours and practices complying with the ends of 'governmental' expectations. These expectations, as observations of the programmes showed, were in fact contradictory for students to be compliant with the hierarchical cultures of schooling and social norms, as well as for students to develop a self-regulatory capacity and responsibility, aligning them with the expectations of the enterprise culture of neoliberalism (Gooptu, 2013). Interestingly, within the site of the LSPs, the two ends appeared to come together, with gaining greater knowledge and control of the self linked to learning to be responsible for one's behaviour in relation to certain traditional–patriarchal norms, such as accepting and being deferent to adult authority, complying with school expectations for individual performance and even shaping oneself in accordance with gender norms.

Explaining this conjoinment of enterprise culture and continued patriarchal cultures in a different context as the coming together of neoliberalism and neoconservatism, Ruddick (2007) has drawn attention to how governmental reason produces a moral imperative upon youth to skilfully manage and navigate the landscape of structural inequalities and risks in new ways. Young people are expected to respond within these conditions not just in material ways but also through affective adjustments and affective reworking of their subjectivities

---

[9] From SS_Content_Final Version_Class IX, C09_S01_All Are Creative (2010, p. 1).

(Cairns, 2013). Interventions such as LSE play an important role in guiding youth to remake themselves along these lines. Similarly, it is also important to note how these liberal pedagogies within the Indian context facilitate self-understanding and choices in line with patriarchal structures of caste, class and gender, as will be shown in the next chapter. Within the progressive context of the LSE classroom, individuals' relationships to oneself and the larger sociopolitical structures of governance is first brought to one's awareness (Fendler, 1998) and then worked upon to transform an ethical and moral understanding and care for the self and to develop self-knowledge and action in accordance with normative expectations and reasons of markets and social norms. In the following chapter, I describe the kinds of subjectivities that are produced within the Indian context as a result of this second kind of self-development.

CHAPTER 6

Ends of Discipline
Curricular Transactions and Social Reproduction of Identities

The story of 'Warm Fuzzies' and 'Cold Pricklies'[1]

A long time ago, there was once a kingdom in which all people had one good practice. Whenever they met each other, they would put their hands into a small bag and take out an object, which they would hand over to the other person first, and only then come to the point of their visit or business. This object was called 'Warm Fuzzy'. On receiving this object, the receiver would immediately start feeling a warm, tingling sensation of happiness. Everyone had a 'Warm Fuzzy' to exchange. So, suppose I was angry, and I came to meet you, I would give you a 'Warm Fuzzy', and take a 'Warm Fuzzy' from you. Then both of us would have a warm sensation and my anger would have disappeared. That's why everyone was happy in this land.

One day, a witch called Henrietta, happened to fly over the land. Seeing everyone so happy in the land, she resented it. So, she decided to do something devious. She disguised herself, and came down to the land. There, she met an old woman named Bretalina.

---

[1] A story related at a life skills session conducted by Dr Chandrika Bavegadi at a government high school in south Bengaluru (on 11 February 2012).

On seeing her, Bretlina immediately took out her 'Warm Fuzzy' and gave it to her, as was the custom of the land, when greeting someone. But Henrietta took away Bretlina's 'Warm Fuzzy' and did not give anything in return. She misled Bretalina by explaining to her that there was a shortage of 'Warm Fuzzies' in the land, and advised her to keep them for herself. Thus, spreading the word across the land, Henrietta brought unhappiness to the land.

Instead of spreading 'Warm Fuzzies', people of the land started spreading 'Cold Pricklies.' When someone came or visited them, they would turn their faces, instead of reciprocating and greeting the person. They would be selfish and unkind all the time with each other. This continued until the time that a little girl from the land started thinking about what was happening. She understood that people had been misled and explained to everyone that they could never run out of 'Warm Fuzzies', since on giving one they would always get one in return. In this way she returned the lost peace and happiness to the land.

In the previous chapter, I considered the specific pedagogic devices applied within LSE classrooms to 'visibilize' the self and bring one's behaviours under voluntary control, and through this process, under the control of authorities. In this chapter, I discuss how classroom transactions were sites within which targets of the programme (i.e., students as well as the facilitators conducting the programmes) were given to understand their selves in specific ways, and then discuss the specific ends to which their behaviours were sought to be shaped.

6.1. Classroom Transactions, Enabling a Specific View of the Self

In the vignette given above, the story of 'Warm Fuzzies, Cold Pricklies' related by Dr Chandrika Bavegadi, an independent psychologist and life skills trainer, to a class of ninth standard students is given. The story, which was meant to teach children about the use of 'positive strokes' (i.e., ways of enhancing self-esteem), was used by Dr Bavegadi to draw her students' attention to a range of social expectations for individual behaviour. These expectations included middle class social conventions of polite communication, which demanded the use of words such as 'good morning' and 'thank you'; parental and school expectations from students to take greater responsibility towards academics by self-regulating leisure activities such as television viewing; expectations for greater participation in domestic responsibilities by families and social expectations within and outside school, for the regulation of sexual behaviours.

Stating that the 'Eighth and ninth standards are an age of 'Whys' and 'I'', she pointed out to the students of a government high school in south Bengaluru that students only desired 'Warm Fuzzies' during this age. Presenting television as one of the 'Warm Fuzzies' that students desire, she asked them to think of the following situation: 'If I see T.V. today, what will happen tomorrow? I won't tell you to study, but you think and decide.'[2] Similarly, drawing their attention to the topic of sexual attraction (and presenting it as a 'Warm Fuzzy'), she told them, 'In this age there will be boy-girl attraction, but the problem is the consequences.' Pointing out that every choice has consequences, she asked them, 'Why don't we use our choice with respect to this?' Children responded in a chorus, stating it was because they don't think about these consequences. She then summed up the discussion stating, 'Because like T.V., it gives us immediate pleasure, so we don't think.' The result, she argued, was 'trouble, trouble tomorrow'.

That LSPs were about drawing attention to specific behaviours in order to change them, rather than about 'skills', was unmistakable from repeated observations of classroom transactions. Activities and reflective exercises for students to engage with their thoughts, beliefs and actions to bring about self-directed changes were largely conducted in a tokenistic manner, as the session with Dr Bavegadi shows, with the outcomes of such reflections pre-given to students in the forms of rhetorical questions, advice, instruction, tone and intonation of speech, gestures and body language. In some cases, despite engaging students in activities and encouraging students to respond to questions around their behaviours, facilitators also summarized the 'right' behaviours to

---

[2] What could be seen here was how 'Warm Fuzzies', which was a term used to signify forms of self-reinforcements to increase one's self-esteem, were differently interpreted within the session to imply hedonistic behaviours.

be learnt from the exercise. An example of this was a seen during a session conducted by Gautam, a facilitator from IP, at the aided minority Tamil medium school in east Bengaluru. After playing a game called the 'Yes game' with students, in which one child must find an object hidden by the rest of the group, by following the cues given by the group, Gautam discussed with students the lessons learnt from the activity. After eliciting responses from students regarding what they had liked and disliked about the game, he concluded the session by drawing students' attention to the following point:

> In the 'yes game', if you tell the child searching for the object the wrong route he can't reach the goal. In the same way only if we follow our parents and teachers, we will be able to reach our goals. We have to listen to elders and teachers. Otherwise you will go off on the wrong path.[3]

As evident from Gautam's summary of the activity, children were not even offered an opportunity to reflect about the lessons they might have gained from the activity. Rather than listening to student's voices and interpretation of the activity, Gautam drew out the lessons to be learnt through the activity, reinforcing certain normative expectations placed culturally (both, through the school culture, as well as the larger social-authoritarian culture of Indian society)[4] upon young people, in relation to their agencies and in accepting the authority of adults and teachers.

In another session, Vrinda, a facilitator from MFCL, did away with the reflection wholly and instead used the session to identify students' behaviours and how this would lead them to success or failure.

---

[3] Classroom observations made on 17 February 2012.

[4] See Saraswathi and Pai (1997) for a discussion of ethno-theories of parenting in Hindu society. While there is not much literature on parenting among Muslim families of India, Harriet Becher's (2008) work on south Asian families' parenting practices, and Hem Borker's (2018) work on Muslim girls' education, shows how religion gains significance in parenting practices and expectations for children's behaviours to be shaped in accordance with the principles of Islam and through obedience and respect for elders' authority.

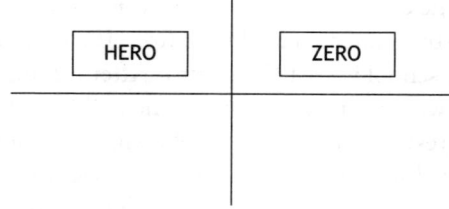

Figure 6.1 *'Heroes' and 'Zeros'*
Source: Maithreyi, 2015.

Reprimanding ninth standard students of a composite government school in north Bengaluru for making noise in her class, Vrinda drew the picture given above (Figure 6.1) on the board.

Pointing to the two columns respectively, she told the class that those who keep making fun in class, tease and fight with others, create trouble or commotion will all become 'zero', while those who take care of their homework, finish their classwork, stay quiet, mind their own business will all become 'heroes' in the end.[5] Other sessions by Vrinda and her colleagues were also similarly fashioned, with the first few minutes of the class focused on playing games as an end in themselves and a second longer section designed to advice students on how to be and behave.

Descriptions and expectations of individuals, rather than the activities and reflections, became the primary focus of sessions. Specifically, as the examples of Dr Bavegadi's, Gautam's and Vrinda's classes show, pedagogic transactions were also structured to first construct learners' identities as 'broken' and needing to be 'fixed' (Butterwick & Benjamin, 2006). Making a note about LSE, social skills and employability programmes in general, critical scholars such as Butterwick and Benjamin (2006) and Ainley and Corbett (1994) have drawn attention to how these psycho-educational interventions are designed so as to position learner identities as wanting, so that they can be guided by

---

[5] Classroom observations made at a government high school in north Bengaluru (22 November 2012).

'experts' to be remade in specific ways. Further, they have pointed to how measures for behaviours and identities of marginalized youth within these programmes are always drawn from Western middle-class norms and embed a capitalistic orientation but are presented as supposedly neutral and universal. As Ainley and Corbett (1994, p. 367) have argued, these norms then expect individuals to 'make good use of their time, to get on with other people, to present themselves well, to be responsible, to stay solvent and to cope in the most normal circumstances,' all of which were also expectations placed on students and lower middle-class facilitators within my field sites, '...when the 'normal' circumstances are those of poverty, homelessness, domestic instability and high local youth unemployment'.

In a similar fashion, disregarding the contexts from which young people at these government and low-cost schools came from (described in detail in Chapter 3), they were constructed within sessions as impulsive, hedonistic and irresponsible. As Gautam's and Dr Bavegadi's sessions, described before, showed, children were seen as incapable of planning for their futures, particularly in relation to education and employment. In the facilitators' narratives, this was equated with a lack of similar kinds of investments made by the children and their families towards education, as seen within middle-class families. (This 'lack' was both with respect to the material and affective forms in which investments in education had to be demonstrated, by being interested, persistence, persevering and planning towards successful educational outcomes.) Further, the commitment to education also had to be demonstrated by adopting the middle class' strategies and behaviours to secure education and future employment. (See also Chapter 4 for more detailed accounts of how organizational accounts framed students in these government and low-cost schools as at risk for educational failure, dropout and unemployment.) While facilitators such as Dr Bavegadi constructed students as given to pleasures such as television viewing and sexual attractions, as an indicator of this, others such as Vrinda would reprimand them for their appearance, questioning why they could not take the trouble of spending rupees five to wash their clothes and come neatly to school. All of these behaviours together were positioned as examples to show how students and their families showed little interest in schooling and did not understand the value of education.

Along with academic values, personal cultures of the non-elite students and facilitators also came under review within programme spaces. Teachers within the schools also presented deficit accounts of students' personal selves, particularly pointing to the 'culture of poverty' that they came from; wherein parents had no time to teach them 'life skills' unlike within middle-class homes. For example, Sindhupriya, a teacher from the Tamil minority school in east Bengaluru explained, the students in her school needed LSE to learn manners, like how to give respect, to lead life and learn good from bad. Another English and crafts teacher, Suma, from a government high school in south Bengaluru, argued that middle-class parents teach their children 'moral values', which is lacking in the students of these government schools, because of which LSE was important. Thus, students and their families were not just positioned as behaviourally and academically deficient, but also morally deficient, and LSE was seen as necessary to compensate for all of this.

As these various accounts also show, learning to be gained from the LSPs were largely cultural, drawing upon middle-class values and norms for behaviour. In fact, the emphasis on learning middle-class behaviours was nowhere more significantly highlighted than in the trainings organized for facilitators, most of whom also belonged to non-elite social backgrounds as the children. To provide just one example of this, further I describe one occasion where I was able to observe this cultural disciplining of facilitators.

In this incident that took place during a two-day training programme facilitated by IP's international curriculum and training expert, Christiana Munro, a theatre-improvisation activity was underway. The activity involved having two members of the group start the task by performing an act or scene, which was to then be extended, modified or changed by other members of the group, who would take turns replacing one actor at a time. Thus, the activity essentially involved a situation of collaboration, interpretation, teamwork and creative extension through which the impromptu skit could be moved forward.

During one such round of the activity, two facilitators (Dhanush and Gautam) started the act by pretending to be two children playing cricket. This was then modified by another facilitator (Nandini), who replaced one of the 'children' as a teacher reprimanding the child for playing cricket during class time. Another facilitator (John) replaced the other 'child', playing the teacher's husband, ordering her to cook food. Finally, Jishnu, a new recruit to IP, replaced the 'wife', acting as the 'husband's employer at a hotel, ordering him to serve the prepared food.

While the performance took on the manner of a slapstick comedy and had the audience laughing at how the actors had managed to outwit each other, Christiana and some other middle-class members of the group reprimanded the actors for 'putting each other down'. In response, facilitators John and Dhanush tried to explain to them that everyone had enjoyed the performance. They further tried to argue that none of the actors themselves had felt insulted because of the rapport and close camaraderie shared amongst themselves, which allowed them to take such licenses with each other. However, Christiana intervened here stating that even though they had enjoyed themselves during the performance, some of them, such as Nandini, may have been unconsciously hurt in this process. She argued that Nandini may think about this more deeply when she went back home and further stated, 'There are other reasons why we do theatre than to make jokes.' Pointing to another act in which a middle-class, female volunteer had added to an ongoing scene by tying a *rakhi*[6] to the other actor, who was a lower-class male facilitator, Christiana provided this as an example of personal transformation that was the goal meant to be achieved through these activities.

Significant to note here is how an understanding of personal relationships among the facilitators was sought to be corrected,

---

[6] *Rakhi* is an amulet or band tied by sisters onto their brothers' wrists in some communities in India. The band symbolizes their bond of love, as well as the expectations of protection by the sister and the commitment made by the brother to uphold this. The tradition was largely practised in north India, though in contemporary times it has become a popular cultural festival practised commonly across many communities and religions in the north and south.

without attention to intra- and inter-class differences in understanding of relationships. Rather than focusing on a structural critique of power within patriarchal relationships (e.g., adult-child/ student-teacher relations; gendered family relationships; class relations of hotel manager and employee) that the first group of trainers had established, and using this to reflect on social inequalities and self-identities,[7] Christiana and others criticized Dhanush and his team based on a middle-class understanding of humour and social decorum in relationships. Instead Christiana valourized the second performance, ignoring the class and caste implications of the act, in which a middle-class female actor had symbolically neutralized the threat of a male (caste/class) 'outsider'[8] through a benevolent act of rendering him her brother through the traditional act of tying a *rakhi* and invoking his protection towards her.[9]

As this example shows, rather than using this opportunity to bring the group to reflect upon, critically think about, analyse and question certain stereotypical beliefs that had been revealed during performance (e.g., the emphasis on academics and the devaluation of other aspects of childhood, such as play; gender, caste and class relations; work relations), the activity seemed to have mainly ruffled a middle-class sensibility around interpersonal relations and the licenses that can be taken within this. Thus, Christiana's primary reaction was towards the behaviour of 'putting down of others' that she had perceived the facilitators to have engaged in, rather than the everyday normative expectations for children, women and workers that they had displayed.

Further, what is also important to note in this example, as with the various sessions for children described before, is how, in setting certain expectations for behaviour, individuals were already discursively

---

[7] Though Christiana did attend to the imbalance of gender relations.

[8] That is, the lower caste and class male, who is implicitly imbued as dangerous within public discourses. See Chakravarti (1993), Jeffrey (2010) and Phadke (2007).

[9] See Iyer (2017) and Sinha-Kerkhoff (2003) on the symbolic value of celebrating Raksha Bandhan in contemporary India.

constructed and guided to understand themselves in particular ways. For example, denying the facilitators' understanding of their relationship as friends who could take certain licenses with each other, Christiana presented Nandini as deeply hurt at an unconscious level that she herself had not yet understood. Presenting this as the normal and expected reaction, Christiana not only established expectations for a certain kind of middle-class propriety and decorum in interpersonal interactions but also gave to Nandini a certain way of understanding her own self.

Thus, as stated before, I argue that presenting individuals with a specific understanding of themselves was one of the many ways in which programmes 'disciplined' subjects. Along with this, they also prescribed the appropriate choices to be made in overcoming those aspects of the self that arguably hindered the making of 'successful' choices. Making this amply clear, managers such as Joel Mathias (the former head of the Programme Delivery and Management team at IP) even argued: 'We're not telling children don't stand up and talk. But there's a way to do it. We are correcting their behaviour and saying 'give respect, take respect'.'[10]

Thus, the life skills classes themselves never became a space for deliberation, co-construction of knowledge or critical questioning of ideas and notions associated with the self, bodies or social norms and expectations. It remained a space within which conventional norms and expectations got reinforced, albeit in interesting ways. Through the use of activities such as stories and games, conventional and didactic methods of disciplining used by regular schoolteachers were replaced while delivering the same content. Interestingly, students also concurred that life skills facilitators differed from their regular teachers not in what they taught them but how they taught the same messages to them in a friendlier manner. (Students had in fact internalized their social positions of subordination within the adult–child/teacher–student relationships, which were also marked by hierarchies of caste and class differences between teachers and students, and even

---

[10] Personal communication, 3 March 2012.

took for granted teachers' authority over activities that involved creative expression.)

Schools' and the LSE organizers' rationales for intervention associated students' immaturities linked to their bio-developmental stage of youthfulness with cultural codes for behaviour drawn from the middle classes; thus establishing discipline, obedience, educational choices, along with manners and morals as relevant subject matter of intervention. Class-specific social–cultural deficits re-positioned as general factors that place young people at developmental risks were put forth as rationales by programmes to reshape their behaviours in line with neoliberal developmental agendas of schooling and employment, as I will further explain. While no single rationale dominated the agenda of programmes, programmes appeared to be catering to several different ends—of funders seeking demonstrable educational outcomes, schools and teachers expecting more disciplined and manageable classrooms, managers with a vision of transferring 'middle-class merit' among the poor and disadvantaged as a means to empower them to overcome their structural barriers, and even catering to entrenched patriarchal expectations of society.[11] Thus, a range of behavioural objectives and expectations were set on students, teaching them 'how to live life' by being a good student, a flexible and adaptable worker desired within the neoliberal workplace, an ideal citizen embodying bourgeoisie social values and behaviours, and the appropriately gendered subject, having internalized society's patriarchal norms.

Further, through an analysis of the curricula of the different organizations, I will in fact demonstrate how the neoliberal ethic of self-management through individual choices and regulation of behaviour combined with a patriarchal understanding of the self, thus sustaining older social relations in new forms. Together, all of these learnings sought to teach young people their multiple roles and place within the social order.

[11] This is in contrast with LSE programmes that target specific behavioural problems; for example, substance use, HIV/AIDS, etc. The lack of a specific subject matter of training led to the programmes being pulled in different directions to meet different stakeholders' needs.

6.2. Meeting Developmental Targets of Schooling and Education through LSE

A primary objective that the LSPs focused upon was to ensure that students attending their programmes complied with the developmental targets of education and the cultures of schooling. Significantly, knowledge around LSE put forth by agencies such as UNICEF and UNESCO (that are the primary influencers on LSE at the ministerial, programme and policy levels [UNICEF, 2012]) have drawn attention to its potential for 'reforming traditional education systems *which appear to be out of step with the realities of modern social and economic life*' (WHO, 1999, p. 2) and have advocated for the development of knowledge, values and skills that can allow young people to gain control over one's own life, to continue learning and to participate fully in society. LSE has in fact been conceptualized as an 'approach' that can address the problems affecting education systems and academic outcomes by attending to the ancillary behavioural problems (e.g., of violence or health choices), while also laying the foundation for skills that are in demand in today's job market (UNICEF, 2012; UNESCO, 2004; WHO, 1999). While developmental discourses around LSE have sought to thus broaden an understanding of what it means for young people to be educated, on field, the programmes observed appeared to largely prepare students for meeting conventional objectives of attendance, academic learning outcomes and discipline and, more specifically, to understand one's role as a student and the expectations placed by schools upon them.

The emphasis on the conventional targets of schooling can partly be explained by the pressures that government and aided schools (largely perceived to be 'failing' and under public scrutiny to produce better outcomes as an indicator of their quality) laid on the organizations to improve school outcomes. However, it is important to locate these expectations of programmes by schools as well as the interest within the LSPs themselves on schooling targets, within the larger context of developmentalism in education and the changing emphasis on education. Targeting developing nations and urging states to intervene in social and economic institutions to achieve (economic) development

(Wong, 2017) since the 1990s, global economic and policy discourses have associated education with the targets of reducing poverty, improving economic growth and improving health outcomes (Bennell & Furlong, 1998; King, 2007; Tarabini, 2010). Global development agencies and frameworks have been influential in setting these goals for education across the world, even in the Global South (King, 2007). The landmark World Conference on Education for All (WCEFA), jointly organized by the UN agencies, laid down a mandate for all children to be enrolled within school and complete basic education (primary or education of a higher level as determined by individual nations). Completion of basic schooling was linked to improvements in learning outcomes, 'life skills'[12] and behavioural changes through provisions of information, knowledges and skills. Interlinked economic, political and social outcomes from economic growth and good governance, addressal of environmental concerns, increase in popular participation, gender parity and development of individual capacities to gain greater control of one's life were all sought to be achieved through EFA (Buchert, 1995; WCEFA, 1990).

Specially, a vision of 'education for all' as 'schooling for all' (Balogun, 2008) has pervaded the national and international imaginary, and is even accepted by non-governmental agencies as fundamental to poverty reduction and growth strategies (Tarabini, 2010). As discussed earlier (in Chapter 3), within this context, the GES is seen as a site that must deliver on these several counts—from incorporating poor and marginalized students into the state and international structures of development to supporting the aspirational developments of a globalizing nation by preparing the right kind of manpower and delivering on the Minimum Levels of Learning targets set by international agencies, which have become the measure of a nation's progress. Prinsloo and Louw (2006) further point out that tied to these ends, schooling and education seek to create the individuated and self-referential individual, seeking to increase one's own marketability and gain the cultural and mobility capital required to participate in the global economy.

[12] Though the WCEFA declaration and framework repeatedly makes mention of 'life skills', the term is nowhere defined in the document.

Thus, the philosophical goals and enterprise of education have been replaced by narrow targets and indicators to measure school participation, such as marks and attendance that have indirectly been tied up with economic goals such as reduced burden on states through improved health indicators, economic participation indicators and reduction in delinquency and crime (Fendler, 1998; Sadagopal, 2006). While the latter changes require deeper shifts at the behavioural level, progress towards these developments continues to be measured through indicators such as school attendance and completion rates, minimum proficiency achieved in reading and mathematics, participation of youth in formal and informal learning, proportion of youth with information and communications technology skills and so on.[13]

One reason for this is the difficulties in measuring behavioural change that is dependent on a number of factors such as knowledges and skills but also more tacit factors such as motivations and beliefs. While programmes such as LSE have been proposed as an 'approach' to learning by influential developmental agencies to bridge overt school knowledges and underlying behavioural change, the difficulties of reliably assuring and measuring changes underlying behaviour have been noted by several experts. For example, Givaudan et al. (2007) have noted that while LSPs show positive effects for knowledge and intentions that are related 'precursors' to behaviour change, their impact on behaviour change itself has been less reliable. Hodge et al. (2012) have similarly noted how LSE evaluations have seldom been able to fully measure the whole range of underlying psychological development that contribute to behavioural outcomes.

With measurable learning outcomes and targets having become significant within the present audit culture within education (Lingard, 2010; Morley, 2010),[14] also significantly determining the flow of aid, especially to developing countries in the Global South (Goldstein,

---

[13] These are the kinds of indicators adopted for evaluation and monitoring of the SGDs on education (see UNESCO, 2018).

[14] Audit culture describes the increasing subordination of state practices under practices of NPM, in order to ensure greater accountability and transparency of public institutions through the adoption of calculative processes of 'performance indicators' and 'benchmarks' (see Lingard, 2010; Shore, 2008).

2004), reliable measures to report the outcomes of LSE has been imperative for both organizations as well as nations to report and present to donors and funders. The struggles in developing a reliable measure to report to funders and schools, regarding the impact of their programmes, was also felt by the organizations conducting LSPs on the field. As discussed earlier (in Chapter 4), anxiety over producing positive results following their interventions led some organizations such as VYB to rehearse or practice answers to paper-and-pencil-based tests on topics such as critical thinking with children before the evaluation. Through such practices, organizations converted the spontaneous and contextual application of skills into rote learning for test-taking, similar to other forms of learning measured at school. In other cases, such as at IP, the anxiety to produce reliable results of behavioural change resulted in facilitators' own performance appraisals being linked to school goals of achieving 100 per cent results; thus facilitators were to be evaluated on their performance of teaching LSE based on school results.

Overt indicators of attendance and marks had to be thus adopted as default measures to guarantee schools and funders of the programmes' impact, in the absence of other reliable indicators to measure behavioural change, which also require longer durations to demonstrate visible differences. In this process, programmes such as LSE have also become avenues through which discourses such as EFA, 'right to education' and the educational targets of the SDGs have come to be reiterated; thus, also establishing specific form of education and educational participation as 'hegemonically aspirational' for the non-elite. Mainly, schooling and school knowledges and behaviours have been positioned as the avenues to overcome various structural disadvantages, not just through access to the academic knowledges that schools have to offer but also through the tacit middle class capital of mannerisms, dress and discipline that form the hidden capital of schools (Sriprakash et al., 2020).

In fact, the discursive value placed on schooling, by the LSPs, was visible in classroom transactions, conducted by facilitators such as Yamuna (from VYB). In her introductory session on 'What are Life Skills?', for eighth standard students in a government school in south

Bengaluru, Yamuna clearly oriented the discussion towards classroom behaviours, explaining life skills as 'nothing but good behaviours to be a *good student or good human being*'.¹⁵ Validating the different answers given by students in response to the question she had posed, Yamuna explained that LSE was about learning 'how to behave with elders and teachers', 'how to behave in class', 'how to be clean', 'how to be disciplined' and how to perform the academic tasks demanded within class, such as learning tables, and so on.

The conflation of being a 'good human being' with being a 'good student' is unmistakable from the account presented above. Having established 'life skills' as such, the following curricular transactions further established the salience of the targets of schooling. Curricular analysis showed how one of the first topics taught by VYB to eighth standard students, on self-awareness, was structured to 'responsibilize' young people in relation to their social roles as students. Here, excerpts from the self-awareness module is reproduced verbatim to demonstrate this.¹⁶

> Self-awareness includes recognition of our personality, our strengths and weaknesses, our likes and dislikes especially our emotions. Developing self-awareness can help us to recognize when we are stressed or under pressure. It is also often a prerequisite for effective communication and interpersonal relations, as well as for developing empathy for others.

Establishing an understanding of the concept as described before, there were just two main activities and a set of corresponding facilitating questions given as a part of this module. The first activity, called 'Roles I Play', sought to 'create an awareness and positive perspective about the roles that the student plays', particularly drawing attention to their 'role of a student and the responsibilities attached to it'.¹⁷ The stated aim of this activity was to convey the importance of

---

¹⁵ Classroom observations made on 16 July 2012.
¹⁶ From the soft copy of the curriculum document shared with me by Ranjit Rao (the head of operations at VYB's Inspire project) via email (dated 25 May 2013).
¹⁷ Reproduced verbatim from the curriculum document.

school and education to children. The second activity called 'Your Strengths, Your Opportunities' sought to draw children's attention to their personal strengths, weaknesses and opportunities through which they could perform their roles as students successfully.[18] Thus, the primary emphasis within the self-awareness module appeared to be on developing an understanding of one's roles and responsibilities, particularly in relation to that of being a student.

Further, even when guided to make a 'Strengths, Weaknesses, Opportunities and Threats' analysis within the classroom, the focus was on drawing students' attentions towards their own behaviours, rather than towards structural–environmental factors that could be significantly disabling. For example, during classroom transactions, discussions around behaviour related to individuals' roles as 'students', such as attendance, performance at school and so on, were linked to individual responsibility and motivation to achieve these, rather than to obstacles posed by structural factors. With a large majority of children coming from working-class homes, as described earlier, and many employed in part-time work, the difficulties this posed for academic participation never became a point of discussion within the programmes. Even when facilitators encountered specific cases of children who had dropped out because of a hostile school environment that did not take into account these factors about their lives, counselling was employed (as part of the LSE programme) to motivate the child to return to school. Instances such as this were reported by facilitators such as Yamuna (of VYB), who presented the case of a high school student, Chetan, who was on the verge of dropping out due to the difficulties of managing school and work. Sharing details about Chetan's circumstances, she stated that he worked early mornings as a newspaper boy and would thus come tired to class, where he would fall asleep. After having been scolded and humiliated for this by the teacher several times, Chetan had decided to drop out, when Yamuna intervened and counselled him to continue in school. Similarly, in other schools, I met other children who were unable to

---

[18] The full details of the activity, along with the specific facilitating questions used are presented in the appendix.

attend school regularly, either due to financial difficulties or other duties or chores at home. Ignoring these real contexts of their lives, despite which students persisted, what was evident from observations on field were how LSPs were co-opted in responsibilizing students in ensuring the ends of school and developmental agendas of funders, by guiding them to uncritically internalize the value of education and their roles as students.

Thus, instead of making students critically aware of themselves in relation to the caste, class, gender, discourses of development and social and political economies, the LSPs encouraged middle-class attitudes towards education. Disregarding the structural barriers that operated upon their lives and posed challenges for mobility, it urged students to acquire the middle class 'educational merit' to become successful and escape their circumstances of poverty. As seen from the discussion of VYB's self-awareness module, the goal appeared to be that of narrowing one's understanding of oneself, locating outcomes of schooling as internal to the individual self. School-going behaviours were presented as problems of rational decision-making on the part of the individual. Aligned with the developmental goals and requirements of various national and international agencies, particularly large, global charities and corporate foundations (e.g., General Electric, Michael & Susan Dell Foundation, Akshaya Patra, etc., that are ardent advocates of education) that were also funders of many of these LSPs, to improve learning outcomes in school, the programmes also uncritically advocated education as the solution to a wide range of problems from poverty to inequality. Thus, they also appeared to work towards aligning children with this understanding, disciplining them to understand themselves in relation to the global discourses on education and development. LSPs thus functioned as 'technologies of self' and 'technologies of government' through which the neoliberal responsibilization of youth in relation to welfare objectives such as education could be undertaken.

Thus, the first set of responses by students interviewed across different schools to the questions 'What is the meaning of life skills?' or 'What did you learn in the life skills class?' were always about learning how to live or how to study. For example, during a life skills class conducted by VYB, I spoke to a group of four eighth standard girls amongst whom I was sitting during the class. On enquiring about what life skills meant to them,[19] the girls responded immediately stating that it referred to 'good behaviours'. When I probed further and asked them why they needed life skills, the girls responded by saying that they needed it to share their emotions and difficulties with their friends. Further, they added that it was important in order to learn to give respect to elders and to be disciplined. Trying to further understand their responses, I asked them if this wasn't taught by other teachers and elders too, to them. In response to this, one girl replied that while others told them to give respect to elders and to be disciplined, in this class they were taught how to be disciplined and to give respect. Thus, students' responses showed 'disciplining' knowledges, on how to be and behave according to expectations of schools to be the paramount concern that the programmes dealt with.

In another instance, a group of tenth standard girls from a government girls' high school in east Bengaluru explained that the LSE programme taught them 'learning about life'. They added that the aim of the programme was to teach them 'how their life should be' and to study well. Significantly noticeable from students' responses was the normative emphasis laid on them through the programmes on *how to be*. Stating that during the course of the programme they had learnt about themselves, learnt to solve family problems, overcome stage fear and to study well and score good marks, students rarely emphasized the experiential process of developing a skill or in coming to understand aspects of themselves and mainly pointed to the messages given during classes. Even when students identified certain processual knowledges—for example, how to solve problems or sharing of emotions, interestingly they reported that programmes taught them the appropriate responses under these circumstances, rather than skills, to undertake these activities.

Such accounts of the programmes as teaching students specific behaviours (rather than skills) were also given by teachers, who

---

[19] Personal communication, 24 September 2012.

reported that the programmes performed the functions of improving academic results and 'discipline' (i.e., by improving obedience, respect, completion of academic tasks, punctuality, regularity and so on). During personal interviews, teachers like Ragini, the high school mathematics and science teacher at the Tamil-minority aided school in east Bengaluru, pointed out that LSE programme conducted by IP at their school was helping them manage students better, by making students more disciplined and helping them achieve their academic goals.[20] Pointing out that the school had allowed IP to conduct their programme first on a probationary basis, she stated that IP was allowed to continue as a result of the impact they were having on academic goals. Specifically, she stated that the programme had helped to secure a pass percentage of 93 per cent the previous year. She argued that children too had become more disciplined when compared to other schools, as a result of these programmes. Rather than evaluating the programmes in relation to skills such as critical thinking or problem-solving that was meant to be taught through the programmes, to make children more reflective, responsible and self-regulating, teachers discussed the ways in which the programmes were enabling their own goals and the school's conventional goals of academic outcomes and behaviour.

Catering to these expectations of schools, organizations also attended to targets such as attendance, pass percentage and discipline, which were discussed regularly during classroom sessions, during internal meetings and trainings, and were even adopted as measures by organizations to evaluate their own programmes. In some cases, organizations specifically catered to these objectives of creating the ideal subject of schooling by including components that catered more directly to academic outputs. For example, VYB's LSE programme also included a component to inculcate basic academic foundational skills (such as knowledge of alphabets and numbers, grammar and conjugations in high school students), as this was lacking in many students in government schools even at the high school stage. In addition, VYB also had a 'dropout prevention' programme. As part of

---

[20] Personal communication, 2 August 2012.

this, they instituted 'support groups' within each classroom, encouraging group members to monitor each other on aspects of attendance, behaviour and completion of work. Each group also had a group leader, who reported to the facilitators, who tracked children on these dimensions.[21] Thus, clearly moving away from an emphasis on just self-regulation and skills for self-awareness and critical decision-making through which these ends (choosing to remain and continue in school) were to be assured, organizations such as VYB used external and explicit methods to ensure that the conventional expectations of schools were met.

6.3. LSE and Cultivating 'Employability'

While academic outcomes were one area of impact that organizations sought to achieve through their programmes, another area of focus of programmes, in line with economic discourses of human capital theory and its impact on education, was the preparation of a 'skilled workforce', with the right skills to fit oneself in accordance with the expectations of a neoliberal economy, in the future. Developers of these programmes, such as Devesh Arya, purporting to address the mismatch between 'skills' and 'job' created by the education system, thus sought to train students attending IP's LSE in attitudes of 'adaptability' and 'flexibility' required for the global economy. Arguing that investments in technical skills for the future was a 'waste'[22] and that 'soft skills' such as communication and initiative were the essential skills required for jobs, Arya and others put forth their LSPs as 'empowering' youth to 'escape their cycles of poverty', while also contributing to the nation's growth.

The rationale for training of youth in a new set of 'soft' rather than 'hard' skills needs to be viewed within the context of increasing neoliberal reform of vocational education that has been adopted by the state and advocated by developmental agencies. Within this context of

---

[21] Rajesh Sridhar, personal communication (23 February 2012).
[22] A detailed account of this comment, made by Arya, the CEO of IP, has already been given in Chapter 4.

reform, improving individual's 'employability' has come to be accepted as a better way to bring the poor into the social and economic mainstream than through the redistribution of wealth (McGrath, 2010). These reforms that have positioned individual skilling as the panacea to all problems of development have in fact glossed over the structural limitations to employment, such as jobless growth, seen even in the context of India and instead have privileged the extractive practices of capitalism that require individual's social relations and affective labour to reproduce itself (Hardt & Negri, 2004; Hochschild; 1983; Warhurst & Thompson, 1998; in Maithreyi & Prabha, 2019).

The LSPs observed, in fact, contributed to this growing social perception that central to getting and keeping jobs were the learning of a set of behaviours, mannerisms and attitudes, related to communication, creativity and enterprise that comprised the 'middle-class merit' that had made them successful. Thus, despite identifying their programmes as 'empowering', the organizers of LSE were in fact contributing to the phenomena of 'deskilling' underway in the current context of advanced capitalism. Further, such views failed to take into account how technical and domain-specific knowledges are central to securing white collar, middle-class jobs within the IT, finance or media industries that the programme organizers had themselves worked in previously and to provide working class youth opportunities for real mobility. They, therefore, were central to the very discourses and practices through which class gets reproduced.

Further, they also failed to acknowledge the investments that disadvantaged youth (must) make in acquiring such cultural capital (refer Jeffrey et al., 2004; Vasavi, 2013–2014), in the hope of acquiring better jobs and futures. As other scholars have noted, while rural and working-class youth are pushed to make these personal investments in acquiring education and 'hard' skills, what is freely available and offered to them, pushed by corporate, governmental and non-governmental networks of governance are programmes such as LSE that seek to prepare them to comply with various socio-economic institutions, markets and the workplace. Within such programmes that emphasize particular kinds of personal skills for development, what gets left out are the critical skills of negotiation, awareness and knowledge of rights, abilities to critically examine and question conditions of labour and so on.

The result of such dismantling of vocational, technical, and critical–liberal education systems through state and international policies, and the replacement of 'hard' technical skills (that represent domain specializations and offer workers bargaining power), with life and social skills, represents a move to render workers bereft of their negotiating power, as several scholars such as Ainley and Corbett (1994), Jackson and Jordan (1999) and others have noted. The emphasis on 'soft skills', as opposed to 'hard skills', it has been argued, leads to the creation of conditions of greater job insecurity (owing to the lack of specific domain knowledge that can anchor workers to specific jobs or industries, within which they can grow through accumulated experience and established networks). The absence of accumulated technical skills and experience allows workers to be flexibly moved, transferred, retrenched and retrained based on industry and economic demands. Further, in this process, soft skills become important to create new cultural sensibilities, individualize and 'de-unionise mentalities', manage conflicts that may emerge in this process and cultivate a sense of loyalty to the organization first (Jackson and Jordan, 1999).

Arya's own LSE programme embedded these underlying rationalities. The programme, which focused on training children in five key areas, as a way to prepare them for future jobs, defined these skills (like VYB) in particular ways, through a structuring of the content and the curriculum. The five focus areas of IP's programme (Table 6.1) were 'interacting with others', 'overcoming difficulties and solving problems', 'taking initiative', 'managing conflict' and 'understanding and following instructions' (all of which are key areas sought to be managed within the workplace and that contribute essentially to organizational work flow). Together, these five focus areas were said to cover the entire range of 10 life skills identified by the WHO.[23] While IP claimed to have covered the entire set of skills under these

---

[23] As stated by Joel Mathias (former head of Programme Delivery and Management at IP; Personal communication, 3 March 2012).

Table 6.1 IP's Curricular Focus Areas

Interacting with Others	Overcoming Difficulties and Solving Problems	Taking Initiative	Managing Conflict	Understanding and Following Instructions
Group poem	Non-dominant hand drawing	Morning mirror	Erasures	Blind drawings
Body tracing	Concrete poems	Sensitivity line	Puppet making	Sound circles
Alien conference	Anchors	Find the leader	Puppet show	
Gender circles		Collage poem	Teasing tableau	
Newspaper fashion show				

Source: Adapted from IP's arts-based curriculum sixth-eighth standards, for 2012–2013.

five broad domains, it is important to note how specific skills, such as empathy, managing stress or emotions, that deal with individual well-being and contribute to the personal quality of life did not get represented or become key areas of focus within the programmes. Looking across the (arts) curriculum more closely,[24] I will discuss two broad themes of leadership/taking initiative and communication to demonstrate how the skills were presented in specific ways so as to enable the 'soft skills' required within the workplace.

Examining the lessons under the theme of 'taking initiative', what was evident was how students were discursively encouraged to take initiative to change their behaviours, particularly in order to shed the habits, routines and practices developed within their communities and among their peers. For example, a close reading of the curriculum document showed that the first three sessions (after the

---

[24] IP, as mentioned before, had two programmes—one that was arts-based and another that was sports-based. I mostly visited their arts-based sessions and hence am drawing my analysis from the arts curriculum.

initial 'Goals and Agreements' session, already discussed earlier) were to focus on three different activities, all of which were to conclude with a reflection over how students would adopt behaviours that were different from what they saw or experienced within their own communities. The first activity, called 'Morning Mirror', which required students to stand in a circle and have every student closely observe and imitate the fifth person in the circle from them, adopted the following questions for reflection: after initially asking students what happened in the game, the second part of the conversation was to ask them to think about the 'mirrors' in their communities that established trends, expectations and peer pressure to conform to certain kinds of behaviours. In the final part of the reflection, students were encouraged to think of what they would do differently from their communities in order to 'experiment' with what had been discussed in class (around the pressures of conforming to community expectations or norms).

The second activity, called 'Find the Leader', required one child to leave the room. In his/her absence, a leader was selected for the group, who would lead the group in performing certain actions (e.g., clapping, touching the nose, tapping the shoulder, etc). Upon the first child's return, the group had to follow the leader in performing the actions initiated by him/her, while the child who had left the room had to carefully observe and identify who was leading the group. Following the activity, in which students took turns becoming the leader, the reflection questions asked them to first discuss what it was like to be a leader, following which they were asked to reflect on how they could develop strategies of being a leader to help themselves in life. Finally, the reflection was to conclude by having students commit to something new that they would be willing to try that week to demonstrate their leadership abilities. Specifically, the question posed was 'What would you be willing to try this week? Will you try developing one of these plans and report back to us?' thus indicating that the expectation was for students to take initiative over (or lead) themselves.

Finally, the third activity involving initiative and leadership was called 'Sensitivity Line' and required a set of five to six student-volunteers to stand in front of the class with their backs facing the class. The volunteers were asked to randomly turn around to face the class one by one and start a story. As one student is facing the class and talking, another child was expected to randomly interrupt the first child and continue the story, while the first child had to immediately stop and turn back to the original position. After several such rounds of interruption, the next level of the game was to be played in which students were given topics such as 'My ideal community is…' or 'If I really knew I was creative I would…', on which they had to turn around one by one and talk. During this round however, students were not expected to interrupt each other and were expected to wait to turn around and discuss the topic only after the previous child had finished. The reflection that followed expected students to discuss their understanding of their personal presence and how this could be channelized within public speaking in schools and communities.

Taking the three activities together, what can be seen is the emphasis on self-reflection and regulation that has been identified in the curriculum document as 'leadership' and 'initiative'. Further, the expectation for leadership and initiative placed on children is in relation to differentiating themselves from their peers and communities, by identifying peer influences, proposing ways in which they could differentiate themselves from these activities and thinking of what would comprise their 'ideal communities'. Further, in the last activity, what was sought to be reinforced (according to the curriculum document) were the abilities to work together and develop awareness. Awareness, as is evident from the activity, appeared to be regarding the implicit communication codes to recognize appropriate situations in which one can speak; for example, learning to speak without interrupting others, learning cues for when one can speak and so on (hinting at learning tacit rules within a workplace or school, such as knowing to speak only when spoken to, as expected of those in subordinate positions). Thus, seen together, the three activities on 'taking initiative' appeared to emphasize the development of self-control, while also learning new cultural codes for behaviour that are removed from one's own social cultures. With several instances of classroom transactions and trainings for facilitators (as the one discussed earlier) showing how programmes sought to inculcate middle-class norms for social participation in children and facilitators, initiative and leadership to distance oneself from one's own background were unmissable from the set of reflection questions posed across the first three lessons of IP's LSE module.

Similarly, skills such as communication were also presented in specific ways so as to prepare students for their subordinate roles within workplaces in the urban, service economy. For example, in training youth in communication, the curricula mainly represented the sub-skills of 'listening', 'public speaking' and 'taking and giving instructions', which appeared in 7 of 19 session plans in the facilitators' training manual (for 2012–2013). While the skills of 'listening/active listening' appeared across six sessions, 'public speaking' and 'taking and giving instructions' appeared in one session each. From this, it is already evident that the primary understanding of communication that was sought to be developed was with respect to listening to others and receiving and giving instructions. Other forms of communication, such as assertive communication, questioning (e.g., stereotypes, normative expectations), negotiating, debating, technical or formal communication (all of which can be critically empowering in contexts of unequal relations of power), did not receive much focus within the curriculum.

To provide a clearer explanation of what specifically became the interest within the communications module of IP's curriculum, I present here a discussion of an activity called 'Blind Drawings' given in their curriculum.[25] The goal of the activity, as listed in the curriculum, was to help

1. Identify how to communicate accurately or properly;
2. Listen attentively while following instructions; and
3. Give instructions clearly.

The activity required children to work in pairs, sitting back-to-back against each other. Each child of the pair took turns at calling out a set of instructions to the other child, so that he/she could reproduce

---

[25] See Appendix 2 for more details of the activity and session.

the drawing the first child had made using basic geometrical shapes, while the other child tried to follow these instructions as carefully as possible. Following this, children's attention was drawn to the problems of communication (both in listening as well as giving instructions) due to which the drawings may have been erroneously reproduced.

What is seen here is how communication—a complex process of interpersonal interaction, reciprocation, negotiation and strategization—that intrinsically embeds relations of power/knowledge, is depoliticized and reduced to a set of objective procedures. The activity, which involves a simplistic transmission, reception and reproduction of a set of value-neutral commands does not capture any of the undercurrents of real-world communication situations, even one that may involve a situation of communication at the workplace. For getting a task done at the workplace may also involve differential relations of power, social dynamics, interpersonal histories, organizational hierarchies, and work pressure and politics; all of which may affect the acts of 'listening' and 'instructing'.

Further, the goals and questions for reflection presented as part of the activity also clearly showed how the onus was on the individual to examine his/her skills of listening or communicating (e.g., 'Were you drawing close or far from the original?' 'What kinds of communication were you using?' 'Where was the communication not working properly'; 'What can we do to communicate more clearly and to listen to understand?') and correct it, rather than on understanding it as a dynamic process of interaction.

As such instances of curriculum and classroom transaction showed, the primary focus of the curriculum seemed to be towards cultivating a specific habitus in youth in order to make them more amenable to the modern workplace. In fact, placed together, the goals of discipline, obedience and hard work emphasized in relation to becoming the ideal student, and the skills for enterprise and initiative to distance oneself from the provincial influences of the home and adopt the appropriate behaviours of listening and following instructions expected of the workplace—together showed how school and economic imperatives were merged in producing the responsible, future-worker citizen desired under current economic contexts.

6.4. Understanding of the Self in Accordance with Patriarchal Norms

A final form in which programmes sought to shape students' understanding of the self was in relation to gender. While expectations set on poor and marginalized youth to comply with the standards and norms of schooling and economy exposed the patriarchal values that underlie LSE, nowhere was it more strongly visible than in the production of gendered conceptions of the self through the programme. Further, in contrast with the expectations of distancing oneself from the traditional–parochial influences of local cultures and contexts, in order to embody the ideal student and worker selves, gendered identities were reproduced within the programmes by drawing on the local norms for behaviour. As Kumar (2017) argues, girls, who are seen as the 'carriers of culture', have been excluded from the gaze of modern education which requires a fundamental split between the home and the school (an exception that was made even under colonial apparatuses of governmentality, when the question of girls' education was treated with a vagueness and indifference, according to him). In a similar fashion, the ideal girl-student and citizen, even in the context of the LSPs, required the adoption of gendered identities as conceptualized socioculturally within the larger community and society.

This became apparent during the roles and responsibilities activity (of the VYB curriculum, discussed earlier). That these sessions became a vehicle to forward certain normative and patriarchal constructions of the self was apparent from the response given by an eighth standard student, Jency, from the government school in south Bengaluru, and the facilitator conducting the session. Jency, in response to the task of listing out one's responsibilities as a son/daughter, had written the following account:

> A boy should be a suitable son to his mother. He should do the work that she sets for him. He should earn a good name from the people around. It is not enough if he just does what he is told, but he should also stand on his own feet, and support his mother and family.

A girl means she should do the work assigned to her by her mother. She should preserve and uphold her tradition and must remain within her limits. She should study and try to take care of everyone. She should take responsibility for all the work.[26]

As the account clearly shows, Jency presented a normative account of gender roles that revealed the internalized patriarchal norms and expectations of society. Yet, the interest within the class was not on critically examining these ideas on the social limits set for girls, or the burdens of economic provisioning and family care that had to be taken on by boys. Rather than discussing what implications these have for the formation of identities, the facilitator's interest was on getting children to complete the task of enumerating one's responsibilities as part of specific roles. Thus, the facilitator only acknowledged Jency's responses for having successfully met the session's objective but did not undertake a further discussion about these responsibilities and roles.

Similarly, even during Dr Bavegadi's session at the south Bengaluru government school (described earlier), it was noticed how certain gender stereotypes were reinforced in her discussion of children's behaviours and in her attempts at bringing them to reflect upon themselves. Speaking of the ways in which children may give others 'Cold Pricklies' (i.e., hurt others, or bring them sadness), she pointed to instances at home, when girls complained on being given a chore to do by their parents, stating the following: 'When there is a brother at home, you fight saying why doesn't he get any work, and only I get?' seeming to suggest that such a reaction would amount to an inappropriate behaviour. Again, instead of enabling girls to understand or challenge the forms of patriarchal expectations placed upon their selves, Dr Bavegadi appeared to be validating social expectations that contributed to the establishment of differentiated roles for girls and boys, specifically in relation to tasks such as performing and taking responsibility for domestic chores.

Other instances of such gendered forms of 'disciplining' students included Deepika's experience within the LSE class discussed earlier

[26] On 29 August 2012.

(in Chapter 5), wherein she was gently guided to learn to refrain from demonstrating her real emotions of anger and pain in violent contexts such as that of eve-teasing. In fact, the high point of this particular discussion in which Deepika was dissuaded from standing up and calling out her aggressors came when Sunil, her classmate, interjected to convince Deepika of the futility of her actions, stating, *'Nayi suriyana pathu kolachcha suriyan ku edhuvana aaguma?'* ('If a dog barks at the sun, will the sun get affected?') Sunil's response, which received a thumping ovation from his classmates, sealed off the discussion on the appropriate behaviour for girls to adopt in situations of (sexual) danger, reasserting male power over women's bodies. This theme, that is, of girls learning to avoid the dangers of sexual predation and the normalization of men's power in taking over their bodies, was in fact repeatedly encountered across other schools as well, with LSE facilitators expected to teach girls appropriate ways to behave. For example, at a south Bengaluru government co-educational high school, a special class was held by the LSE facilitator, Yamuna, for girls, based on the demand made by the regular teachers' of the school, following their perception of liberal relationships between boys and girls in the school. During the session, Yamuna and some of the other regular teachers advised girls and dissuaded them from allowing boys to be too free in their interactions with them. Teachers pointed out to the girls that allowing boys to open and check their bags was giving them too much room and pointed out that they must be reprimanded for such behaviour and kept at a distance. Similarly, girls were also advised to walk straight home after school, with their heads bent down and making no eye contact with anyone on the streets.

In fact, gender norms were reinforced and validated through facilitators' own practices and behaviours. As discussed earlier, facilitators such as Nayanika (from VYB) were explicitly dissuaded by schools and teachers from developing close emotional bonds with male students. Facilitators' or programme staff's internalization of gender norms further remained unexamined, as is clear from the example of the theatre improvisation activity discussed earlier, in which a female volunteer symbolically invoked the protection of a male facilitator.

Such instances showed how programmes appeared to deliberately remain silent and blind to questions of gender norms, inequalities, discrimination and violence.

In fact, instances such as these (as well as other discussions that reinforced social hierarchies between students, teachers and employers) made visible how programmes remained sites within which patriarchal expectations intersected with neoliberal constructions of the subject; thus, requiring youth to become entrepreneurial in directing one's own self to align with the larger patriarchal culture. Within this context, the ideal self was one that was selectively skilled—'educated' in discipline and social skills of docility, flexibility and adaptability but technically de-skilled, malleable according to hierarchical–patriarchal–gendered norms of society and the economy. Through field data, I have shown how contradictory goals of discipline (i.e., self-discipline and self-responsibilization desired by the programmes and obedience to external forms of authority desired by the schools) sat together within the space of LSE and were seamlessly woven together, to achieve the overall effect of a 'deskilled', uncritical self that must accept, adapt and adjust to various demands placed upon it. Thus, such instances not only presented examples of 'responsibilization', but also pointed to strong practices of disciplining of the self in line with normative expectations of school and society, which were far from the goals of empowerment that these programmes speak of.

What implications did these contradictory 'disciplines', imposed on youth, have? What kinds of subjectivities did it help develop? I turn to these questions in the next chapter, looking at the 'disconnects' that emerged between the global programme ideals and the local contextualization of the programmes. These 'disconnects' also opened up spaces for negotiation and resistance by actors, which I examine, in keeping with a Foucauldian analysis of power. As Tania Murray Li (2007) has argued, governmental power is neither homogenous nor complete. She further states that the '…the analytic of governmentality draws our attention to the ways in which subjects are differently formed and differently positioned in relation to governmental programs (as experts, as targets), with particular capacities for action and critique' (p. 276).

Hartman (2003) helps us understand this point further, when he notes that

> Critique, as a kind of 'limit-attitude,' becomes for Foucault the means by which a subject can positively resist power through a testing of the limits of domination and subjection. If power operates in terms of the 'conduct of conduct,' or in the modification of action by action, critique allows us to view the field of possible action in terms of its possibility, and not only in the terms given us by power and knowledge.
>
> Through critique, through (and only through) the critical engagement with institutions and practices, we can more effectively resist our governance and our docility. (p. 11)

Examining the nature of these 'disconnects' that emerged from the differences in worldviews held by the different groups involved, I attempt to thus show the internal limits of these pedagogies of discipline and how they were simultaneously adopted and resisted through the ways in which youth engaged with the programmes. I argue that the resulting encounter produced specific forms of subjectivities and social contexts that did not strictly replicate patriarchal–neoliberal imaginaries for cultural transformations via youth subjects.

CHAPTER 7

Cultural Disconnects and the Possibilities for Subject Formation

Having laid out the international and national contours of LSE in the previous chapters, here, I attempt to go beyond the empirical description of the field. That is, reflecting on the LSPs, their linkages with larger structures and discourses of regulation, and the multiple stakeholders' (i.e., the students, facilitators and managers of the LSPs) interpretations and actions in response to the discourses and practices of LSE, I offer a theoretical exposition on the regulation and formation of subjectivities. Departing from the earlier chapter that focused mainly on the contexts and conditions through which young people were subjected in specific ways, in this chapter I examine the 'responses', that is, the set of historically situated, symbolically mediated, ongoing dialectical processes of possibilities and counter-possibilities through which social systems and actors get formed (Ortner, 1994; Postill, 2010). In taking into account these 'responses', I also examine LSE itself as a 'response' to other local conditions and factors, thereby examining its material and dialectical constitution as a globally influential discourse.

7.1. Local Contexts, Global Discourses and 'Cultural Disconnects': Understanding Responses from the Field

LSPs, as they unfolded in practice, had to contend with multiple realities (some of which, such as adaptation to the school culture, has already been discussed earlier). Here, I draw on some examples from the field to demonstrate another issue that emerged in practice, that is, of how certain 'cultural disconnects' emerged in translating what essentially appeared to be middle class cultural practices and socialization techniques onto the field.

By 'cultural disconnects', I refer to the differences in the understanding of the programmes between the facilitators and children (who were the recipients of the programmes) and the international experts, developmental agencies and middle-class managers of local organizations, who sought to transform and 'empower' disadvantaged children through these. In presenting these 'disconnects', I argue that they emerged not just as a result of the poor training and monitoring practices of the organizations but, more importantly, as a result of differences in 'cultural capital' (Bourdieu, 1986). In order to demonstrate what I mean by this, I start with some illustrations of these 'cultural disconnects' observed and then examine the result of these 'disconnects'.

7.2. Middle-Class Cultures, Capital and Disconnects

The following anecdote is from an event that was observed during a TTP by IP.[1] The training which was conducted for a private English medium school, Millennium Education Society (MES), was led by two lead facilitators—'Sasha' (Shashidhar) and Jaffar. While Sasha was an experienced, middle-class, freelance personality training consultant and voice-over artist who had worked with IP as a consultant 'lead facilitator' for over two years, Jaffar was a recently trained lead

[1] On 2 February 2013.

facilitator. Jaffar belonged to a lower-middle-class background and was a former (school-based) arts teacher, who had joined IP a few months earlier. I discuss this particular training handled by these two lead facilitators from different backgrounds in order to highlight the differences in their facilitation style and the ways in which they oriented their audience. (I use this as an example to demonstrate how 'cultural disconnects' emerged in the course of translation of these programmes on field.) Here, a short excerpt of the first day of training is presented.

Diary Entry: February 2, 2013, TTP for MES

After a round of morning warm-up activities, Jaffar started the next session saying, 'Think of how you can *use* what we did in the morning *with children*'. Sasha immediately rephrased this, saying, 'For that you should first see *how this will be of use to you*. Then only we can take it to the children'.

A little while later, Sasha, who was conducting a session on understanding the goals of IP's LSE programme, asked the teachers what is meant by 'life skills'. Some answered that it meant 'personality development'. When Sasha pushed them to think further by bringing them to focus on the two words - 'life' and 'skills', one teacher pointed out that it means 'How we *should* live life'. Immediately Sasha rephrased this saying it is about 'the skills *we need* to lead life'. Giving an example he explained, 'If there is a fire here, we need skills to escape and help others escape. Everyone may be ready to pour water to put out the fire, but that needs life skills.'

During another activity called 'River of Life', in which participants had to share intimate details of their life's journey, Jaffar asked the group, 'how did you feel after sharing your story?' Teachers responded stating that they had realized that others' problems were bigger than theirs, and thus they could use this activity to give children an opportunity to talk about their lives as well. Even though Jaffar tried to draw their attention to aspects of their own selves, the conversation kept slipping towards children. So Jaffar summarised the discussion stating, 'The goal of this activity is to be able to bring out what children have in their minds. They might have so many problems.'

This led to a teacher speaking of the various kinds of activities that might be useful to have children speak about their problems. At this point Sasha intervened and reminded the group that the goal was for them to *think about themselves*. He asked them to reflect about aspects such as the creation of a 'safe space' that had been necessary to create an atmosphere of trust and sharing, where they could share their feelings.

What appeared to be conspicuously noticeable throughout the training described above (as during several other instances observed on field) was the difference in outcomes emphasized by the two facilitators. While Sasha and other middle-class employees and volunteers (like myself) associated the programme and its participative pedagogies and experiential moments of learning with a process of self-introspection, personal transformation and change, non-middle-class facilitators (like Jaffar), teachers and children associated it with specific content to be learnt through the programmes. For example, in replying to Sasha's question on the meaning of 'life skills', teachers described it as learning how one *should* lead life (implying certain standards and social norms prescribed by society). In contrast with this, Sasha presented life skills as the 'skills' internal to oneself and, thus, drew attention to the need to learn how to manage these skills to manage oneself.

A similar kind of 'disconnect' could also be observed during the facilitation of the 'River of Life' activity. While Jaffar, during reflection, appeared to move away from a discussion on the internal aspects of the self and sought to summarize how the activity was to be conducted with children, Sasha reoriented the discussion to the self. Jaffar appeared to be at a loss when it came to having a 'vital conversation' around the phenomenology of trust and sharing that was the basis of the activity.[2] However, at this point Sasha brought back the conversation to the creation of a 'safe space', by drawing attention to participants' personal attitudes and effort that had facilitated the opening up of the self. He thus took the conversation beyond the level of the

---

[2] 'Vital conversation' is the term used by the organization to describe a deeply introspective and emotionally charged discussion on sensitive topics related to the self.

immediate relief felt by the teachers to see how and what had enabled this experience, and how experientiality was central to the process of learning. Focusing continuously on the need to be self-reflective during the session and trying to explain this philosophy to the teachers, Sasha also made the following comment: 'The way I behave is my life skills. If I develop life skills in me, I can develop it in children. If there is a lack of life skills in me, it is difficult to develop it in children.'

Central to these ideas circulated by the middle-class organizers and managers of the programme was the notion of working upon the self. Life skills were not seen as 'rules of thumb' or guides; neither were they seen as that required only by children, to be given through instruction. Rather, they were seen as particular and specific experiences of 'concerted cultivation' that provide opportunities for examining one's self and bringing aspects of it into conscious awareness.[3]

This understanding of the skills was also seen in the narratives of most founder/directors of these LSPs, including Devesh Arya, the founder and CEO of IP, as can be seen from the excerpt below:

> I asked myself what was my strength. It was to think creatively. I started thinking of all my experiences [that had enabled this], all of which came from non-academic experiences. That's how I started these programmes. Experiences of supporting a friend who had an accident, struggling through projects, going blank in a debate competition, rejecting a neighbour who had been affected by cancer when he became sick—these experiences started standing out for me. I realised all these were experiential in nature, and these were the moments that were unique and gave me those insights. I wanted to create these powerful experiences for children to help them build insights. I started these programmes purely from that space.[4]

As Devesh's account shows, life skills were understood to be more than 'skills' and as experiences of reflecting upon the self and engaging

---

[3] Vincent and Ball (2007), drawing on Lareau (2003), describe 'concerted cultivation' as the use of language and reason as strategies to pin down aspects of the self, talent and identity.

[4] Personal communication, 28 May 2012.

in a process of 'conscious self-making'.[5] Thus, trainings were also meant to focus on the creation of such experiences. Further, training for facilitators and adults were meant to simultaneously help them achieve an emergent understanding and recognition of the strategies, practices and environment through which this process of 'conscious self-making' could be brought to fore, rather than on teaching strategies or providing instructions on how to conduct a class.

IP was in fact one of the few organizations that invested heavily in building this culture of conscious self-making through introspection among its entire staff (even among those who were not directly in contact with the children or involved in training)—a practice that seemed to stem from a more complex account of behavioural change held by IP. As the following comment by Arya, put to his team during training, showed this practice seemed to be motivated by a belief that unconscious and unexamined aspects of the self could influence the ways in which one behaved. Stating the following to his facilitators at a training programme,

> When you are doing art in a class, and a child comes up and says I don't want to sit next to that girl because she's a Dalit, and you say it's ok, you don't have to sit, then your bias is coming through.[6]

he argued: 'Therefore, there is a need to explore one's self, who am I, and where I come from. Then come skills' (Personal communication, 15 May 2014).

Thus, in order to adequately familiarize and transfer this culture and practice to facilitators, IP organized a series of trainings for them during the academic year 2012–2013. This included an intense, four-day training programme that included sessions on organizational goals

---

[5] 'Self-making', as used by Vincent and Ball (2007), refers to the idea that the child must become someone of categoric value through a process of choice-making and realization of one's potential. I use 'conscious', as an adjective here, to refer to how the programmes are specifically designed to bring these processes to the level of awareness and verbalization.

[6] Personal communication, 15 May 2014.

and vision,[7] sessions for self-introspection and personal transformation, and 'teach back' sessions in which facilitators could practice their skills of facilitation.

In addition to this, there were other occasions on which facilitators received training along with the other members of the organization, such as when the master trainer, Christiana Munro, visited India in October 2012. Other than trainings, there were also occasions when facilitators could receive clarification or discuss the pedagogy of facilitation. These were called 'Curriculum Feedback Sessions' (of which there were three held—two with the internal managerial team of IP and one with Christiana Munro when she visited India). During these meetings, the team discussed the relevance of the curriculum and the facilitation practices to children, and received clarification on how activities were to be conducted and on the aims and objectives of the activities and sessions.

However, despite this rigorous training and investment in bringing about a personal transformation in the facilitators, as well as in their knowledge of facilitation, what was largely visible was the loss-of-transfer of this culture. While facilitators mastered 'content knowledge' (e.g., psychological terminologies, programme jargon) and imitated overt behaviour and mannerisms of the middle class (which included dressing style, mannerisms such as greeting each other with high fives, handshakes or hugs, adopted personal accessories such as leather-bound organizers with which to plan their sessions/schedules), the actual tacit skills and knowledges required for facilitation were often missed out.

To provide an example of what I mean by this, I present another session conducted by Devyani and Sonu (two newly trained lead facilitators of IP) during an annual training programme, conducted for the staff and volunteers of IP, in the presence of Christiana. The session was conducted with the intention of achieving two aims: first, it was meant to be an internal training programme for the entire organization in order to ensure that a common understanding of

---

[7] From where the earlier example given by Arya to his team has been taken.

the programme was available to all its staff and volunteers and to train them in the philosophy and pedagogy that IP subscribed to. Second, this session was also specifically meant to provide Devyani and Sonu, who had recently been trained as lead facilitators, with an opportunity to practice their skills and receive feedback from the master trainer, Christiana.

Devyani was a senior programme coordinator at IP who had been involved in their Youth Centre and mentoring programme for over six years. Having come from an impoverished home, Devyani had first encountered IP as a 'mentee' and had received mentoring support from IP in making important life choices such as selection of a career, decisions about continuing education and so on. Devyani had then started volunteering with IP in 2007, after completing her tenth standard. She had been assigned the task of going into disadvantaged communities and identifying youth like her, who could benefit from IP's mentoring and LSE programme, and convincing their families and motivating the youth to attend the programmes, as she was seen as having the knowledge, personal experience and language required to convince members from these communities.[8]

Sonu, the other facilitator, also came from an impoverished background, and was a migrant from Orissa who had come to Bengaluru in search of better job prospects. Sonu worked as a senior coordinator in the administrative team at IP and was in charge of technical and logistical support (which involved ensuring the availability of resources, food, water required during outdoor trainings), distribution of required material for sessions to facilitators on the instructions of the admin-in-charge, stock-taking and other clerical jobs involving payments related to the bank, electricity bills, etc. Pointing out that IP had a tradition of providing training in life skills to all its employees (including the administrative staff), Sonu informed me during an informal conversation that he had initially resisted this, considering it irrelevant to his job. It was only following the CEO, Arya's intervention, that he had been convinced to attend the training. However, having attended the training once, Sonu had felt that his 'mind had been opened up'. This

---

[8] As reported by Devyani (Personal communication, 20 April 2014).

course of events had also opened up his mind to the possibility of training for, and becoming, a 'lead facilitator' and ultimately starting an organization similar to IP, independently, back in his hometown.[9]

At the annual in-house training event (that took place in October 2012), Devyani and Sonu were given the task of facilitating sessions on personal transformation for a mixed group of middle-class staff and volunteers and 'non-middle class' facilitators of the organization. The particular activity that was to be conducted was a game called 'Lava Pit' that was used to build skills of teamwork, communication, critical thinking and stronger interpersonal relations.

For the purpose of the activity, the group was divided into two teams, and each was given the task of crossing an imaginary lava pit (i.e., an imaginary space designated in the middle of the room). Each of the teams were provided with a set of 'magic carpets' or mats (that would allow them to cross the pit without getting burnt by the lava). However, the number of mats provided was lesser than the number of team members and the numbers required to cover the entire length of the pit. Thus, each team had to strategize in a manner that would allow them to cross the pit with all members safely. For this, they had to accommodate themselves on as few mats as possible (staying physically in contact with each other), while freeing up other mats to place them ahead so that they could step on these as they moved forward. During this process, if members stepped into the 'lava', failed to remain physically connected to each other or left some members out, the team was asked to start all over again. Finally, the goal was to complete the task before the other team.

While this was the nature of the activity to be facilitated by Sonu and Devyani, a series of 'disconnects' could be observed right from the start. First, instructions with respect to the goals and restrictions placed on the players while completing the activity were so weakly explained that it allowed the two groups to take creative licenses with respect to the performance of the activity. For example, instead of the activity leading to an atmosphere of competition between the two groups to

[9] Personal communication, 19 October 2012.

find the most effective team-based strategies to finish the activity first, it led to an atmosphere of cooperation and subversion of rules with the two groups helping each other, instead of competing to outdo each other. The two groups coordinated their movements and pooled in their mats in order to increase the total pool of mats available to both teams to cross the pit. Further, since mats were exchanged in such a manner that each team moved a few steps at a time and then gave their extra mats to the other team to also move forward, both teams finished the task at the same time and, in the process, also missed out connecting physically with their own team members.

Following the activity, during reflection, middle-class members of the group such as Sonali (Programme Anchor from IP's managerial team) and Carmen (a college student and volunteer from the US), noted that the activity had been 'chaotic', no one had been listening to each other and that ideas had not been shared with members within their own groups. Other middle-class members such as Tim (a retired schoolteacher and volunteer from the UK) noted that the groups had been 'closed' and that he had felt left out. Tim also noted how another volunteer, Stephanie's suggestion, on how to strategize to achieve the goal had never been paid attention to.

In contrast to this, the non-middle-class facilitators, who had dominated and led the activity, had enjoyed the boisterous atmosphere in which the activity had taken place and the improvisations (of exchanging mats across the groups) they had made under the circumstances. For the facilitators, the game had been an instance of displaying their camaraderie, with most of the activity having been dominated by instructions and plans they had called out to each other across the groups. In this process, they had left out some of the other middle-class members in their own groups to follow suit.

Thus, what emerged dramatically during the reflection process was the difference in experiences that the middle-class managerial group and volunteers had in comparison with the experiences had by the facilitators. These differences in experiences were further compounded by other factors such as the formation of in-groups and out-groups (as reflected in Tim's account, with Tim and the other middle-class members of the group forming the minority out-group). This also had implications in terms of the comfort experienced by different group members in terms of personal and physical space. For example, Sneha (one of the founding members and volunteers of IP) described her experience in the following manner:

> I feel very protective about my personal space. I did not feel safe in the space because there were new people I was meeting for the first time and I was asked to come physically proximate to strangers for an activity.

All these observations made by participants raised several opportunities for reflecting over questions of 'safety', space, group dynamics, gendered and class-based experiences of discomfort, experiences of feeling left out or not being heard and even an occasion to reflect over the creative improvisations made. However, Devyani and Sonu were largely unable to delve deeper into these experiences and engage participants in a process of self-reflection. Though Sonu had mastered and demonstrated the behavioural knowledge and skills of being a good and engaged 'listener' (which is one of the tasks that is emphasized of a facilitator and taught to them), he was unable to actually reflect an understanding of the points being made. Though he adopted the right body language (i.e., with his head tilted on one side, nodding in response to the comments made by the speakers and providing feedback with periodic responses such as 'okay', which appeared to demonstrate a keen interest in what the speaker had to say), he was unable to reflect respondents' thoughts back to them, or to the larger group, stimulating them to dig deeper into the nature of the problem. While he tried to prolong the reflection by constantly saying, 'More...anyone?' he was unable to pick up on the previous point and recast it into a provocative thought or question that would further the discussion.

Similarly, Devyani responded to Tim and Sneha's comments by redirecting the focus onto children, rather than provoking the group to examine themselves, stating, 'It is very beautiful the way Tim and Sneha have put these points. Are these things what happen with our young adults as well?' Again, her use of the term 'young adults' revealed the manner in which Devyani had been able to internalize the language of the organization (which also referred to adolescents as 'young adults', giving the impression of valuing the agency of their students), while being unable to master the tacit skills of facilitation which required engaging individuals deeply with their own selves.

These points on how reflection was conducted by the two facilitators can be compared with how the same activity (i.e., Lava Pit) had been facilitated by Arya (the CEO of IP) and Diana (the Associate Manager of the Programme Delivery Team at IP), for teachers of a private English medium school called Excellence Academy.[10] During this training, Devesh and Diana sought to throw back at the group the thoughts and actions that had emerged in the course of the activity in order to help them reflect on themselves. For example, following the 'Lava Pit' activity, Arya, who conducted the reflection, drew the teachers' attention to points during the activity when they had not followed the rules (unlike Sonu and Devyani who did not comment upon this).

Informing them that he had noticed this, Devesh pointed out to the teachers that he was not looking at it from a perspective of 'cheating' but was trying to understand their perspective. Asking them questions such as, 'Did you feel it was not important to follow rules?' and 'Did you feel that there were weak members in the team?' Devesh brought around the discussion to questions of 'What does it mean to win?' and whether it was acceptable to win by bending the rules or leaving team members out. Having elicited responses from the group about members who were in a 'sari', and who were slowing down the group's progress because they found it difficult to jump over to the next mat, Devesh related this to real-life 'handicaps' and disabilities, bringing the group to introspect on whether the following conclusions could be deduced from their action: 'So you're saying you can leave behind a [handicapped] person to reach a goal?' Stating that 'one [aspect of the game] is the goal, and the other is how you get to the goal', Devesh was able to elicit responses from teachers'

[10] On 23 April 2012.

with respect to how, while the goal was important, how one got to the goal must also be paid attention to.

Similarly, Sanjana, the programme anchor of the design and development team at IP, who was also present at the training, made a thought-provoking intervention to the ongoing discussion stating, 'It is easy to break the rules when no one is watching. When this repeatedly happens we become less guilty [of breaking the rules].' This prompted one of the teachers to share her self-realization of how this had been true in her case with teaching. With no one monitoring her classes on an everyday basis, she pointed out that she had gradually become more and more lax in her duties as a teacher and had become less uncomfortable about this over a period of time.

Thus, what could be seen from the two different instances of facilitation with the same activity was how the two sets of facilitators oriented the group members to different lessons to be learnt from the activity. While Devesh and Sanjana sought to bring the teachers to internally examine themselves, Devyani and Sonu, on the other hand, seemed to shift the focus outwards, towards the children that they would be working with.

This was despite having been introduced to the 'culture of self-making' through several forms of training and the extended period of time spent with the organization, in the case of facilitators such as Devyani. In fact, other facilitators, both at IP and the other organizations (where the training processes were, however, not as strong as IP's), oriented to the programmes similarly, thus clearly presenting how programmes failed to transfer the middle class 'cultural capital' or ways of relating to the self as a 'project-in-the-making' (Vincent and Ball, 2007) to others not belonging to similar class backgrounds.

7.2.1. Class, Self and 'Strategic Opportunizing'

To further explain these differences and discuss the divergent outcomes and formation of subjectivities, that were in contrast with the aims of the LSPs, I draw upon Bourdieu's (1986) analytical concept of 'cultural capital', which describes the non-material forms by which class differences and inequalities are sustained. According to Bourdieu (1986), non-economic and embodied forms of wealth, such as experiences of socialization and education, that are the work of time and specific cultural practices of upbringing, endow individuals with particular kinds of minds, bodies, selves, tastes, mannerisms, lifestyles and dress that provide the crucial material necessary to sustain class distinction beyond monetary wealth. In its objectified form, this also consists of various 'objects of culture' (such as books, paintings, art, instruments, technology), certifications, degrees and scholarships, that confer status and are not equally accessible to all. Central to this notion of 'cultural capital' is the hidden, congealed and embodied forms of knowledge transferred through hereditary processes or exchanged within specific social networks (e.g., family, friends, school, community, religious, etc.), that are otherwise difficult to transmit or acquire due to their tacit and embodied nature. According to Bourdieu, it is these forms of 'capital' that essentially allow social differences to be reproduced and maintained within society.

More recently, studies by Annette Lareau (2000, 2003), Carol Vincent and Stephen Ball (2007) and others have drawn on this concept to show how child-rearing strategies in middle-class and working-class homes differ, affording children different 'cultural capital' and base for socio-economic participation and success within dominant institutions (that favour particular kinds of selves). For example, in her book *Unequal Childhoods: Class, Race and Family Life*, Lareau (2003) argues that middle-class parents invest in strategies of 'concerted cultivation' (that require greater direct and indirect resources such as income or time off from work and leisure) and engage children in age-appropriate activities. Part of these strategies also involve the use of reasoning and questioning as ways to pin down aspects of identity and create a sense of autonomy and entitlement of the self. On the other hand, she has noted that White and African-American working-class families invest in strategies of 'natural growth', which emphasize food, shelter, safety and love as the prerequisites for healthy development, leaving other aspects of development (such as leisure) to children themselves. Working-class parents were also found to use more directives and physical punishments in correcting children's behaviours, rather than engaging them in a process of examining and introspecting one's self, which has implications for the sense of autonomy and entitlement experienced by these children.

These differences noted by Lareau in fact seemed to have clear overlaps with the differences in ideas about children's socialization, shared by the middle-class organizers of the LSPs (who emphasized autonomy and self-examination on the part of the child) and the facilitators and teachers in government schools (who seemed to favour strategies of 'natural growth', as will be shown further). Similar observations have also been made by other scholars about the middle class in the Indian context, who have been noted to provide their children with experiences of 'concerted cultivation' through engagement in various paid curricular and extra-curricular activities, in a bid to foster a sense of individuality and competition in them (refer Ganguly-Scrase and Scrase, 2012; Nambissan, 2010; Saraswathi and Pai, 1997). In fact, Saraswathi and Pai (1997) note that while the traditional 'ethno-theory of (child) development' has favoured a view of learning as maturation (as seen among the working class in Lareau's study) and did not favour the use of praise, rewards and reinforcements for this, present practices of socialization among the middle class shows a heavy investment in educational and extra-curricular activities that support children's individualistic and materialistic expressions. This shift in attitudes of child rearing that offers the child more autonomy and opportunities for self-expression reflects the new 'middle class modernity' that has been a consequence of their greater cultural contact and affinity with the West and its cultural and educational resources and experiences.[11]

In contrast with this, 'modern' ideas about self-making appeared to still be absent among those who belonged to the lower classes, or to provincial contexts, such as the children and teachers from government schools (an observation that has been made by other scholars, such as Nita Kumar [2007] also). Thus, for example, government

---

[11] For a socio-historical account of middle-class formation in India, refer Baviskar and Ray (2011), Deshpande (2003), Fernandes (2006) and Joshi (2001).

schoolteachers such as Jyothsana Nayak, a Hindi teacher at the government school in south Bengaluru, explained the LSP in the following manner: 'In government schools, parents don't talk to children. They only provide for clothes and food. Children need someone to talk to. Then they will get relief and feel like doing something'.[12] Echoing Lareau's 'natural growth' strategy, what Jyothsana seemed to understand as significantly absent from the homes of the children she worked with was affection or emotional support. She therefore saw the programmes as fulfilling this requirement of 'natural growth', in addition to providing good advice.

Absent from Jyothsana's account was an idea of 'life skills' as training to engage the child with one's self and develop insights into their attitudes, behaviours and beliefs. Even facilitators such as Vrinda (from MFCL) and Yamuna (of VYB) explained the programmes in a similar fashion. While Vrinda explained to me that their role was one of providing guidance and advice, and that the success of the programmes ultimately depended on whether children took up these strategies and applied it to their lives,[13] Yamuna explained that her role was one of providing emotional and personal support to those children that no one else (i.e., neither parents nor teachers) had time to care for.[14]

These different ways in which stakeholders have oriented to the LSPs and discourse has contributed simultaneously to the 'failure' and 'reproduction' of the developmental work of producing 'entrepreneurial selves' through programmes such as LSE, particularly in the Global South. To explain this further, I offer the conceptual idea of 'strategic opportunizing' and argue that actors I engaged with were strategically and opportunistically responding to the programmes, and the larger life situations that they found themselves in. Actors' attempts at 'strategic opportunizing', I argue, is what simultaneously contributes to the failure and reproduction of the global neoliberal culture

---

[12] Personal communication, 6 August 2012.
[13] Personal communication, 15 November 2012.
[14] Personal communication, 23 March 2012.

of entrepreneurialism and self-responsibilization. That is, in the face of an assemblage of discursive socio-cultural practices and techno-scientific rationalities that have produced new standards for 'being' (e.g., 'modern', 'successful', 'educated', 'flexible', 'adaptable', 'skilled', etc.) and that have consequently marked their own cultural ways of being as 'coarse', 'dull', 'backward' or 'uncultured' (as discussed in the earlier chapters), I argue that actors 'responded' in two ways: first, by taking stock of their own selves and making sense of themselves against these new discourses (i.e., about how one is and how one ought to be); and second, by selectively appropriating these discourses in order to stay relevant in the current scenario. I explain this further by discussing how each group of actors made sense of the life skills discourse.

Actors' interpretations and negotiated responses to the programmes is also critical to understanding the circulation of *neoliberalism with a small n*, rather than as a 'grand narrative' or theory: that is, through novel configurations of relations of government, whose outcomes are contingent and unpredictable. Such an analysis is also consistent with a Foucauldian analysis of power, within which limits to governmental action is intrinsic to the nature of the power itself, as power is seen not as a totalizing and central force but as capillary and distributed equation of relations with 'acting subjects' (Li, 2007). Li (2007, p. 277) points out that therefore, 'any governmental intervention risks producing effects that are contradictory, even perverse. For this reason, reflexivity and calculation of risk are intrinsic to government.... Yet this does not mean that transformation is (always) successful.'

The in-built critique of power within frameworks of governmentality is also what, Li (2007, p. 276) argues, 'opens critical terrain for ethnographic analysis'. Drawing on these insights for analysis by previous governmentality researchers, in the following section, I examine actors' (i.e., at individual and collective, local and global levels) negotiated, strategic and opportunistic production of selves to unpack the discursive structures of neoliberalism, which are constituted as a series of 'responses upon responses' (or as Foucault argues, actions upon actions), thus making the production of subjects and effects of governance tenuous and constantly evolving.

7.3. Facilitators and the Production of a New Professional Status

As a way to explain the aforementioned point, I start with accounts presented by the facilitators, which offers an insight into how they understood the LSPs and their own selves in relation to it. Belonging to modest, lower middle-class or lower class, rural and/or agricultural backgrounds, associated with small towns and universities, the facilitators that I speak about were those that Nita Kumar (2007) describes as the 'provincial other' to the urban, globalized, corporatized and 'modern' India. As members belonging to these 'provincialities', they were those who have occupied 'inferior positions' within organizational and institutional discourses, and were recognized by the organizations as not sufficiently educated in 'modernity' and 'bourgeoisie culture' that require a particular facility with practices of self-making in space and time (N. Kumar, 2007).

Even when many facilitators, in organizations such as VYB and MFCL, had exposure to a 'modern' discipline such as psychology,[15] they had mostly not imbibed its cultural ways of understanding the self as a 'bounded, rational and autonomous entity' (Burman, 2007; Fendler, 1998; Rose, 1999) and did not apply its techniques of self-making to their own lives. In fact, many of these facilitators had not even heard of LSE before joining their respective organizations. Consequently, they were also those whose knowledge was devalued in all three organizations, and the ones who occupied lower roles within the organizations, with little decision-making powers or opportunities for creatively contributing towards curriculum development. In their functions, they resembled what Giroux (1988) has noted about teachers as being 'high level technicians' in the neoliberal economy, who have been separated from the processes of knowledge creation and generation, and are required to merely follow the blueprint for education laid down somewhere else (Sarangapani, 2011). Based on this understanding, facilitators were also constructed by the organizations as 'recipients' of the programmes who had to be educated in 'life

---

[15] Some facilitators even had a masters-level training in the subject, because of which they had been recruited by their organizations.

skills', monitored and evaluated. In the face of these constructions of their selves, I now present the set of responses put forth by facilitators such as Kaveri and others, in making sense of their lives.

Providing explanations such as 'We've never grown up with [these skills]' but are 'opening up a little' because of this, what facilitators such as Kaveri seemed to be doing was attempting to make sense of themselves. Comparing herself with the children that she worked with, Kaveri attempted to explain to me about how these skills were important for the children in government schools to gain confidence and to ensure a level playing field for them, when compared to others from the middle class. Pointing to how she herself had never received such opportunities due to the absence of such training during her school days, she sought to explain how she and government school children (like her) lacked confidence because of this. Thus, she argued that they were also afraid to speak in front of 'private school children' and brought their 'culture' (of being loud, rash, withdrawn, disrespectful or addicted to drugs) into school.[16] Stating 'They [government school children] should also improve like private school children. When they leave school, they should know how to be in society', she made a case for the LSP. She pointed out that while these skills should have come automatically to them, it was important to place these 'openly in front of this generation of children', so that they may also benefit.[17]

Similarly, others such as Yamuna (a facilitator from VYB) also appeared to be making sense of her non-middle-class self and that of the children in government schools in a similar manner. Stating the need for these programmes specifically for children in government schools, she explained,

> ...government school children require life skills more because they don't know anything, have no discipline, won't wear uniforms; ... they come like free persons. They are the rebel kind. They don't know that they need to wish the teacher. Government schools don't teach them how to behave or about interpersonal 'talking'

[16] In contrast with this, Kaveri believed that middle-class children left their 'culture' behind, since they were 'bold'.
[17] Personal communication, 31 July 2012.

[*sic*] skills. They come from slums so we need to educate them. In private schools, they are already taught so many things.... There may be family problems like parents not looking after well (in private schools), but these kind of problems are not there.[18]

From the narratives of facilitators, what appeared in common were the ways in which they came to evaluate and understand their selves and the children they worked with, comparing it with the bourgeoisie standards of the new economy, workplaces, educational settings and society. In relation to these standards, there was a recognition of their own selves as lacking knowledges that were important for mobility and success. Thus, for example, facilitators such as Bharath (from IP) explained to their students:

I was poor. My parents struggled to put me through school. Someone like this (pointing towards me) taught me art, clay modelling, acting, dance, and today it has helped me get a job.[19]

Recounting to his class about how he got his present job by impressing his managers with his mimicry skills, Bharath sought to highlight the 'hard skills' that the programmes could offer, thus compensating for the poor outcomes that schooling had offered him, as would be the case for the children he worked with.

In 'responding' to these programmes and their discourses in this manner, I argue that facilitators were not just trying to make sense of themselves in relation to the new demands and expectations placed on individuals through these educational discourses to become more 'skilled'. I argue that they also 'responded strategically' in another sense, by 'opportunistically' using the discourses and practices of these very programmes. That is, facilitators seemed to be adopting and applying the language and practices associated with these LSPs to themselves, in order to stay 'relevant' and access certain kinds of training, identities, jobs while also rejecting parts of it and substituting it with other ends.

[18] Personal communication, 31 March 2012.
[19] Observed at a session for eighth standard students at Tamil minority school in east Bengaluru on 22 August 2012.

Facilitators such as Bharath and Sonu continued to see value in these forms of cultural training programmes offered by the middle class, for the opportunities for mobility it could provide them. Understanding the specific opportunities it could afford them (such as getting trained and certified by international experts such as Christiana Munro), Bharath even stated the following to me, on one occasion: '*Adu ondu training sikkidare, naane training shuru maaDuttini*' ('If I could get that one training, I will start my own training programmes').[20] Similarly, others such as Sonu also expressed these desires of starting his own organization with the skills he could gain from working at IP.[21] In these instances, facilitators appeared to be drawing on the very discourses of 'skills training' and the particular ideas of an entrepreneurial self that has gained currency in the present context, and that threatened to render them irrelevant, 'unemployable', 'uneducated' and 'inconsequential' to fit in and survive within this climate.

Yet, when I describe these 'responses' as opportunistic, what I also mean to show is how, on the other hand, they appeared to use this space and training for very different ends, training children in a different set of knowledges. That is, they appeared to be conducting the sessions without necessarily adopting the discourse and practices of LSE in its entirety, which is what led to the 'disconnects' observed on the field (as noted earlier). For example, the knowledges and skills that they emphasized for children were ones of support and advice on how to be 'disciplined' (by following external norms, rules, conventions and authority), additional vocational or technical skills that could secure them jobs (like mimicry that had enabled a job for Bharath) and the language and cultural jargon available to children from the middle class.

That practices of self-introspection and self-making were less valued by the facilitators compared to learning to respect authority, learn specific skills and take away pieces of cultural jargon was repeatedly evident from how facilitators conducted their classes and the

---

[20] Personal communication, 22 September 2012.
[21] Personal communication, 18 October 2012.

knowledges they emphasized. For example, it was apparent in classroom transactions undertaken by Vrinda (a facilitator with MFCL), who repeatedly explained to her students, 'We will teach you also to go on the right path. If you go on that right path, very good. Otherwise, I can only say it's your bad luck'.[22] Others such as Yamuna (of VYB) focused on presenting 'jargon', specifically in English, such as learning the spelling of 'psychology', learning the full form of 'WHO', learning terms such as 'copers', 'spewers', 'exploders'[23] and so on, that was understood as the cultural capital of the middle class. Similarly, other facilitators such as Arunoday from MFCL emphasized learning the names of the 10 life skills in English. Insisting that children should have these names at their fingertips, he provided them with the following warning: 'Next class if you don't learn the 10 life skills, there will be no punishment. But I won't give you entry into class'.[24]

Further, all these forms of novel information presented to the children had to be copied, memorized, repeated and reproduced in subsequent classes. Thus, for the facilitators, as much as for the children themselves, this English jargon itself inspired awe and represented the power of middle-class 'knowledge', therefore often becoming the main part of the lesson and take away from the classes. Often, sessions would include a game in which the children and the facilitator, together, would try to use this 'jargon' learnt, for example, by identifying people in the group through categories they had learnt in the classes, such as 'spewers' or 'copers'.

Further, while using this language, explanations and (sometimes) even the activities and pedagogic practices (e.g., questioning) of the programmes would be put to more conventional ends of teaching children obedience or respect for elders, as can be seen from the following examples. The first example is from the session by Gautam, playing the 'Yes game' (described in Chapter 6), after which he went

---

[22] Personal communication, 25 October 2012.
[23] These were categories mentioned in the facilitators' manual, in the lesson on anger management, to describe people based on their differences in their expression of anger.
[24] Personal communication, 15 November 2012.

on to summarize the lessons to be learnt from the game, which were mainly related to following parents and teachers to be able to reach the goal. He concluded this lesson saying 'Study hard and somehow pass'.

In another session, Yamuna, the facilitator from VYB, conducted a class on decision-making for students of ninth standard at a south Bengaluru school[25] again using this as a way to draw attention to appropriate classroom behaviour. A part of this session is presented here.

Yamuna: I will tell you a story. Listen carefully. This is about 10 frogs which lived in a river. A few of the frogs, about five of them, think of moving to another river to get better food. So how many frogs left the river?

Students (in chorus): five…10….

Yamuna: I said five frogs were thinking (emphasizing this) of going to another river. I did not tell you how many went to another river. So thought has not taken action here.

(Turns to the black board and writes 'Decision' on the board. Students, in chorus, start shouting 'memory', in response to this. She continues to write 'Decision → Action-Oriented', then turns and addresses the students.)

Yamuna: You all, before coming to the ninth this year, would have thought you have to study well. You have to make it action-oriented. If you haven't converted it into action it will get cancelled. Next topic let us take, 'Thinking of being good'. Every decision has good and bad consequences. What are the good consequences of being a good student?

Student 1: Girls are always called good. Boys are called bad. (Children start laughing)

….[26]

Student 2: We will get good marks.

---

[25] On 13 December 2012.
[26] Portions of the transcript omitted due to constraints of space.

Student 1: We should do our work, complete our work. We shouldn't bring a bad name to our school.

Student 3: We will have a good name with teachers. There will be discipline. We will get good marks.

Yamuna: So these are the good consequences of this decision. What are the bad consequences that come from it? ...

Student 4: Responsibility becomes more.

Student 5: We can't make noise in class.

Student 6: We will have less freedom.

...

Yamuna: Next step—you have to assess whether there are more of good or bad consequences to the decision. If you have taken a decision you have to think of its consequences also. You should think if I should go ahead or not. If good is more you should go with that; if bad is more you should not go with it. That decision, who needs to take? You only. You only know—or should I take (the decision)? So choice is yours.

In another session, conducted for a group of eighth standard students at the south Bengaluru government school, Yamuna drew her class' attention to the following expectation for behaviour at school.

Yamuna: Can we talk to teachers and parents like we talk to our friends? ... When you have a doubt can you just ask like this (adopting an aggressive tone and gesture)? There's a way to ask no? What approach should we use?

Students: We must fold our hands and tell the teacher 'miss we are unable to understand. Can you please explain it?'

Yamuna: So you shouldn't ask rashly, but softly. Then teacher will feel like answering. Otherwise she will think I have so much experience and she (student) is talking to me so rashly [*sic*].

What can be seen from these aforementioned transcripts is the coupling of the 'questioning' method with conventional techniques, such as, the use of 'directives' to reinforce traditional notions of 'discipline' (that are very different from the notions of 'self-disciplining' that were emphasized by the programme managers. These practices in fact resemble the traditional socialization goals mentioned by Saraswathi and Pai [1997], as noted earlier). Questioning, here, served as a means to elicit the 'right' answers that were important to reinforce conventional discipline, rather than to allow for children's agencies to be expressed or selves to be explored.[27] Rather than involving children in gaining experiential knowledge of the self through reflection and exploration of one's thoughts, behaviours, actions, beliefs and conflicts involved in decision-making, the focus was on providing an algorithm for decision-making and on testing its recall as seen in the first example by Yamuna, as though decision-making itself was a simple process of applying rules. (This is also what seemed to be implied in Vrinda's comment discussed earlier.)

Thus, what the facilitators appeared to value as 'skills' were not the tacit skills of self-making but the overt forms of discipline, punctuality, regularity and neatness that they saw in middle-class children. They also valued the additional extracurricular skills of art, drama and sports that the middle-class child had access to, and the familiarity with certain forms of language use, particularly in English that children from the middle classes had. While interpreting 'life skills' in this manner, by coupling existing ideas of child development with more progressive ideologies and techniques, what was also interesting to note was how facilitators appeared to be constructing themselves as a new class of professionals, who formed the much-required bridge between the middle classes and their visions for a 'developed' and 'sanitized' society and the populations that they sought to 'reform'. Pointing to their knowledge of both these worlds, I argue that facilitators, themselves youth, managed to stay 'relevant' in the current environment (instead of being rendered irrelevant, due to too much education for traditional jobs and not the right kinds of education for the new corporate and service sectors that have opened up in the new economy).

---

[27] It thus appeared to mimic the 'textbook culture' of the classroom that Krishna Kumar (1988) and Sarangapani (2003b) refer to.

Facilitators tried to stay relevant by strategically adopting the very language and discourses of the programmes but still achieving very different outcomes (as a result of their own standpoints from which they interpreted these discourses). Therefore, I use the term 'opportunistic' in describing their responses to imply that they used the knowledges got from the programmes not in its spirit but only as a means to other ends. One part of these ends was to strategically build and negotiate their own identities and positions of power/knowledge vis-à-vis the organizations, other dominant institutions (such as schools, workplaces, the economy) and the larger neoliberal enterprise itself, that has come to define who and what constitutes 'authority' and 'knowledge'.

That is, while facilitators were being constructed as 'lacking knowledge' and 'culture' by the managers (due to their class positions and social status), facilitators sought to reverse this perception by constructing themselves as the real 'experts' and as the adults who genuinely cared for the children from these disadvantaged groups. In addition to this, more than one facilitator, in their accounts of themselves and their organizations, constructed the management as lacking experience and the real expertise required to work in the schools and communities that they worked in. Presenting themselves as having the real knowledge about these communities, some such as Kaveri[28] and Nayanika[29] pointed to the unrealistic ideas of the management with respect to the programmes, challenging those from the middle class to attempt conducting a session at these schools. They sought to point out to both the lack of actual skills required to manage children within government schools, as well as the resilience required to work within these materially challenging conditions as factors that would make them unable to perform in these contexts. Others such as Gautam (a facilitator from IP) clearly expressed their frustration with what they viewed as unrealistic techniques and practices that were unsuited to the context and tasks of managing and educating these children, stating the following.

> They (managers) insist on freedom. But class can't work if we give them full freedom. The last 10–15 minutes when we have to deliver

[28] Personal communication, 26 June 2012.
[29] Personal communication, 23 March 2012.

the message, it's very difficult for us. Without discipline it is not possible to control the class.³⁰

Similarly, other facilitators such as Santhosh (from IP) also spoke of how novel pedagogic practices, such as that of 'reflection', were also unsuited to these contexts, arguing that while they [facilitators] were getting paid to undertake these practices and apply it to themselves, children were not similarly motivated or interested in this.³¹

While it may be argued that challenges such as these posed to the LSE programme, by the facilitators, partly arose from the differences in 'cultural capital' that limited their abilities to undertake participative and introspective learning practices, it can also be said that in trying to achieve what the facilitators believed were the 'real skills' or knowledges that were of value within this context, they were in fact also carving out a niche identity for themselves. Though recognized (post their training and jobs in these organizations) as 'life skills trainers', and more importantly as 'life skilled' themselves and as having a meta-level knowledge of life skills (by schools or other organizations that they applied to, drawing on the language and personal culture learnt in their respective organizations),³² they in fact continued to reproduce traditional practices and discourses on 'disciplining youth'.

However, these 'opportunistic strategies' employed by the facilitators, I argue, were also self-limiting and 'partially blind', in that they were not informed by the depth of cultural knowledge required to understand how their own strategies of offering alternate skills and knowledges were limiting for themselves as well as for the children (because these were not the skills relevant to the new economy and the modern reflexive society). Further, I argue that these 'responses' were 'blind' also because they were undertaken without a recognition of how this contributed to the sustenance of the neoliberal logic of individual enterprise (in their aspirations of becoming like the middle class and adopting certain

---

³⁰ Personal communication, 17 February 2012.
³¹ Personal communication, 19 October 2012.
³² Here, I refer to the aspects of dress, language and personal mannerisms (such as handshakes and hugs) that some facilitators reported having adopted, following their association with their respective organizations.

aspects of their selves) and, as a consequence, led to a reproduction of their class and social status (for without the cultural capital of the middle class they could never find entry into their worlds).

Yet I contend that this was also no different from how the children related to the programmes, or even how the middle-class managers did (despite the different understanding of 'life skills' that they seemed to have). That is, I argue that these other groups were also 'strategically opportunizing', using the programmes albeit in different ways, thereby resisting and contributing to the reproduction of the neoliberal logic, as I will discuss further.

7.4. Students and 'Strategic Opportunizing': The Production of a 'Culturally Better-Educated Subject'

While the ultimate target of the 'life skills' project and the reforms it seeks to achieve were the students from disadvantaged and poor communities, it is important to explain why these young people appear so little throughout the book. This is partly a result of how students appeared on the field—merely as targets to be acted upon by various authorities. Thus, they became available only through these encounters.

Access to students was always mediated by teachers and schools, who structured the interactions and responses of students. This was most evident during visits made to government schools with no on-going programmes, to interact with students and understand what they had learnt through earlier available programmes. On one such occasion at a government boy's high school in south Bengaluru, requests to interact with children led to the interaction with children being held in the staff room, where the boys were brought and the entire interaction was supervised and regulated by the school. Children were called into the staff room and told to tell me about the life skills that had been taught to them, with constant cues from the teacher-in-charge, who also sought to jog their memories and provide clues to the answer. Following her lead, children simply repeated her answers. This was the case with most encounters, and getting access to children's voices and their understanding of the programme became difficult. Children mainly appeared as characters fitted into the organizations' and schools' plans of 'education' and 'development' with little discussion in any of these spaces about what life skills meant to them. It is within this context that children's responses to the programmes must be understood.

As has been explained before, within the context of the larger social–patriarchal set-up of society and school, children (particularly those belonging to disadvantaged families) were seen as 'unknowledgable', 'uncultured' and requiring 'disciplining' and guidance. This was evident not just from the accounts of children offered by teachers, facilitators and the managers but was also visible through actual classroom observations. Within this context, children's responses were sought to be reshaped according to conventional (adult) wisdoms. An instance of this was provided in the previous chapter on how a young girl's response to eve-teasing was sought to be remade according to traditional norms that prescribe for girls to be demure and avoid situations of confrontation. Children too learnt to relate to themselves according to the expectations of teachers, society and schools, as could be seen from another instance described earlier, wherein a young girl described herself in relation to the duties (of preserving tradition) prescribed by societal (gender) norms.

Thus, based on these experiences and relations with teachers and other adults, and the structure of the school and society, children responded within the context of the programmes too, as students who must 'answer when asked' and 'be told what to do'. While the space of the LSP differed from the regular classroom, by offering students a friendlier and relaxed atmosphere, children continued to understand these spaces as marked by the authority of teacher and related to the classes and activities in a conventional manner. By this, what I mean is that they continued to see themselves as individuals lacking both the ability and authority to contribute to classroom discussion or the construction of knowledge. Thus, even on occasions in which children were given opportunities to express themselves, such as during artwork or theatre activities, children would resist 'performing' themselves[33] and instead would demand the 'right' answers from the facilitators or myself. Thus, during theatre activities such as 'Morning Mirror' (discussed earlier, in Chapter 6), children demanded that they be shown exactly what to do (*'Neengo pannungo miss. Adhaye naango seyarum.*' ['You do it miss, and we'll do the same.']). Clearly, unsure of the expectations here (due to the novel nature of the activity) and uncomfortable with taking the lead in interpreting and self-directing what was to be done, they expected the facilitator or me to perform for them, so that they could then imitate this. I specifically describe these responses by children, seen on many occasions, as 'imitation' because it often led to a scenario of identical representation (of an act, artwork or piece of writing). To illustrate this point, I describe a check-in activity called 'alien conference',[34] wherein children were given the task of imagining how they would look or act as aliens. The idea of the activity was to teach children empathy for those who were different and the ability to communicate and interact despite differences.

In the activity, participants were paired up in groups, and one partner of each team had to act as an alien, while the other would act as a translator. While conducting the activity in the aided Tamil medium school, Bharath, the facilitator from IP, had actually modified the activity which required students to imagine that one was from another planet and describe three things about the planet. In order to illustrate what was expected of students in the activity, Bharath first provided an example by holding up his palm with his middle finger and ring finger held together and with the other fingers parted, telling them that their bodies might look different. Then, Bharath asked me if I would be willing to demonstrate a scene wherein he would behave like an alien and I would translate his actions and talk. Accepting this request, together we acted out a scene in which I explained to the children that the alien was extremely hungry and was looking for food and found the children

---

[33] That is, by presenting their own ideas, beliefs and thoughts through the activity.
[34] Observed on 27 November 2012.

to be particularly appetizing. The children had a good time laughing at our act and then kept asking us to repeat it. But when encouraged to perform a scene of their own, immediately some responded saying 'No let's do something else'. Finally, after much coaxing and encouragement to shed their inhibitions and perform in pairs, only two students—Narendra and Murugan volunteered to do this, performing the same act as we had. Since after this, no one else was willing to try this activity, Bharath asked them to sit in their own places and show how they would behave as an alien. Here too most children were hesitant. Only Narendra stood up and made some robotic moves. After this, Bharath went row by row, forcibly asking children to perform as an alien, and most children made a similar screeching sound with their throats to show that they were aliens.

What this session and others like this demonstrated was not just that children were reluctant to perform without a script (i.e., without being told exactly what they must do); but when they did volunteer to perform (like Narendra and Murugan had, who also happened to be the only two boys in a class of about 20 children), they reproduced the same actions and story that had been presented to them by the facilitator, Bharath, and me. Further, some such as Soundarya, from the same school and class, informed us that she had even performed the alien 'skit' back at home and had received appreciation for this; thus demonstrating how a creative improvisation lesson had been converted into a fixed script by the children.

Key to understanding these responses by children within the programmes is the point about 'expectations' that I made earlier. That is, what appeared to be happening within the programmes (as within the context of regular schools) was that children learnt to respond according to the expectations set for them, thus rarely expressing (or performing) their own minds or displaying their creativity. This could in fact even be seen in the ways in which children responded to questions about the programme, or when asked about what 'life skills' meant to them. Most children voiced adults' ideas about 'life skills' as 'good behaviours' or as 'important aspects of life' (*jeevanige bēkaada anshagaLu*), as 'giving teachers respect' (*gurugaLige gaurava koDuvudu*), as what is good for the future or as lessons on how to be, on maintaining discipline and staying silent in class, on not hitting others or using foul language and keeping the classroom clean.[35] I present these set of responses given by children, as representing adult voices and expectations, for two reasons. First, when probed further, on how these skills would be useful or 'good' for the future, children were largely unable to explain the relevance of these skills to their lives. Thus, they appeared to be repeating what was told to them without having understood or arrived at these conclusions themselves.

Second, I make this point since, when probed further, children's second set of responses appeared to show how they related to these programmes in a completely different fashion. Children mostly spoke of the programmes as a space for fun, games and stories that made it different from the regular school. They referred, mainly, to the specific activities that they had enjoyed during the course of the programmes, such as artwork, games or sports, rather than speaking of behavioural goals such as 'obedience' and 'discipline', or other tacit skills of self-making.

Even ex-students of these programmes, such as Chandrasekhar and Sonia, who had completed school and were working or studying further, were only able to remember the games and stories that they had learnt in the classes. Others such as Valli, who worked as a telecaller for Vodafone, from within the cramped space of her single room house after completing SSLC, noted that these programmes had no relevance to their work and lives, and stated, 'We did it then and it is over. No use now'.[36]

Thus, these responses that were in stark contrast with the first set of responses given by children on the usefulness of these skills to life seemed to suggest that they were responses derived from elsewhere. In fact, even during classes, children sought to maintain this distinction between school and 'life skills classes as games and fun', by enthusiastically participating in the activities but withdrawing during the processes of discussion and reflection. During reflection, children often used strategies such as pointing to the facilitator that it was late

[35] These responses are drawn from a number of focus group discussions conducted with children across five schools.
[36] Personal communication, 14 March 2013.

and time to go home, to avoid reflection; or they would simply answer with the response, 'same as her/him' (meaning their answer was similar to whoever had answered before), to avoid the reflection process. In other cases, they would plead with me to intervene and stop the class stating that the class was 'boring', or would directly tell the facilitator, 'sir *arukarengo.*' (Spoken in colloquial Tamil, this literally meant 'sir don't put blade' or 'don't bore me'.)

In fact, on some occasions, children would also jokingly reprimand the facilitator, pointing to him or her that they were engaging in the same kinds of behaviours as their teachers (that is, of giving advice, telling them how to behave), thus, clearly seeking to make a separation between the LSP and the school routines. (On other occasions, they admitted to me that the facilitators were presenting the same messages as their teachers, but in a friendlier manner.) That they likened the discussion and reflection to regular school tasks became clear when, on several occasions, I came across children pulling out their class work or homework books and working on these lessons, in the midst of a life skills class, when no interesting activity or game was being carried out.

Thus, contrasting these two different sets of responses by children about the programmes, I argue that the initial responses given by them was not an indicator of their 'voicelessness' or lack of agency, but an indicator of how children positioned themselves within these institutional contexts and practices that set expectations for behaviour but to which they also responded strategically. That is, I state that children's initial responses about the programmes, as a training in 'good behaviours', can be seen as strategic response to satisfy schools' and other authorities' expectations for conformity and 'disciplining' of children and youth.

While responding in this manner by providing the expected answers on how to be and behave, even on given paper and pencil tests conducted by the organizations to measure the impact of the programmes (that will be described further), students however did not seem to apply these lessons in practice and within their everyday lives. Therefore, despite the articulations about discipline, respect and harmony that children learnt to voice, across the schools, teachers and facilitators rued the behavioural problems related to discipline, class cleanliness and 'respect', or even more serious behaviours such as smoking or elopement that they continued to encounter. For example, some schools such as the Tamil medium school in east Bengaluru even blamed the facilitators and the LSP for giving children too much freedom that they believed was making them 'rash' and 'bold'. In other instances, even the facilitators, such as Sneha (of VYB), reported on how children only appeared to be paying lip service to the lessons, such as abstinence from smoking, taught to them. She pointed out that while they had stopped smoking in her presence, due to the fear of being reprimanded, they continued to smoke behind her back, clearly showing how children had not internalized these messages.[37] Thus, it seemed that children's responses to the programmes was 'strategic', in order to avoid certain negative consequences or in order to appease teachers, facilitators and other adults with power over them.

Similarly, it could also be seen how the messages related to social behaviour and personal attitudes, such as on empathy, and agreements such as 'participating fully and not putting others down' had little impact on their day-to-day interpersonal relationships or communication styles. This became particularly visible during one class when Asma, a student from the Tamil medium school, shared her fear of being teased and ridiculed by other children of the class for being different, with me. That is, being one of the few Muslim girls among the majority Tamil-speaking, Hindu children in this school, Asma felt alienated and hesitated to express her cultural knowledge and ways of being within this space. During one LSE class, when children were asked to share their 'favourite' actors, films, songs and so on, as part of the activity underway, Asma hesitated to share this in front of the class, and turned red when her friend Priya drew the facilitator's attention towards her, stating that she had not shared her responses to these questions. Asma, who became very conscious and tense and visibly tried to turn the attention away from her, later explained to me about why she had been hesitant to share her likes and dislikes. In a Tamil-minority school, where children mostly discussed Tamil cinema and emulated superstars like Dhanush and Vijay from the Tamil film

---

[37] Personal communication, 17 March 2012.

industry, she felt that her beloved actor Salman Khan and favourite song, *Chance pe Dance*, would only invoke ridicule. Thus, even while the programmes were meant to teach children values such as empathy and tolerance for difference through modules on self-awareness and interpersonal relations, instances such as these clearly presented a case of how these lessons were not imbibed by the children.

Similarly, it was also noticed how on other occasions children made fun of Asma, or isolated her, having their own in-groups of Tamil-speaking friends. Others, such as Kannadiga students (who were also in a minority in the school), were similarly teased and bullied by the Tamil children, who formed the dominant community in the school, and they too would hesitate to come up and perform in front of the class. This was until a new, male, Kannada-speaking facilitator from IP was appointed to their class. Though previously the class was led by a female Kannadiga facilitator, Kaveri, the classroom dynamics only changed after Bharath's appointment, since unlike Kaveri who was unable to assert herself against the large number of Tamilian children, Bharath asserted his authority as a male teacher, privileged and valued the cultural knowledges of the Kannadiga students and would regularly invite them to perform in front of the class.

Though children did not apply the messages given by the programmes in the manner that they were intended, in defining themselves (i.e., by adopting the behaviours of discipline, obedience, respect and so on), children appeared to be 'opportunistically' using the material of the programmes in defining themselves in an alternate manner. The main takeaway for the children from the programmes were the 'real' skills it provided, either to manage academics or get employment. Thus, some groups of children at the Tamil-minority school pointed out to me that these programmes should also be made available to the tenth standard students (who did not receive the LSE classes as the board exams took precedence over extra-curricular activities), as they felt that it would also improve their memory and concentration and in turn aid with their studies. Another important use they saw with respect to the programmes were the technical skills that they could acquire from some of them. For example, some children saw value in learning computers (which was earlier a part of IP's programme) and sports (which would allow them an opportunity to enter the state-level or national-level competitions).

Simultaneously, children also creatively 'appropriated' parts of the programme in producing their own identities. That is, children used these 'new knowledges' that they received access to—such as psychological terminologies like 'consciousness' and 'sub-consciousness' or the spelling of 'psychology', information on 'how dreams are produced', or terms such as 'spewers' and 'copers'—to present themselves as 'better educated' than their peers. Children like Soundarya (of the Tamil-medium school) reported that they performed the skit taught in the life skills class (referring to the alien theatre improvisation game that Bharath and I had played with them) and received much praise for this. Children thus used the stories, games, songs and other activities learnt in the course of the classes to demonstrate their superior 'cultural knowledge' compared to peers in community, who went to other schools and did not receive these LSPs.

They noted how such knowledges, as well as skills such as football and art, had helped them win both material benefits (such as an award for free medical treatment at a local hospital that one child at the Tamil-medium school had received), as well as immaterial benefits (such as bringing prestige to the community). Noting how they did not know how to draw or play sports such as football earlier, they pointed out to the development of technical skills through which they were able to construct themselves as 'educated'. Further using these skills, children also reported playing the role of 'mentors' and 'teachers' within their communities, offering examples of how they occupied positions of responsibility, such as teaching younger children in the community or of using their 'skills' of music and storytelling to pacify younger children who had been left in their care. Thus, these skills were also means by which young people 'resisted' the identities given to them by schools, the life skills organizations and the developmental discourse as 'irresponsible', 'lacking knowledge' or as being 'uncultured' and as destined to 'fail', and thus being 'at risk'.

While resisting the dominant discourses that constructed the young people in these disadvantaged contexts and producing novel identities for themselves, it is also important to note how students' responses were partially blind and self-limiting. By rejecting the very knowledges (i.e., the skills and attitudes of self-making) of the middle classes, students in the government and aided schools partially resisted the neoliberal project of cultivating enterprising subjects. But by also failing to adopt the very capital of the middle classes required for their own mobility, they also participated in the reproduction of their own social positions, while also disrupting the neoliberal educational project of developing entrepreneurial citizens.

7.5. 'Managers' and the Production of 'Distinction'

Finally, I come to the 'managers', who, despite their desire to bring social change, appeared to be doing something else in practice. 'Managers' is the term I use for the young group of 'social entrepreneurs' (most in their late 20s and early 30s), who were mainly responsible for conceptualizing, developing and operationalizing the LSPs observed, by drawing on their access and connections to their global social networks of expertise and aid. I refer to them as 'managers', not so much as an indicator of their designations, but more with reference to their attitudes of 'governing' the lives of the poor. That is, this was a group (irrespective of their official designations) that actively sought to intervene in the lives of the poor, using managerial solutions to problems of poverty and development (Ilcan & Lacey, 2011) that focused on various techniques to manage life itself, in order to help them escape from their cycles of poverty and to 'socially vaccinate' them against life's 'risks'.

While often these were individuals from the middle class (particularly, what Fernandes [2006] calls the 'new middle class'), with no prior formal training or engagement with educational, psychological or clinical work or practice and no formal authority[38] or accreditation in

---

[38] In fact, many of them were operating within government run schools outside the purview of the state education department and had no interface with or permission from the education department to conduct these programmes.

life skills training itself, the group largely consisted of individuals who were adequately familiar with the 'cultures of self-making', having previously worked in corporate firms and the 'new workplace' (Urciuoli, 2010). Applying their childhood experiences of 'concerted cultivation' and the cultural knowledges of 'soft skills' and 'managerialism', drawn from their work experiences in the corporate sector, the 'managers' designed, planned and implemented the programmes along the lines of these experiences. Arguing that through these programmes they sought to 'give back' to society; founder-directors, and other members of these organizations, such as Devesh Arya, presented their visions as one of contributing to individual development and national growth, as can be seen from the account given here.

> Twelve to 14 million people graduate from the country but don't get jobs.... There are 12 to 14 million jobs as well, but not people. The education system is not preparing us for the future.... We said 'the education system is good. We are not going to change the education system.' We see a lack of life skills. Why life skills? Because when you have life skills you will be able to deal with life's challenges on your own. You'll find a way to deal with life's challenges.[39]

What was evident in managers' discourses, such as the one aforementioned, was the neoliberal assumptions of 'work-productivity-growth' promoted by neo-classical economics (Vasavi & Kingfisher, 2003), which see appropriate 'skills' as the key to both individual and national development (Gibb & Walker, 2011). These 'skills' were the ones that sought to make individuals aware of their 'roles and responsibilities', of 'how to be and behave' with self-responsibility and social consciousness (as seen from the presentation of messages such as the importance of particular forms of education, or campaigns, such as conserving energy through the use of CFL bulbs). Rather than helping individuals understand and demand for their rights and entitlements, teaching them to critically examine the nature of citizenship or questioning the state's role in development, equity and access, managers equated personal transformations with changes in one's own self, beliefs and behaviour. Thus, for example, managers such as Sukumar, G. (of MFCL's LSE

---

[39] Personal communication, 15 May 2012.

programme for government schools) explained to me that 'in today's 'globalised' world nothing else matters except skills'.[40] Structural constraints, such as caste, class, gender and related problems of access to infrastructure, education and employment, and inequities in wealth distribution, that marked children's lives in the government and aided schools and contributed to a reproduction of these inequalities, never found voice within these managerial discourses.

Despite this, however, I argue that responsibilizing marginalized youth for future outcomes was not the only way in which the managerial middle class associated with the programmes were responding. That is, despite the neoliberal vision of achieving development through skilling programmes for marginalized youth, I argue that the managers were less concerned with the outcomes of the programmes themselves. Rather, their real response appeared to be one of building the organization as an identity, which would stand as an identity for themselves (as I will explain further). Thus, they appeared to be responding to a different global condition—one of global expansion of the middle classes (Kharas, 2017) and the need to maintain identity and status within this context.

Within the current economic scenario, a number of scholars, such as Ball (2006), Fernandes (2006), Leichty (2003), Sancho (2015), Ganguly-Scrase & Scrase (2012), Mahajan (2021) and others, have drawn attention to the increasing base and diversity within the 'middle class', that threatens 'their "imagined futures" and those of their offspring…from the "unmanaged congestion" in the old and new professions and in management positions (Jordon et al., 1994)' (Ball, 2006, p. 38). Responding to this threat, as scholars such as Sancho (2015) and Mathew (2016) have sought to show, investments in 'cultural capital' such as private school and English-medium education have not only become important strategies for the middle class to retain its class status but have also become strategies for other groups to acquire a middle-class status. Others such as Fernandes (2006) and Sriprakash et al. (2020) have drawn attention to how, within the newly liberalized political economy and restructured spaces of labour market and society in India, there is a growing clamour from those below (i.e.,

---

[40] Personal communication, 7 June 2012.

the lower and middle levels of the middle class) to acquire the cultural trappings and symbolic capital required to get a foothold into the elite segments of this class.

It is within this context that I argue that the LSPs served as personal resources for the managers, rather than as tools to reproduce the neoliberal agenda of development. With members of the middle class being those who most depend on 'cultural capital' (as noted by Deshpande, 2003), I argue that the production of the LSE discourse and programmes served as differential strategies of 'cultural production' that could help them retain a distinction from those above and below (Leichty, 2003). Demonstrating this below, I describe how the programmes were structured to meet different ends from the ones described above (that only formed a part of their talk, but not practice, and hence, also represented another instance in which the language of the programmes was 'opportunistically' employed).

For when viewed from the outside (through the critical lens of a researcher), organizations largely appeared to be 'entrepreneurial' ventures of self-making for the middle-class managers, through which they also inadvertently 'disrupted' the neoliberal project of responsibilization, partially. The year-long ethnographic observations showed how implicit organizational goals and visions focused on growth and expansion of the organizations as an end in itself, with very little focus on the child and his/her cultural change.

This was evident from the manner in which everyday practices, decisions and activities were framed around the goals of developing the organization as a 'brand' (that would also stand as an identity for the individuals associated with the organizations), rather than on cultivating the 'enterprising' and 'self-responsible' future worker and citizen. Organizational goals and annual plans were therefore, often, described in terms of reaching targets, building a 'brand', scaling, economizing and gaining more visibility, as can be seen below from the accounts of various managers given below.

> 'Our vision is of empowering children from vulnerable backgrounds through life skills. The mission is to reach 2,40,000 children by

2014. The organisational goal is to empower 50,000 young adults by training 500 adults in IP's life skills philosophy.... We have to build a brand image that says "life skills means IP".' (Devesh Arya, during the presentation of annual plans, goals and objectives, 20 April 2012)

In another instance, during a personal interview (20 September 2012), Pavan Raghunath, the former HR and soft skills team manager at VYB, admitted to me that they wanted to 'productize soft skills'. The question they were asking was, 'Can life skills be delivered by all?' since they found that psychologists were expensive and funding for these kinds of skills was not high. Arguing that NGOs could not afford the cost of psychologists, he pointed out that they were looking at a model wherein anybody could be handed a 'tab and a user manual, and you were good to go' (i.e., to teach soft/life skills).

Thus, within organizational plans and goals, such as those presented before (or the teachers' training programme discussed earlier), the chief focus was on efficiency of delivery and reach, not the quality or depth of knowledge and training required to achieve change. Efficiency and cost-effectiveness of delivery models and scalability of programmes took prime precedence within organizational discussions, and the emphasis was on growing in organizational size.

Weekly team meetings and discussions also focused on completion of targets, updates on work progress, new partnerships and so on, rather than on understanding or addressing the 'cultural disconnects' seen on field, or on finding ways to improve the pedagogic process, in order to bridge these gaps and address other 'field' related problems. Thus, the 'field' appeared to be a site that was just to be acted upon and as a site of delivery for the programmes; while field realities were never factored into organizational processes and did not find much space within organizational discourse. In fact, in organizations such as IP, weekly team meetings did not include the facilitators; thus clearly demonstrating how the 'field' did not figure in the weekly stock-taking and planning processes of the organization.

Impacts of the programmes on the various behavioural transformations expected in students, when measured, were also rudimentary, correlational or superficial and focused little on the actual transformation of the child. For example, all three organizations justified the positive impacts of their programme through the collection and analysis of data on attendance and pass percentages. This was the main indicator used with donors and schools, to justify and receive support for their programmes. While organizations such as IP even presented results such as an increase in attendance on the days that their LSE programme was available in schools (since children attended school so that they could be a part of the fun and games of the life skills classes), they however did not critically interrogate these results and examine whether such attendance amounted to any real change in the cultural mindsets of children and parents; or whether such results could also be sustained in the event of these programmes being discontinued. Therefore, it also seemed that the programmes were not working towards bringing about an internal change and self-discipline in the child, as much as they were working towards ensuring temporary changes and benefits, which provided evidence and support for the positive effects of the programmes. Long-term effects did not figure as a concern in most programmes, evident from the fact that most did not maintain a record or follow up on the children who had received their interventions.

Even when specific life skills were measured to present evidence for the benefits of these programmes, evaluations relied on rote knowledge rather than internal changes in the self. For example, VYB administered a paper-and-pencil test to assess improvements in children's creativity and critical thinking skills following their intervention in schools. The test administered for creativity took into account the number of 'uses' that children could list for a given object (e.g., pen) and did not consider other dimensions that have been identified within psychological literature for creativity, such as flexibility, originality, elaboration and functionality of responses (refer Kim, 2006; Torrance, 1966; 1974).

Further, as was witnessed during a team meeting prior to the administration of the test, the facilitators were instructed by the team leader, Nayanika, to create an intense atmosphere of competition, by comparing each of their classes to other classes and the number of responses that children had given there, so that children would compete to give the maximum possible responses.[41] Similarly, with respect to the critical thinking test used by VYB, examples such as the following were used to test this domain, with these questions having also been previously discussed in class.

I find a sealed, addressed envelope lying on the road
  a. Throw it into the dustbin
  b. Put it in a post-box
  c. Give it to my schoolteacher
  d. Give it to any person walking by

I watch an advertisement which says by applying Fair and Lovely for just a month the skin becomes fair and glowing:
  a. First I go and buy it, because I want to look beautiful
  b. I don't believe in this
  c. First I will ask others and if it is working for them then I buy it
  d. Don't do anything

Prior to the administration of the test, facilitators were similarly advised by the team leader to adequately revise these topics to ensure that the children score well. While on the one hand, such strategies revealed the manner in which 'processes' or experiential aspects of learning got reduced to item-response formats, testing declarative knowledge rather than procedural knowledge, on the other hand, they also revealed the 'textbook' culture of learning (Kumar, 1988) that was adopted by the programmes (as also discussed earlier), focused on strategies of 'coaching', memory and 'performing' the right answers.

While paper-and-pencil tests was one form of evaluation used, which was inadequate to measure the rich, complex dynamics of the classroom and individual learning, IP used an observation checklist that measured five parameters of interaction—'overcoming difficulties', 'solving problems', 'taking initiative', 'managing conflict' and 'understanding and following instructions'—based on their five life skills. Designed and tested by two British psychologists, the checklist was to be used by each facilitator to rate children individually, in their

[41] On 23 February 2012.

respective classes. Based on behavioural observations such as 'does X carry out tasks without being told', 'does X show sensitivity to others' needs and feelings', facilitators were required to mark each child on a scale of 1–5 (5 indicating the highest performance, representing independent functioning on the part of the child). This was carried out at the beginning and end of the academic year.

As was observed when facilitators used the checklist in the classroom, they often randomly scored the checklist and were unable to explain the scores given in many cases, either because they did not understand what was to be evaluated, or because there were too many children in the classroom and they could not pay full attention to each one. Further, as was reported by the statistical analyst employed by IP to analyse the impact of their programmes, the results from the checklists often showed contradictory data, which was however not being attended to by the organization. Arguing that IP had mostly been averaging the responses as an indicator of change, Jayanthi, the analyst pointed out that while the overall averages seemed to be showing an improvement from the baseline, facilitators had, on many occasions, given a lower score at the end-line compared to the baseline, leading to a negative result. These results had not been systematically analysed.[42] She also noted that, in some cases, all questions on the baseline and end-line tests would carry the same score (e.g., all questions on the baseline checklist would be marked '2', and all questions on the end-line would be marked '5'), out of fear that results that showed a lack of improvement might reflect poorly on the facilitators' performance.

Discussion over these questions around practice, scoring and disconnects were often brushed aside by the managers, in favour of arguments about 'scale'. For example, after a combined observation of a life skills class at the government school in south Bengaluru with Ranjit, the programme manager at VYB,[43] we had a discussion on assessing the impact of programmes. Revealing his concern about the impact of the life skills component of their programmes, Ranjit pointed out that while the academic learning programmes could be measured in

---

[42] Personal communication, 28 May 2012.
[43] On 13 December 2012.

terms of input and output, they were unsure of what output was available to measure the life skills component. Even when I spoke about the need to pay attention to the process of change as an indicator, he argued that these 'outcomes' would not sit well with the donors and seemed unconvinced of this himself.

Similarly, during a meeting with another manager, Aamir Raza (the MD of MFLC) and his programme team, the conversation veered towards the pedagogy adopted by MFCL, the lack of experientiality within the programmes and the translation or usefulness of the skills and values to the lives of children in the government schools that they intervened in. Raza responded to the questions that emerged during this discussion stating:

> The challenge is there needs to be a meeting point of idealism with practicality, and I think that's a conscious battle that MFCL has to constantly keep fighting. And, I truly believe that something's better than not trying it through…because the Indian challenge is numbers. It's alarming, it's scary for me to think about those 1.7 million schools [sic] now, churning out those children. And everyone of them means a life… and by the way these are ones who went to school. There are lots of them who don't even go to school. Now the thought of what they are going to be doing in life…because what skills their parents have had…if they pass out 100 percent of their children, it's not enough for them to lead a life because the world has changed so dramatically…it has to be with some structured programmes. So, as much as I might like a CFL,[44] but that is not a solution to India's educational problems because CFL is the ideal. Interestingly some of Krishnamurthi's schools are struggling to find facilitators'.[45]

Further, even on occasions when facilitators sought to raise these 'disconnects' with the managerial group, these did not seem to become central concerns or points of discussion as could be seen from some exchanges between the management and the facilitators. For

---

[44] A school following J. Krishnamurthi's educational philosophy and experiential learning approach in Bengaluru.
[45] Personal communication, 13 August 2013.

example, during a curriculum feedback session with Christiana (the international life skills trainer hired by IP), Gautam—a facilitator, tried to point out to her that he had been finally able (after several sessions) to get children to understand that 'Sir questions *kēLuttaare*' ('Sir will ask questions'), after the activity is over. He argued that while they were now participating in reflection, they were still not able to relate these questions to their lives. What Gautam seemed to highlight through this account was how the metaphorical nature of the activity and reflection were not relatable to the children's experiences within everyday life. He also sought to point out to the difference in the structure and format of programmes, that required students to participate by putting forth their own ideas and knowledges, which was very different from the expectations of obedience and submission to authority within schools that students were used to. Christiana responded to this, stating that he should then give a story from his own life as an example, after which the children should be invited to share similar examples. Gautam pointed out, 'If it comes from them only, we will know if they have learnt. Otherwise they will just listen to what we have said', drawing on his experiences from the classroom. But Christiana brushed this insight aside, still arguing about how this practice would work.[46]

This disconnect between lesson plans and content and children's lives was also seen across other organizations, which similarly continued to use culturally inappropriate metaphors as part of their activities. For example, in the story of 'Warm Fuzzy and Cold Prickly' discussed earlier, 'Warm Fuzzy' was used to indicate a warmth and pleasantness in interpersonal interactions; while 'Cold Prickly' was used to refer to coldness and hostility in interpersonal interactions.[47] This, however, could not convey the full import of the message to children who mostly were only familiar with their mother tongue, Kannada, and had little access and facility with English language and to the cultural content and orientation of its use.

[46] On 18 October 2012.
[47] The term 'Warm Fuzzy' was situationally used to represent both the socially desired behaviours that were to be inculcated in children (e.g., polite speech, social greeting), as well as to represent certain pleasurable behaviours that children indulged in (e.g., excessive television viewing, as explained in Chapter 5).

Taking these practices of the organizations into account, what can then be seen is how the middle class, who developed and conducted these programmes, appeared to be strategically using these discourses in defining their own selves and carving out niche identities for themselves, rather than in ensuring programme success. From examining internal processes of the organizations, and the importance accorded to the various activities such as cultural contextualization of the curriculum and programme evaluation (key parameters for understanding the real effects of the programmes), the picture that emerged was one wherein neoliberalism's practices and discourses were subtly upturned, yet sustained, through 'appropriations' (Rockwell, 1996) made for different ends.

What I mean by this is that while the managers did not actively seek to create the neoliberal subject through their pedagogic practices, they still articulated a 'culture of enterprise' and appropriated the neoliberal educational discourse in order to create 'distinction' for themselves. Carrying out these programmes as 'experts' in the self-skills that they applied to their own lives (and that others did not have), they, thus, reproduced their class identity and status through the means of these programmes. Their organizations in fact served as a platform for them to build this distinction in relation to the other classes, by offering a set of 'skills' that was not available within the everyday cultures and experiences of these other classes. Further, through the practice and discourse of LSE, they were also contributing to the larger educational discourses and practices that emphasized neoliberal values of individual enterprise and self-work as important to success. Despite the narratives of 'empowerment' that formed a part of their everyday discourse, there was no real attempt either to address structural limitations within discussions, or to pay more careful attention to the 'disconnects' that led to a failure of transference of skills.

Further, important to achieving this 'distinction', recognition and unique identity was the success of the organization, which came to represent both—their 'entrepreneurial spirit' and 'social consciousness' (that served to distinguish them from other white-collar workers in the middle class). Its success was also important as their own means of sustenance was tied to it (i.e., having quit their previous positions within the corporate sector, the organizations had come to represent full-time employment for them).

Thus, planning and strategizing not only for visibility and brand recognition but also for funds and expansion, through different strategies of advertising and networking, became a large part of the day-to-day activities, and were seen in routine practices such as customizing experiences and relationships with corporate firms, increasing visibility and raising funds through regular events organized such as marathons and runs, participation and organization of conferences, involving schools and various forms of educational technology providers, and so on. These strategies were also carefully planned, as seen from how appointments of individuals to key positions were made at IP. While IP used individuals such as Ruma, with specific experience within multinational corporate investment firms such as Goldman Sachs, for their corporate volunteer engagement and fundraising portfolios (since she had the right knowledge of such firms to provide customized and uniquely identifiable experiences for them, according to her),[48] appointments of facilitators (i.e., those who delivered the life skills classes to children in schools) did not require a background in psychology or education, but were required to belong to social backgrounds and communities as the children themselves.

What these strategic plans deployed by the organizations, thus, revealed was how individuals who managed the programmes had appropriated the neoliberal discourses in making their own selves and in establishing their identities as 'enterprising' and 'successful'. Yet, while sustaining its logic in constructing their own identities and distinction, they also subtly, unexpectedly and partially upturned its effects, by allowing the programmes to be appropriated to other ends on the field. Thus, I argue that their 'responses' have also been 'opportunistic' in having appropriated the neoliberal LSE discourse only so far as it has helped them make themselves.

Examining these various 'responses' and actions of the groups of young people that were involved in the LSPs, the chapter thus draws attention to the dialectical process of subject formation. Rather than presenting identities as subjected to governmental reasons and ends, I have tried to show how identities are produced in the interactions

[48] Personal communication, 17 April 2012.

between projects of governance, their appropriations and resistance. Further, I draw attention to how youth identities are produced through the convergence of multiple rationalities—economic, educational, cultural, as well as through convergences of ideologies that occur at various levels from the local to the regional and even the global.

Thus, I also argue for the importance of seeing youth as agents, participating in the processes of their own subjectification, while also resisting and reworking the structural and discursive forces that shape them. This calls for the adoption of dynamic and fluid categories and lenses to study youth and their inter-relations with social phenomena, particularly in relation to global processes such as neoliberalism and its multiple forms.

CHAPTER 8

Conclusion

'If you don't know computers you can still run life, but life skills are skills that one cannot live without'.[1]

—Dr Chandrika Bavegadi

The statement given above presents the response of Dr Chandrika Bavegadi, an independent psychologist and LSE trainer, to my question, 'What are life skills?' During the course of the personal interview I conducted with her, at her modest two-bedroom house in south Bengaluru, which doubled as her office, it was unclear what skills she was referring to, or to whose lives they mattered. However, gaining IT skills, that is seen as the passport for mobility and a global middle-class status and that remains a dream and aspiration for millions of Indian youth was clearly not considered as important to life, by her. While Dr Bavegadi responded from her middle-class location of 'having arrived', for several young people in the government schools that she worked in, this, and other academic, technical, vocational skills that remain hard to access, were in fact the skills desired and were the key takeaway from programmes. These 'hard skills' were as important to these youth as the 'soft skills' that the LSPs had to offer, if they were to be able to benefit from the 'high skills' IT, finance, technology, media and hospitality industries that have opened up following liberalization.

[1] Personal communication, 24 January 2012.

Post-liberalization, India has witnessed several changes and transformations, visible in the explosion of cities, the expansion of the urban service economy and infrastructure, proliferation of malls, brands and consumptive cultures, growth of media and entertainment, and the rise of a 'new middle class' (Fernandes, 2006; Gooptu, 2013; Bhatia & Priya, 2018). The period has also witnessed an intense remaking and making of identities and social relationships (Bhatia & Priya, 2018; Mahajan, 2021; Mathew, 2016), as more and more individuals have accessed and have been incorporated into markets and global chains of production. Education, training and skill development that have always been sites for acquiring cultural capital and regulating youth identities have gained a renewed importance within this context, as sites for the preparation of a global citizenry and workforce (Vasavi, 2015), as well as sites to acquire the tacit capital required to enter the 'new middle classes' and distinguish oneself from traditional moorings within caste and society (Mathew, 2016; Sancho, 2015; Sriprakash et al., 2020). Schools and educational institutions, as sites of confluence, of local communities and cultures, state structures and rationalities, and global systems and frameworks of knowledge production, are also spaces within which child and youth identities are being made and remade through the contradictory expectations of these global imaginaries, and local pressures and anxieties.

Contextualizing my observations on the rise of psychotherapeutic education and an entrepreneurial skilling culture in this context, along the lines of which even school-going youth are being sought to be measured and remade, through programmes such as LSE, the aim was to discuss the regulation and production of youth identities, in this book. Examining how youth have come to be produced as a category to be known and managed by various authorities, I also however have paid attention to how knowledges and practices of identification and regulation of youth are mediated by and negotiated within the local context. While predominantly, youth, even within the Indian context, are popularly understood through the categories and definitions set by frameworks of psychology and economics produced in the Global North, I have examined how youth identities come to be shaped through local discourses and practices that include young people's own conceptualizations of themselves. This perspective offers something new, as it urges social theory to move beyond viewing youth as a social category produced only through governmental reason, grand narratives and knowledge systems of Western liberalism, or structural contexts of the political economy. Rather, it argues for the need to understand how social categories such as youth emerge through the inter-linked processes and practices of social transformation and subject formation and, thus, calls attention to the co-production of social contexts and identities that both subject and are subjected to diverse relations of power.

Though emerging perspectives on youth, from multiple fields, such as sociology, anthropology and geography, have contributed to challenging universalizing and determining discourses of psychology and economics, by identifying differences in youth experiences, much of this literature has also contributed to, or focused exclusively on, the development of new kinds of interventions, modification and contextualization of interventions around youth. Knowledge production within these disciplines, on the problems of social exclusion and difference, have also offered avenues to reconstitute 'institutionally structured relations of class, gender, ethnicity, (dis)ability and geography as complex, but quantifiable, factors which place certain youth at-risk' (Kelly, 2000). As critical scholars such as Coppock (2011) have shown emerging psycho-educational interventions within this context, thus invite the individual to self-actualize within the constraints of what he/she is expected to become as an adult. Development interventions that are structured to aid this process identify the 'right' forms of education, skills, attitudes and behaviours to help individuals succeed despite being poor or disadvantaged. 'At risk' discourses attached to the targets of such intervention find them wanting in 'merit', and schools and educational institutions are thus urged to do more, to develop the enterprising, flexible, risk-taking individual, who can maximize his/her potential within a 'properly enterprising form of free market economy' (Down, 2009).

The restructuring of school knowledges and the emphasis on providing 'whole school' and 'whole child' education also thus needs to be seen as outcomes of knowledge production on differences and disadvantages among youth. Against this context, psychologization of the school curriculum is considered necessary, in order to ensure the standardization of schooling outcomes, including the production of homogenous selves suited to the requirements of the global political economy. A network of agencies, drawing attention to students' mental health and its effects on educational outcomes, have thus recommended experiential learning pedagogies, activity-based learning, games and fun within the school curriculum, as observed within the life skills classrooms, as means not just to introduce new and progressive approaches and formats to improve learning outcomes, but also as governmental technologies for reorienting youth to the individual cultures of the neoliberal economy and society, in which success, failures and deficits are associated within individual psychology and (self) work, rather than structurally located.

While drawing on literature that has critically contributed to an understanding of youth regulation and governance through projects of development and education, as well as literature that has focused on the multiplicities of youthhood, the book additionally draws attention to the phenomena of youth identity production—that is, it draws attention to how youth identities are produced through the interlinked processes through which structural and discursive contexts, social identities and subjectivities bi-directionally influence and co-constitute each other. I sought to demonstrate the negotiated production of youth subjectivities in the interactions and transformations seen between local, provincial contexts, international developmental agendas and progressive pedagogic interventions, and through youth action. The overall implications of these productive efforts, I have tried to argue, simultaneously feed and detract from the neoliberal project of the self and expansion of an enterprise culture.

Analysing the LSPs in the Indian context, through which young people are being subject to and are remaking their own identities, I have attempted to capture the forward and backward linkages of this social change. Locating the impetus for LSPs amidst the paternalistic culture of state interventions, youth policies and institutional contexts of schools in India that reference a different moral economy, and the simultaneous transformations of the economy and economic expectations and political pressures on schools to prepare youth for a global economy, I have drawn attention to the specific disconnects that have emerged between the discourses and practice of these programmes. Particularly, in the context of the government school—a site of welfare governmentality, largely perceived to be failing and subjected to a range of performativity tools, new managerial practices and interventions by the middle classes—LSE needs to be seen not just as 'technologies of government', but for the multiple productive affordances it offers. As programmes to empower the poor, it simultaneously sets the frame for understanding young people's behaviours (as 'risky' or 'failing') and regulate it according to middle class social standards. Further, introduced within the context of a 'failing' state education system, it is also seen as critical to the state school's own survival and remaking. Thus, appropriated by the government school to its own ends, LSE has also been provincialized to fit with the traditional expectations of schooling and society to reform the 'culturally poor' child according to the social, moral and intellectual values and behaviours of the dominant castes and classes within the predominantly Hindu society. Rather than producing the self-regulating and responsibilized youth-subject sought within the Anglo-American contexts of LSPs, LSPs within the Indian context thus appeared to be aligned according to the schools' goals of cultivating gendered forms of discipline, obedience and respect in accordance with the larger authoritarian and patriarchal culture.

Further, structurally, LSE also serves as a site through which caste–class structures and hierarchies could be justified and maintained, allowing the young, globally oriented, entrepreneurial middle class to create 'distinction' for themselves, from others within the globally expanding middle classes. This distinction is produced through the re-identification of the class-based knowledges and behaviours taught through these programmes as 'merit' and the skills important for success in life, and the missing factors responsible for the poverty and failure of those within the lower classes.

The identification of these personal cultures of the middle classes, such as their investments in education, practices of concerted cultivation, dress and mannerisms, as 'life skills' thus also justified the interventions of lay members of the middle classes within the state schools. While these interventions, seen as important not just to compensate for children's home backgrounds but to help children manage and improve in school despite it served to 'responsibilize' disadvantaged youth, and allowed schools and state systems of education to transfer their responsibilities of ensuring students' well-being and outcomes to the external agents and students themselves.

Further, it has also allowed for the discourses and outcomes of schooling and education to be significantly shaped by the middle classes, through their backward and forward linkages with schools, teachers, students and parents, on the one hand, and policy makers, aid organizations, businesses and other NGOs, on the other hand. In this manner, life skills discourse and activities have also served to forward middle-class interests and ideas of development but, more importantly, also contribute to deflecting the potential threat to the middle classes, through class revolt or identity-based uprisings, in the context of rising inequalities and state failure in assuring equal educational outcomes. By relocating the possibilities for educational success within individual psychology, by working upon the poor by remaking and recasting their identities, and de-historicizing and de-politicizing social locations of caste, gender and poverty that influence outcomes, LSPs are significant in deflecting attention away from more structural concerns such as that of income inequality, marketization of education and even the current state of jobless growth—all of which contribute to individual success and failures. Through pedagogic practices focused on providing descriptions and explanations for young people's behaviours and placing expectations on them to overcome these identities, rather than on empowering young people to produce knowledge about their own selves, by critically reflecting on patriarchal structures of caste, class, gender, education and economy, the programmes thus seek to draw attention on how individual personalities can be 'fixed' (Butterwick & Benjamin, 2006) in order to overcome structural disadvantage. Drawing on the traditional–patriarchal understanding of youth and the 'cultures of poverty' that they belonged to, both youth and the cultures and knowledges of the non-elite are infantilized and presented as inadequate for the future, particularly by measuring it against middle-class norms for education and employment. The lack of investments made, both materially and affectively on education and employment, through persistence and perseverance, despite the structural odds that belie the possibilities of making such investments, are put forth as rationales for developmentally intervening through programmes such as LSE within schools, to remake the poor and marginalized youth and 'empower' them to succeed. Along with academic values, personal cultures of the non-elite students and facilitators also came under review within these programme spaces, and LSE was seen as a bridge between academic systems and the kinds of behavioural changes expected to be produced through schools. Middle-class organizers such as Raza established the importance of this stating that '(even) if they (i.e., GES) pass out 100 percent of their children, it's not enough for them to lead a life because the world has changed so dramatically…it has to be with some structured programmes.' Such statements by Raza and Bavegadi (given above), demonstrate the strong advocacy for soft skilling through which poor youth are sought to be remade to fit into contemporary structures of the economy and society.

However, while LSE appear predominantly as sites of neoliberal governmentality and youth regulation, it is also important to highlight how these were spaces within which specific agendas for youth regulation, the social power of the middle classes, as well as global discourses and frameworks of neoliberal education and regulation itself came to be partially disrupted, through the reinterpretations and appropriations made by those subjected to these regimes of personal culture. Youth 'actors', such as the facilitators and students, from the non-middle classes, 'responded' to these contexts of subjectification by appropriating its discourses and practice to produce their selves in novel ways, as professionally competent and 'culturally better educated'. While these new identities challenged the deficit discourses put forth by the schools, middle classes as well as developmental networks of aid and knowledge, non-elite youth's internalization and learning from the programmes also disrupted the pedagogic disciplining and remaking of the self as enterprising and entrepreneurial subjects, desired to be effected through the LSPs. These disruptions and formations of alternative identities can be partially attributed to the non-elite youth's own lack of cultural capital to gain the kinds of cultural knowledges emphasized through the programmes; to the middle class youth's own strategic and opportunistic appropriation of the LSE discourse to create distinction for themselves, rather than to impact change in the targets of their programmes; as well as to the strategic and opportunistic forms of use that schools, facilitators and students themselves sought to put the programmes to, for acquiring more overt outcomes such as disciplined classrooms, or access the limited opportunities to gain English language, art, sports and facilitation skills, within the context of a government school, that could directly be converted into future jobs or material wealth.

In examining the phenomena of LSE bottom-up, thus, as a set of 'responses' that constitute and are constituted by the larger discursive field as well as local contexts, the attempt has been to argue for youth identity production as an act of 'strategic opportunizing', under everyday conditions of risks and temporality. These conditions of unpredictability, brought by the complex and dynamic interactions between capital expansions, environmental changes and human actions contribute to a condition of constant flux that individuals and larger systems (such as governments, corporations, cultures, capitalism) are forced to grapple with. LSE itself, within this context, appears to have emerged as a 'strategic and opportunistic response' or solution by states and development agencies, to manage local conditions and contexts that pose a threat to development and various authorities in charge of it (at the local and global levels) through the regulation of subjectivities. Thus, materially constituted by a specific network of actors under specific conditions, I argue that they have also invited counter actions within the field (such as from students, facilitators and managers, in the context of my study). The production of youth identities must be seen in this interaction between macro-structural and micro-material contexts, negotiated at different levels and influenced by multiple discourses—the outcomes of which can neither be fully predetermined or controlled individually or structurally.

Appendices

Appendix 1. MFCL's Oath for Behaviour[1]

Children are made to affirm the following stating 'I know/I will' at the end of each class.

1. Affirm one's strength, responsibility, positive abilities and goals, important to shape their future by incorporating good qualities within them **(on self-awareness).**
2. Accept to be optimistic and understanding of others, help others during their happiness and sadness, by building empathetic relations and being mindful of not hurting others **(on empathy).**
3. Accept to speak with love and respect, share with friends, teachers and parents their good ideas, needs and feelings **(on good communication).**
4. Agree to have good and affectionate relationships with friends, neighbours and parents **(on interpersonal relationships).**
5. Accept that decisions we take play an important role in our lives and agree to take decisions for oneself by consulting with friends, teachers and parents **(on decision-making).**
6. Affirm that all problems can be handled and that one who knows how to resolve conflicts will face the problems they encounter by taking support from others **(on handling conflicts).**
7. Affirm that one will always think about novel things and carry out activities with enthusiasm and creativity **(on creativity).**

---

[1] Translated from Kannada and summarized.

8. Affirm that one has the ability to think about oneself and others and make distinctions between right and wrong on any topic, or on matters about oneself **(on critical thinking)**.
9. Affirm that one will express feelings in accordance with circumstances and apply the skills necessary to handle one's feelings without causing others trouble **(on managing emotions)**.
10. Affirm that one will handle conflicts and pressures that are common to everyday life successfully, by handling them intelligently and patiently **(on managing stress)**.
11. Affirm that one will take care of one's school, neighbourhood, society and environment, and shape one's own future by carrying out their responsibilities and duties in the right manner.

Appendix 2. Blind Drawings[1]

The lesson plan discussed below is for students of sixth–eighth standards. The lesson is one of seven sessions that covers the skill of communication. As per the lesson plan in the arts facilitator's manual, the goal of the lesson is to teach children:

1. To communicate accurately or properly,
2. Listen attentively to follow instructions and
3. Give instructions clearly.

The focus areas of the lesson are on communication, listening, understanding differences in learning styles, working together and taking and giving instructions

Materials required for the session:

1. Paper
2. Colouring pens

Warm-Up (20 minutes)
Check-In: Ask each child to describe a superpower they would like to have and why? Discuss as a group how they were progressing in terms of creating a caring environment and safe space for participation and any modification of goals and agreements required.

Warm-Up Game: 'Pass the sound and face.'
Children stand in a circle, and one child starts the game by making a sound and an expression. This sound and expression have to be then

---

[1] The lesson appears in IP's life skills arts curriculum for sixth–eighth standards, for 2012–2013, and has been adapted from there.

copied by the child on his/her right, who then produces a new sound and face for the person on his/her right to copy. The game proceeds in this manner till all children around the circle have had a chance to copy and produce a new sound and expression.

Blind Drawings (45 minutes)
Instructions are read out to the children, explaining that every child must first produce an abstract picture using basic shapes such as triangles and circles. After completing the picture, they must find a partner and sit back-to-back with them. Each pair also decides which partner will have the first go at describing their picture to the other partner, who must produce the same picture based on the first partner's instructions. After five minutes, the children are told to compare the drawings.

In the second round, the other partner calls out instructions to the first partner to reproduce his/her drawing (sitting in the same manner—back-to-back). But before the second round begins, the partners are told to discuss strategies to improve upon the drawing.

Reflection (35 minutes)

1. Children are encouraged to discuss 'what happened'. That is in spite of whether they were drawing close or far from the original drawing, whether communication strategies were working or not, etc.
2. Following this, they were encouraged to think of 'so what?' That is, to reflect on whether these situations are also common in everyday life, and what would be the result of communication processes not being 'fixed' (improved) in everyday life.
3. The final set of reflections were around 'now what?' or how changes could be made to one's communication styles to communicate more clearly and to 'listen to understand', in schools, families and communities.

Closing (20 minutes)
The game involved children taking turns to complete the picture of a monster. One child starts by drawing out the head of the monster and

writing a few words. He/she then folds the paper so his/her picture is not visible but draws a line to indicate where the next child must start drawing from. Children continue in this manner until the entire monster is drawn out. The last child adds a title to the picture and reads out all the messages.

Check-out: Ask children to demonstrate the sound that the creature/monster drawn would make to bid goodbye to the group.

Appendix 3. Your Strengths, Your Opportunities[1]

The objective of the session was to create an awareness in students about their strengths, weaknesses and opportunities. The required material for the activity were only writing material, and the activity was to be conducted over one-and-half hours.
There were two levels to the activity:

1. The first level follows from the roles and responsibilities activity in which they were made aware of the same. Drawing on these roles and responsibilities, the participants were expected to list out the strengths and opportunities accompanying each role in the following manner:

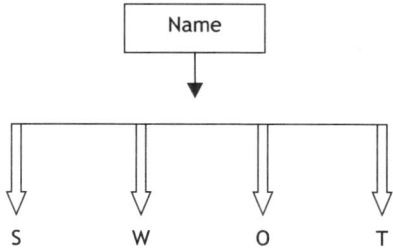

2. At the second level, they were guided to reflect on the opportunities afforded by various strengths listed: for example, having a good voice, being able to make decisions for the class, being good in dance, etc.

[1] The module has been adapted from VYB's life skills curriculum for 2011–2012.

In terms of facilitation, the life skills trainers could encourage children to reflect using the following kinds of questions:

1. Was it was easy for you to write about your strengths and weaknesses?
2. Do you think it is possible to grow beyond your weaknesses and threats?
3. Do you believe that everyone has personal, unique strengths and weaknesses?
4. What was learnt through the activity?
5. How can you apply your strengths to your role as a student in particular?

Bibliography

Abraham, L. (2001). Redrawing the Lakshman Rekha: Gender differences and cultural constructions in youth sexuality in urban India. *South Asia: Journal of South Asian Studies*, *24*(1), 133–156.

Adkins, W. R. (1984). Life skills education: A video-based counseling/learning delivery system. In D. Larson (Ed.), *Teaching Psychological Skills: Models for Giving Psychology Away* (pp. 44–68). Brooks/Cole

Advani, S. (2004). Pedagogy and politics: The case of English textbooks. In A. Chatterjee (Ed.), *Education and democracy in India*. Manohar.

Ailwood, J. (2004). Genealogies of governmentality: Producing and managing young children and their education. *The Australian Educational Researcher*, *31* (3), 19–33.

Ainley, P., & Corbett, J. (1994). From vocationalism to enterprise: Social and life skills becomes personal and transferable. *British Journal of Sociology of Education*, *15*(3), 365–374. http://www.jstor.org/stable/1393149

Allais, S. (2012). Will skills save us? Rethinking the relationships between vocational education, skills development policies, and social policy in South Africa. *International Journal of Educational Development*, *32*, 632–642. https://doi.org/10.1016/j.ijedudev.2012.01.001

Anandhi, S., Jeyaranjan, J., & Krishnan, R. (2002). Work, caste and competing masculinities: Notes from a Tamil village. *Economic & Political Weekly*, *37*, 4403–4414.

Anitha, B. K. (2000). *Village, caste and education*. Rawat Publications.

Arnett, J. J. (2006). G. Stanley Hall's adolescence: Brilliance and nonsense. *History of Psychology*, *9*(3), 186–197. http://jeffreyarnett.com/Arnett% 20new%20website/Articles/Arnett_2006_HP2.pdf

ASER. (2019, 15 January). *Annual status of education report (rural) 2018 provisional*. New Delhi: ASER Centre. http://img.asercentre.org/docs/ASER%202018/Release%20Material/aserreport2018.pdf

Ashton, D., Green, F., James, D., & Sung, J. (1999). *Education and training for development in East Asia: The political economy of skill formation in East Asian newly industrialised economies*. Routledge.

Ashwini, D., Javalkar, P., Thalinja, R., Thakaran, M., Iyer, V., & Mohan, H. L. (2017). *Pathways to absenteeism and school dropout among adolescent girls' in Koppal Taluka, Karnataka: Findings from Sphoorthi Project baseline study*. Bangalore: Karnataka Health Promotion Trust (KHPT).

Austin, J. (2019, 27 April). *Youth cultures*. Encyclopaedia of Children and Childhood in History and Society (2004). https://www.encyclopedia.com/social-sciences-and-law/sociology-and-social-reform/sociology-general-terms-and-concepts/youth-culture#3402800448

Azim Premji Foundation. (2017, March). *Teacher absenteeism study: Field studies in education*. Research Group, Azim Premji Foundation. https://azimpremjiuniversity.edu.in/SitePages/pdf/Field-Studies-in-Education-Teacher-Absenteeism-Study.pdf

Babu, S. S. (2020). Education for confidence: Possibilities of a political education. *South Asia: Journal for South Asian Studies, 43*(4), 741–757.

Bahuguna, N.J. (2007, August 20). No sex education please—We're Indian. *Other News*. Retrieved from http://www.other-news.info/2007/08/nosex-education-please-wereindian/

Bakhtin, M. M. (1986). *Speech genres and other late essays* (Vern W. McGee, Trans). University of Texas Press.

Ball, S. J. (2006). Big policies/small world: An introduction to international perspectives in education policy. In Bob Lingard and Jenny Ozga (Eds.), *The RoutledgeFalmer reader in education policy and politics* (pp. 36–47). Taylor & Francis e-library.

Balogun, O. A. (2008). The idea of an 'educated person' in contemporary African thought. *The Journal of Pan African Studies, 2*(3), 117–128. https://s3.amazonaws.com/academia.edu.documents/7204468/pdf%5Cissues%20and%20perspectives%5Cideaofaneducatedperson.pdf?response-content-disposition =inline%3B%20filename%3DThe_Idea_of_an_Educated_Personin_Contemp.pdf&X-Amz-Algorithm=AWS4-HMAC-SHA256&X-Amz-Credential=AKIAIWOWYYGZ2Y53UL3A%2F20190928%2Fus-east-1%2Fs3%2Faws4_request&X-Amz-Date=20190928T053459Z&X-Amz-Expires=3600&X-Amz-Signed-Headers =host&X-Amz-Signature=fd5a23f0be91f068e04745ca52ed65a580c70876 df9ea5f0bac0d93255948700

Bandura, A. (1977). *Social learning theory*. General Learning Press.

Barry, A., Osborne, T., & Rose, N. (Eds). (1996). *Foucault and political reason: Liberalism, neo-liberalism and rationalities of government*. University of Chicago Press

Batra, P. (2013). Positioning teachers in the emerging education landscape of contemporary India. In IDFC Foundation, *India infrastructure report on education: Private sector in education* (pp.219–231). Routledge.

Batra, P. (2014). Problematising teacher education practice in India: Developing a research agenda. *Education as Change, 18*(1), S5–S18. https://doi.org/10.1080/16823206. 2013.877358

Baviskar, A., & Ray, R. (2011). Introduction. In A. Baviskar and R. Ray (Ed.), *Elite and everyman. The cultural politics of the Indian middle classes* (pp. 1–23). Routledge.

Becher, H. (2008). *Family practices in South Asian Muslim families: Parenting in a multi-faith Britain*. Palgrave Macmillan

Beck, U. (1992). *Risk society. Towards a new modernity*. SAGE Publications.
Benei, V. (2008). *Schooling India: Hindus, Muslims and the forging of citizens*. Permanent Black.
Bennell, P., & Furlong, D. (1998). Has Jomtien made a difference? Trends in donor funding for education and basic education since the 1980s. *World Development, 26*(1), 45–56.
Benner, C. (2002). *Work in the new economy: Flexible labour markets in Silicon Valley*. Blackwell Publishing.
Bhatia, S., & Priya, K. R. (2018). Decolonizing culture: Euro-American psychology and the shaping of neoliberal selves in India. *Theory & Psychology*, (5), 645–668.
Birtchnell, T. (2011). Jugaad as systemic risk and disruptive innovation in India. Faculty of Arts Papers, University of Wollongong. https://ro.uow.edu.au/cgi/viewcontent.cgi?article=2605&context=artspapers
Bloom, P. (2017). *The ethics of neoliberalism. The business of making capitalism moral*. Routledge.
Boradia, A. (2009). *Education of youth and adolescents of India. Education for all-mid decade assessment*. NEUPA.
Borker, H. (2018). *Madrasas and the making of Islamic womanhood*. Oxford University Press.
Botvin, G. J., & Griffin, K. W. (2002). Life skills training as a primary prevention approach for adolescent drug abuse and other problem behaviours. *International Journal of Emergency Medicine, 4*(1), 41–47. http://www.ncbi.nlm.nih.gov/pubmed/12014292
Botvin, G. J., & Kantor, L. W. (2000). Preventing alcohol and tobacco use through life skills training. *Alcohol Research and Health, 24*(4), 250–257. http://www.ncbi.nlm.nih.gov/pubmed/15986720
Bourdieu, P. (1986). The forms of capital. In J. Richardson (Ed.), *Handbook of theory and research for the sociology of education* (pp. 241–258). Greenwood.
Bourdieu, P. (1990). *The logic of practice* (R. Nice, Trans.). Standford University Press.
Brown, P. (1999). Globalisation and the political economy of high skills. Journal of Education and Work, 12(3), 233–251. https://doi.org/10.1080/1363908990120302
Brown, P., & Lauder, H. (2010). Economic globalisation, skill formation and the consequences for higher education. In Michael Apple, Stephen J. Ball, & Luis Armando Gandin (Eds.), *The Routledge international handbook of the sociology of education* (pp. 229–240). Routledge.
Brown, P., Green, A., & Lauder, H. (2001). *High skills: Globalization, competitiveness and skill formation*. Oxford University Press.
Brown, P., Lauder, H., & Ashton, D. (2011). *The global auction: The broken promises of education, jobs and incomes*. Oxford University Press.
Buchert, L. (1995). The concept of education for all: What has happened after Jomtien? *International Review of Education, 41*(6), 537–549.

Burman, E. (2007). *Deconstructing developmental psychology* (2nd ed.). Taylor & Francis e-library.

Butterwick, S., & Benjamin, A. (2006). The road to employability through personal development: A critical analysis of the silences and ambiguities of the British Columbia (Canada) life skills curriculum. *International Journal of Lifelong Education, 25*(1), 75–86.

Bynner, J. (2001). British youth transitions in comparative perspective. *Journal of Youth Studies, 4*(1), 5–24.

Cahill, H. (2015). Approaches to understanding youth well-being. In Johanna Wyn and Helen Cahill (Eds.), *Handbook of children and youth studies* (pp. 96–113). Springer.

Cairns, K. (2013). The subject of neoliberal affects: Rural youth envision their future. *Canadian Geographer, 57*(3), 337–344.

Carnoy, M. (2000). *Sustaining the new economy: Work, family, and community in the Information Age*. Russell Sage Foundation.

Chakravarti, U. (1993). Conceptualising Brahmanical patriarchy in early India: Gender, caste, class and state. *Economic & Political Weekly, 28*(14), 579–585.

Chauvel, L. (2010). The long-term destabilization of youth, scarring effects, and the future of the welfare regime in post-trente Glorieuses France. *French Politics, Culture & Society, 28*(3), 74–96.

Chavan, D. (2013). *Language politics under colonialism: Caste, class, and language pedagogy in Western India*. Cambridge Scholars Publishing.

Chavan, M. (2009). Managing elementary schools. *Vikalpa, 34*(2), 74–77. http://www.vikalpa.com/pdf/articles/2009/34_2_61_90_page.pdf

Chenoy, D. (2013). Public-private partnership to meet the skills challenge in India. In Rupert MacLean, Shanti Jagannathan, & Juoko Sarvi (Eds.), *Skills development for inclusive and sustainable growth in developing Asia-Pacific* (pp. 181–194). Springer. http://dx.doi.org/10.1007/978-94-007-5937-4

Chisholm, L. 1990 A sharper lens or a new camera? Youth research, young people and social change in Britain. In L. Chisholm, P. Buchner, H. Kruger, & H. Brown (Eds.), *Childhood, youth and social change. A comparative perspective*. London.

Cieslik, M. (2001) Researching youth cultures: Some problems with the cultural turn in British youth studies. *Scottish Youth Issues Journal, 2*(Spring), 27–47.

Cieslik, M. (2003). Introduction. In Andy Bennett, Mark Cieslik, & Steven Miles (Eds.), *Researching youth* (pp. 1–12). Palgrave Macmillan.

Cieslik, M., & Pollock, G. (Eds.). (2002). *Young people in risk society: The restructuring of youth identities and transitions in late modernity*. Ashgate.

Clarke, G. (1982). *Defending ski-jumpers: A critique of theories of youth sub-cultures* (Stencilled Occasional Papers: Sub & Popular Culture Series: SP No. 71). Centre for Contemporary Cultural Studies, University of Birmingham, Edgbaston. http://epapers.bham.ac.uk/3008/2/Clarke_1982_SOP71.pdf

Clarke, P. (2003). Culture and classroom reform: The case of the district primary education project, India. *Comparative Education, 39*(1), 27–44. https://doi.org/10.1080/0305006032000044922

Bibliography 251

Coe, C., & Natasi, B. K. (2006). Stories and selves: Managing the self through problem solving in school. *Anthropology and Education Quarterly, 37*(2), 180–198. https://doi.org/10.1525/aeq.2006.37.2.180

Cohen, P. (1990). Foreword. In R. G. Hollands (Ed.), *The long transition: Class, and culture, youth training* (pp. ix-xii). Macmillan.

Cohen, P. (1997). *Rethinking the youth question: Education, labour and cultural studies*. Macmillan Press.

Colclough, C., & De, Anuradha. (2010). *The impact of aid in education policy in India* (RECOUP Working Paper No. 27.). ttps://assets.publishing.service.gov.uk/media/57a08b0aed915d622c000a75/WP27-CC.pdf

Collier, Stephen J., & Ong, A. (2005). Global assemblages, anthropological problems. In Aihwa Ong, & Stephen J. Collier (Eds.), *Global assemblages: Technology, politics, and ethics as anthropological problems* (pp. 3–21). Blackwell.

Coppock, V. (2011). Liberating the mind or governing the soul? Psychotherapeutic education, children's rights and the disciplinary state. *Education Inquiry, 2*(3), 385–399. http://www.lh.umu.se/digitalAssets/77/77528 _inquiry_vo:2_nr3_inkl_.pdf

Craig, D., & Porter, D. (2003). Poverty reduction strategy papers: A new convergence. *World Development, 31*(1), 53–69. https://doi.org/10.1016/S0305-750X(02)00147-X

Crouch, C., Finegold, D., & Sako, M. (2004). *Are skills the answer? The political economy of skills creation in advanced industrial countries*. Oxford University Press.

Cruikshank, B. (1996). Revolutions within: Self-government and self-esteem. In Andrew Barry, Thomas Osborne, & Nikolas Rose (Eds.), *Foucault and political reason: Liberalism, neoliberalism and rationalities of government* (pp. 231–252). The University of Chicago Press.

Cuijpers, P. (2002). Effective ingredients of school-based drug prevention programs: A systematic review. *Addictive Behaviors, 27*, 1009–1023. https://doi.org/10.1016/S0306-4603(02)00295-2

Danesi, M. (2019, 27 April). Youth cultures. *International Encyclopedia of the Social Sciences*. https://www.encyclopedia.com/social-sciences-and-law/sociology-and-social-reform/sociology-general-terms-and-concepts/youth-culture

Danish, S. J., Forneris, T., Hodge, K., & Heke, I. (2004). Enhancing youth development through sport. World Leisure, 3, 38–49.

Dattatreya, M. (2016). *Colonialism and modernity: A study of major Indian critical responses with reference to representative literary texts* (Unpublished dissertation). Department of English, University of Mysore, Mysore. http://hdl.handle.net/10603/146870

De, A., Noronha, C., & Samson, M. (2002–2003). Private schools for less privileged: Some insights from a case study. *Economic & Political Weekly, 37*(52), 5230–5236. http://www.jstor.org/stable/4413020

Dean, M. (1999). *Governmentality: Foucault, power and social structure*. SAGE Publications.

Deshpande, L. (2018). Employee volunteerism in corporate social responsibility and employee engagement in India. *Journal of Social Work, Education and Practice, 3*(3), 26–30.

Deshpande, S. (2003). *Contemporary India: A sociological view*. Penguin Books.

Dev, S. M. & Venkatnarayana, M. (2011). *Youth employment and unemployment in India* (Working Paper No. 2011-009). Mumbai: Indira Gandhi Institute of Development Research. http://www.igidr.ac.in/pdf/publication/WP-2011-009.pdf

Dhotre, S. (2020, 15 August). National Education Policy 2020: A Blueprint for Self-Reliant India. *Outlook* (National, Opinion). https://www.outlookindia.com/website/story/opinion-national-education-policy-2020-a-blueprint-for-self-reliant-india/358711

Down, B. (2009). Schooling, productivity and the enterprising self: Beyond market values. *Critical Studies in Education, 50*(1), 51–64, https://doi.org/10.1080/1750 8480802526652

Duflo, E., Hanna, R., & Ryan, S. P. (2012). Incentives work: Getting teachers to come to school. *American Economic Review, 102*(4), 1241–1278.

Dyer, C. (2009). Cascade training: Learning going missing? *Vikalpa, 34*(3), 77–81. http://www.vikalpa.com/pdf/articles/2009/34_2_61_90_page.pdf

Dyson, J. (2008). Harvesting identities: Youth, work, and gender in the Indian Himalayas. *Annals of the Association of American Geographers, 98*(1), 160–179.

Dyson, J., & Jeffrey, C. (2020, 25–26 June). *Viable lives: Youth action in the contemporary Global South*. Webinar conducted by the Australia India Institute.

Ecclestone, K., & Hayes, D. (2009). *The dangerous rise of therapeutic education*. Routledge

Ecclestone, K., & Lewis, L. (2013). Interventions for resilience in educational settings: Challenging policy discourses of risk and vulnerability. *Journal of Education Policy*, 1–22. https://doi.org/10.1080/02680939.2013.806678

Evans, K., & Furlong, A. (1997). Metaphors and youth transitions: Niches, pathways, trajectories and navigations. In J. Bynner, L. Chisholm, & A. Furlong (Eds.), *Youth, citizenship and social change in a European context*. Ashgate.

Feixa, C., & Nofre, J. (2012). Youth cultures. *Sociopedia.isa.* https://doi.org/10.1177/205684 601282

Fendler, L. (1998, 13–16 August). *Educating flexible souls: The construction of subjectivity through developmentality and interaction*. Paper presented at The Child in a Changing World: Refiguring Early Childhood Education, OMEP Conference, Copenhagen, Denmark.

Ferguson, J, & Gupta, A. (2002). Spatializing states: Toward an ethnography of neoliberal governmentality. *American Ethnologist, 29*(4), 981–1002.

Fernandes, L. (2006). *India's new middle class. Democratic politics in an era of economic reform*. University of Minnesota Press.

Fernandes, L. (2015, 13 August). India's middle classes in contemporary India. In K. A. Jacobson (Ed.), *Routledge handbook of contemporary India*. Routledge.

Fernandes, L., & Heller, P. (2006). Hegemonic aspirations. *Critical Asian Studies*, *38*(4), 495–522.
Finn, J., Nybell, L., & Shook, J. J. (2010). The meaning and making of childhood in the era of globalization. *Children and Youth Services Review*, 32(2), 246–254, doi: 10.1016/j.childyouth.2009.09.003.
Fishbein, M., & Ajzen, I. (1975). *Belief, attitude, intention, and behavior: An introduction to theory and research*. Addison–Wesley.
Flew, T. (2010, 25 November). *Michel Foucault's 'the birth of biopolitics' and contemporary neo-liberalism debates*. Paper presented at the Creative Industries Faculty, Queensland University of Technology, Queensland, Australia. https://www.academia.edu/387691/Michel_ Foucault_ The_Birth_of_Biopolitics_and_Contemporary_Neo-Liberalism_Debates
Foucault, M. (1977). *Discipline and punish: The birth of the prison* (A. Sheridan, Trans.). Vintage Books.
Foucault, M. (1980). *Power/knowledge: Selected interviews and other writings 1971–1977*. Pantheon.
Foucault, M. (1982). The subject and power. *Critical Inquiry*, *8*(4), 777–795. http://www.jstor.org/stable/1343197
Foucault, M. (1988). Technologies of the self. In Luther H. Martin, Huck Gutman, & Patrick H. Hutton (Eds.), *Technologies of the self: A seminar with Michel Foucault* (pp. 16–49). University of Massachusetts Press.
Foucault, M. (1991). Governmentality. In Graham Burchell, Colin Gordon, & Peter Miller (Eds.), *The Foucault effect. Studies in governmentality* (pp. 87–104). University of Chicago Press.
Foucault, M. (2004). *An archaeology of knowledge*. Routledge (Original work published 1969).
Foucault, M. (2005). *The hermeneutics of the subject. Lectures at the College De France, 1981–1982* (F. Gros, Ed., Graham Burchell, Trans.). Palgrave Macmillan.
Foucault, M. (2008). *The birth of biopolitics: Lectures at the Collège de France, 1978–79* (Graham Burchell, Trans.). Palgrave Macmillan.
Frank, T. (1997). *The conquest of cool*. University of Chicago Press.
Freire, P. (1999). Education and community involvement. In Manuel Castells (Ed.), *Critical education in the new Information Age* (pp. 83–92). Rowman & Littlefield Publishers.
Furedi, F. (2004). *The therapy culture. Cultivating vulnerability in an uncertain age*. Routledge.
Ganguly-Scrase, R., & Scrase, T. (2012). Cultural politics in the 'new India': Social class, neoliberal globalisation and education paradox. In Lois Weis, and Nadine Dolby (Eds.), *Social class and education: Global perspectives* (pp. 198–212). Routledge.
Geest, de Febe. (2020, 25–26 June). *'Chalo'! Gendered youth action during urban flooding in a Central Indian Muslim basti*. Paper presented at the Viable Lives: Youth Action in the Contemporary Global South conference.

George, A. M. (2004). Children's perception of sarkar: The fallacies of civics teaching. *Contemporary Education Dialogue*, *1*(2), 228–257.

Gibb, T., & Walker, J. (2011). Educating for a high skills society? The landscape of federal employment, training and lifelong learning policy in Canada. *Journal of Education Policy*, *26*(3), 381–398. https://doi.org/10.1080/02680 939.2010.520744

Giddens, A. (1991). *Modernity and self-identity: Self and society in late Modern Age.* Stanford University Press.

Gillies, D. (2011). Agile bodies: A new imperative in neoliberal governance. *Journal of Education Policy*, *26*(2), 207–223.

Giroux, H. (1988). *Teachers as intellectuals: Towards a critical pedagogy of learning.* Bergin & Garvey Publishers.

Givaudan, M., Van De Vijver, F. J. R., Poortinga, Y. H., Leenen, I., & Pick, S. (2007). Effects of a school-based life skills and HIV-prevention program for adolescents in Mexican high schools. *Journal of Applied Social Psychology*, *37*(6), 1141–1162.

Goldstein, H. (2004). Education for all: The globalization of learning targets. *Comparative Education*, *40*(1), 7–14.

Gooptu, N. (2001). *The politics of the urban poor in early twentieth century India.* Cambridge University Press.

Gooptu, N. (2013). *Enterprise culture in neoliberal India: Studies in youth, class, work and media.* Routledge.

Gorman, D. M. (2003). The best of practices, the worst of practices: The making of science-based primary prevention programs. *Psychiatric Services*, *54*(8), 1087–1089. doi: 10.1176/appi.ps.54.8.1087.

Gough, K. V., Langevang, T., & Owusu, G. (2013). Youth employment in a globalising world. *International Development Planning Review*, *35*(2), 91–102. https://dspace.lboro.ac.uk/dspace-jspui/bitstream/2134/20614/1/IDPR%20 introduction%20 to%20special%20issue%20repository.pdf

Gros, F. (2005). Course content (Graham Burchell, Trans.). In F. Gros (Ed.), *The hermeneutics of the subject. Lectures at the College De France, 1981–82* (pp. 491–506). Palgrave Macmillan.

Hall, G. S. (1951). *Adolescence: Its psychology and its relations to physiology, anthropology, sociology, sex, crime, religion and education* (Vols I & II). D. Appleton and Company.

Hammersly, M., & Atkinson, P. (2007). *Ethnography. Principles in practice* (3rd ed.). Taylor & Francis e-library.

Hansen, T. B. (1996). Recuperating masculinity: Hindu nationalism, violence, and the exorcism of the Muslim 'other'. *Critique of Anthropology*, *16*(2), 137–172.

Hardt, M., & Negri, A. (2004). *Multitude: War and democracy in the age of empire.* Penguin

Hargreaves, A. (1988). Teaching quality: A sociological analysis. *Journal of Curriculum Studies*, *20*(3), 211–231. https://doi.org/10.1080/00220278802 00302Andy Hargreaves

Hartman, J. (2003, 28 February–03 March). *Power and resistance in later Foucault.* Paper presented at the 3rd annual meeting of the Foucault Circle. John Caroll University, Ohio.

Harvey, D. (2005). *A brief history of neoliberalism.* Oxford University Press.

Harvey, D. (2007). Neoliberalism as creative destruction. *Geografiska Annaler, 88 B*(2), 145–158.

Hendren, R., Weisen, R. B., & Orley, J. (1994). *Mental health programmes in school.* WHO.

Hodge, K., Danish, S., & Martin, J. (2012). Developing a conceptual framework for life skills intervention. *The Counseling Psychologist, 20*(10), 1–28. https://doi.org/10.1177/0011000012462073

Holland, R. G. (1990). *The long transition: Class, culture and youth training.* Macmillan Education.

Holloway, W. (2005). Fitting work: Psychological assessment in organisations. In Julian Henriques, Wendy Holloway, Cathy Urwin, Couze Venn, & Walerie Valkerdine (Eds.), *Changing the subject: Psychology, social regulation and subjectivity* (pp. 24–57). Taylor & Francis e-library.

Hochschild, A. R. (1983). *The managed heart.* University of California Press.

Houtman, G., & Wright, S. (2004). Why education matters to anthropology: An interview with Sue Wright. *Anthropology Today, 20*(6), 16–18. http://www.jstor.org/stable/3695259

Hunter, I. (1996). Assembling the school. In Andrew Barry, Thomas Osborne, & Nikolas Rose (Eds.), *Foucault and political reason: Liberalism, neo-liberalism and rationalities of government* (pp. 143–166). University of Chicago Press.

Ilcan, S., & Lacey, A. (2011). *Governing the poor. Exercises of poverty reduction, practices of global aid.* McGill-Queen's University Press.

Indo-Asian News Network (IANS). (2019, 18 September). Delhi govt's entrepreneurship curriculum to deal with joblessness, economic slowdown: Manish Sisodia. *India Today.* https://www.indiatoday.in/education-today/news/story/delhi-govt-s-entrepreneurship-curriculum-to-deal-with-joblessness-economic-slowdown-manish-sisodia-1600321-2019-09-18

Iyer, P. (2017). From 'rakhi' to romance: Negotiating acceptable relationships in co-educational secondary schools in New Delhi, India. *Culture, Health and Sexuality, 20*(3), 306–320.

Jackson, N., & Jordan, S. S. (1999). *Skills training: Who benefits? Training matters* (Working Paper Series 04). Centre for Research on Work and Society, Ontario: York University. http://www.yorku.ca/crws/network/members/Jackson-Jordan.pdf

Jaya, J., & Hindin, M. J. (2009). Premarital romantic partnerships: Attitudes and sexual experiences of youth in Delhi, India. *International Perspective in Sexual and Reproductive Health, 35*(2), 97–104.

Jain, M. (2004). Civics, citizens and human rights: Civics discourse in India. *Contemporary Education Dialogue, 1*(2), 165–198.

Jeffrey, C. (2008). 'Generation nowhere': Rethinking youth through the lens of unemployed young men. *Progress in Human Geography.* https://doi.org/10.1177/0309132507088119

Jeffrey, G. (2010). *Timepass: Youth, class, and the politics of waiting in India.* Stanford University Press.

Jeffrey, P. (2005). Introduction: Hearts, minds and pockets. In R. Chopra, & P. Jeffrey (Eds.), *Education regimes in contemporary India* (pp. 13–38). SAGE Publications.

Jeffrey, C., Jeffery, R., & Jeffery, P. (2004). Degrees without freedom: The impact of formal education on Dalit young men in India. *Development and Change, 35*(5), 963–968.

Jessor, R. (2016). *The origins and development of problem behaviour theory.* Springer.

Johnson, S. (1998). Skills, Socrates and the sophists: Learning from history. *British Journal of Educational Studies, 46*(2), 201–213.

Joshi, S. (2001). *Fractured modernity: Making of a middle class in colonial India.* Oxford University Press.

Kakar, S. (1971). The theme of authority in social relations in India. *The Journal of Social Psychology, 84*(1), 93–101.

Kamat, S., Spreen, C. A., & Jonnalagada, I. (2016). *Profiting from the poor: The emergence of multinational edu-businesses in Hyderabad.* https://download.ei-ie.org/Docs/WebDepot/ei-ie_edu_privatisation_final_corrected.pdf

Kaščák, O., & Pupala, B. (2011). Governmentality–neoliberalism–education: The risk perspective. *Journal of Pedagogy, 2*(2), 145–160.

Kaur, R. (2016). The innovative Indian: Common man and the politics of jugaad culture. *Contemporary South Asia, 24*(3), 313–327. https://doi.org/10.1080/09584935.2016.1214108

Kaviraj, S. (2003). A state of contradictions: The post-colonial state in India. In Quentin Skinner and Bo Stråth (Eds.), *States and citizens: History, theory, prospects* (pp. 145–164). Cambridge University Press.

Keep, E., & Mayhew, K. (1999). The assessment: Knowledge, skills and competitiveness. *Oxford Review of Economic Policy, 15*(1), 1–15.

Kelly, P. (2000). The dangerousness of youth-at-risk: The possibilities of surveillance and intervention in uncertain times. *Journal of Adolescence, 23*(4), 463–476.

Kelly, P. (2001). The post welfare state and the government of youth at-risk. *Social Justice, 28*(4), 96–113.

Kharas, H. (2017). *The unprecedented expansion of the global middle class* (Global Economy and Development Working Paper 100). Washington, D.C: Brookings Institute. https://think-asia.org/bitstream/handle/11540/7251/global_20170228_global-middle-class.pdf?sequence=1

Kim, K. H. (2006). Can we trust creativity tests? A review of the Torrance tests of creative thinking (TTCT). *Creativity Research Journal,* 18, 3–14.

King, K. (2007). Multilateral agencies in the construction of the global agenda on education. *Comparative Education*, *43*(3), 377–391.

King, K. (2012). The geopolitics and meaning of India's massive skills development ambitions. *International Journal of Educational Development*, *32*, 665–673.

Kingdon, G. G. (2017). *The private schooling phenomenon in India: A review* (IZA DP No. 10612). Institute of Labour Economics. ftp.iza.org/dp10612.pdf

Kingsbury, N., & Scanzoni, J. (2009). Structural-functionalism. In Pauline Boss, Willima J. Doherty, Ralph LaRossa, Schumm W. R., & Steinmetz S. K. (Eds.), *Sourcebook of family theories and methods*. Springer. https://doi.org/10.1007/978-0-387-85764-0_9

Kipnis, A. B. (2008). Audit cultures: Neoliberal governmentality, socialist legacies, or technologies of governing? *American Ethnologist*, *35*(2), 275–289.

Kirpal, S., & Brown, A. (2007). The much vaunted 'flexible employee'—what does it take? In Alan Brown, Simone Kirpal, & Felix Rauner (Eds.), *Identities at work* (pp. 211–237). Springer.

Kremer, M., Chaudhury, N., Rogers, F. H., Murlidharan, K., & Hammer, J. (2005). Teacher absence in India. *Journal of the European Economic Association*, *3*(2–3), 658–667.

Krishnan, S. (2020, 25–26 June). Liveable lives in Hindu nationalist India: On caste, youth and suicide. Paper presented at the Viable Lives: Youth Action in the Contemporary Global South conference.

Kumar, K. (1985). Educational experience of scheduled caste(s?) and tribes. In S. Shukla, & Krishna Kumar (Eds.), *Sociological perspectives in education: A reader*. Chanakya Publications.

Kumar, K. (1988). Origins of India's 'textbook culture'. *Comparative Education Review*, *32*(4), 452–464.

Kumar, K. (1991). *A political agenda of education: A study of colonialist and nationalist ideas*. SAGE Publications.

Kumar, K. (2004). *What is worth teaching?* (3rd ed.). Orient Longman.

Kumar, K. (2008). Partners in education? *Economic & Political Weekly*, *43*(3), 8–11.

Kumar, K. (2010). Quality in education: Competing concepts. *Contemporary Education Dialogue*, *7*(1), 7–18.

Kumar, K. (2017). Education and girlhood. *Economic & Political Weekly*, *52*(47), 13–16.

Kumar, N. (2000). *Lessons from schools: The history of education in Banaras*. SAGE Publications.

Kumar, N. (2001). Learning modernity? The technologies of education in India. *Autrepart*, *18*(2), 85–100. http://horizon.documentation.ird.fr/exl-doc/pleins_textes/pleins_textes_7/autrepart1/010026458.pdf

Kumar, N. (2007). *The politics of gender, community, and modernity. Essays on education in India*. Oxford University Press.

Kumar, K. (2008). Partners in education? *Economic & Political Weekly*, *43*(3), 8–11.

Larner, W. (2000). Neo-liberalism: Policy, ideology, governmentality. *Studies in Political Economy*, *63*(1), 5–25. http://spe.library.utoronto.ca/index.php/spe/article/view/6724/3723

Larson, D. (1984). Giving psychology away: The skills training paradigm. In D. Larson (Ed.), *Teaching psychological skills. Models for giving psychology away* (pp. 1–18). Brooks/Cole Publishing Company.

Lau, R. W. K. (2012). Understanding contemporary modernity through the trends of therapy and life-'skills' training. *Current Sociology*, *60*(1), 81–100. https://doi.org/10.1177/0011392111426650

Lauder, H. (2013). Education, economic globalisation, and national qualifications framework. In Michael Young, & Stephanie Matseleng Allais (Eds.), *Implementing national qualifications frameworks across five continents* (pp. 3–6). Routledge.

Lareau, A. (2000). *Contours of childhood: Social class differences in children's everyday lives* (Working Paper No. 19). Berkley Centre for Working Families, Berkley, CA: University of California. https://workfamily.sas.upenn.edu/sites/workfamily.sas.upenn.edu/files/imported/new/berkeley/papers/wp19.pdf

Lareau, A. (2003). *Unequal childhoods: Class, race and family life*. University of California Press.

Leichty, M. (2003). *Suitably modern: Making middle class culture in a new consumer society*. Princeton University Press.

Lesko, N. (1996). Denaturalizing Adolescence: The Politics of Contemporary Representations. *Youth & Society*, *28*(2), 139–161. https://doi.org/10.1177/0044118X96028002001

Lesko, N., Chacko, M. A., & Khoja-Moolji, S. (2015). The promises of empowered girls. In Johanna Wyn, & Helen Cahill (Eds.), *Handbook of children and youth studies* (pp. 36–48). Springer.

Lemke, T. (2001). 'The birth of bio-politics': Michel Foucault's lecture at the Collège de France on neo-liberal governmentality. *Economy and Society*, *30*(2), 190–207. https://doi.org/10.1080/03085140120042271

Li, T. M. (2007). Governmentality. *Anthropologica*, *49*(2), 275–281.

Lingard, B. (2010). Towards a sociology of pedagogies. In Michael W. Apple, Stephen J. Ball, & Luis Armando Gandin (Eds.), *The Routledge international handbook of sociology of education* (pp. 167–178). Routledge.

Lukose, R. (2005). Consuming globalization: Youth and gender in Kerala, India. https://repository.upenn.edu/gse_pubs/30/

Madsen, U. A., & Carney, S. (2011). Education in an age of radical uncertainity: Youth and schooling in urban Nepal. *Globalisation, Societies, and Education*, *9*(1), 115–133. https://doi.org/10.1080/14767724.2010.513589

Mahajan, A. (2021). Contours of lived experiences of children identified as 'gifted' in India (Unpublished dissertation). Manipal University, Manipal.

Maithreyi, R. (2015). Reconceptualising life skills education: A critical analysis of ideas around childhood, 'risks' and 'success' (Unpublished dissertation). Manipal University, Manipal.

Maithreyi, R. (2018, December 14–16). Redefining education through life skills education programmes: Examining the role of public and private entities in the new politics of education. Paper presented at the Comparative Education Societies of India, M. S. University, Vadodara.

Maithreyi, R. (2019). Curricular analysis of India's vocationalisation of secondary and higher secondary education scheme. In R. Maithreyi, Ketaki Prabha, Anusha Iyer, Sridhar R. Prasad, & Jyotsna Jha (Eds.), *A critical sociological analysis of the skills development initiative of India* (pp. 16–42). https://cbps.in/wp-content/uploads/Final-Skills-Full-Report_19-July-2019.pdf

Maithreyi, R. (2021, April 8–9). 'Learning to service' the neoliberal economy: The reproduction of caste/class and gender through vocational education programmes. Paper submitted to the ICAS: MP TM5 Workshop: 'Querying Childhood: Feminist Reframings', Centre for the Study of Developing Societies, New Delhi.

Maithreyi, R., & Prabha, K. (2019). Introduction. In R. Maithreyi, K. Prabha, A. Iyer, S. R. Prasad, & J. Jha (Eds.), *A critical sociological analysis of the skills development initiative of India* (pp. 6–14). https://cbps.in/wp-content/uploads/Final-Skills-Full-Report_19-July-2019.pdf

Manasa, A., Kumar, H. M., & Siddiqui, A. (2018, 14–16 December). An experiment with education-social identity: The case of Swaeroes in Telangana Social Welfare Residential Schooling. Paper presented at the Annual International Conference of the Comparative Education Society of India, Vadodara.

Mathew, L. (2016). *Aspiring India: The politics of mothering, education reforms and English* (Unpublished dissertation). University of Pennslyvania, Philadelphia. http://repository.upenn.edu/edissertations/1885

McGrath, S., 2010. Beyond aid effectiveness: The development of the South African further and training college sector, 1994–2009. *International Journal for Educational Development, 30*, 525–534.

McLeod, J. (2012). Vulnerability and the neo-liberal youth citizen: A view from Australia. *Comparative Education, 48*(1), 11–26. https://doi.org/10.1080/03050068.2011.637760

Michaels, S. (1991). The dismantling of narrative. In A. McCabe, & C. Peterson (Eds.), *Developing narrative structure* (pp. 303–351). Lawrence Erlbaum Associates.

Ministry of Human Resources Development (MHRD). (2012, August). *Vision of teacher education in India: Quality and regulatory perspective. Report of the High-Powered Commission on teacher education Constituted by the Hon'ble Supreme Court of India* (Vol. 1). New Delhi: Department of School Education and Literacy, MHRD, Government of India. https://www.mhrd.gov.in/sites/upload_files/mhrd/files/document-reports/JVC%20Vol%201.pdf

Ministry of Human Resources Development. (2018). *Educational statistics at a glance.* New Delhi: Department of School Education and Literacy, Statistics Division, MHRD, Government of India. https://mhrd.gov.in/sites/upload_files/mhrd/files/statistics-new/ESAG-2018.pdf

Ministry of Human Resource Development. (2020). *National Education Policy 2020*. New Delhi: Ministry of Human Resource Development. https://www.mhrd.gov.in/sites/upload_files/mhrd/files/NEP_Final_English_0.pdf

Ministry of Labour and Employment. (2009). *National Skill Development Policy*. http://www.msde.gov.in/assets/images/NationalSkillDevelopmentPolicyMar09.pdf

Ministry of Statistics and Programme Implementation. (2017). *Youth in India*. New Delhi: Ministry of Statistics and Programme Implementation.

Ministry of Skill Development and Entrepreneurship. (2015). *National Policy for Skill Development and Entrepreneurship 2015*. New Delhi: Ministry of Skill Development and Entrepreneurship, Government of India.

Ministry of Youth Affairs and Sports. (2014). *National Youth Policy*. New Delhi: Ministry of Youth Affairs and Sports, Government of India.

Mitra, A., & Singh, J. (2019). Rising unemployment in India: A state-wise analysis from 1993–94 to 2017–18. *Economic & Political Weekly, 54*(50). https://www.epw.in/journal/2019/50/commentary/rising-unemployment-india.html

Mofrad, S. (2013). Life skills development among freshmen students. *International Review of Social Sciences and Humanities, 5*(1), 232–238. http://www.irssh.com/yahoo_site_admin/assets/docs/20_IRSSH -539-V5N1.161113627.pdf

Mooij, J. (2008). Primary education, teachers' professionalism and social class about motivation and demotivation of government school teachers in India. *International Journal of Education Development, 28*(5), 508–523. https://doi.org/10.1016/j.ijedudev.2007.10.006

Morarji, K. (2014). *Negotiating tensions of development: A critical ethnography of education and social reproduction in contemporary rural India* (Unpublished dissertation). Cornell University, New York. https://www.google.co.in/url?sa=t&rct=j&q=&esrc=s&source=web&cd=2&cad=rja&uact=8&ved=0CCgQFjAB&url=https%3A%2F%2Fdspace.library.cornell.edu%2Fbitstream%2F1813%2F36022%2F1%2Fkm265.pdf&ei=bSvXVKX-CM-1uQS4vQE&usg=AFQjCNGpBDkUqsL3x92 mDfMoGWhDkM_ k9Q&sig2= Kd7W L6QKLDGm79jwol0XPA&bvm=bv.85464276,d.c2E

Morley, L. (2010). Momentum and melancholia: Women in higher education internationally. In Michael W. Apple, Stephen J. Ball, & Luis Armando Gandin (Eds.), *The Routledge international handbook of sociology of education* (pp. 384–395). Routledge.

Morrow, V. (2013). Troubling transitions? Young people's experiences of growing up in poverty in rural Andhra Pradesh, India. *Journal of Youth Studies, 16*(1), 86–100. https://doi.org/10.1080/13676261.2012.704986

Morrow, V., & Mayall, B. (2009). What is wrong with children's well-being in the UK? Questions of meaning and measurement. *Journal of Social Welfare and Family Law, 31*(3), 217–229.

Mukhopadhyay, R. (2011). *Anthropology of the education bureaucracy* (Unpublished dissertation). Manipal University, Manipal.

Mukhopadhyay, R., & Sriprakash, A. (2011). Global frameworks, local contingencies: Policy translations and education development in India. *Compare: A Journal of Comparative and International Education, 41*(3), 311–326. https://doi.org/10.1080/03 057925.2010.534668

Mukhopadhyay, R., & Sriprakash, A. (2013). Target-driven reforms: Education for all and the translations of equity and inclusion in India. *Journal of Education Policy, 28*(3), 306–321. https://doi.org/10.1080/02680939.2012.718362

Mundy, K., & Murphy, L. (2001). Transnational advocacy, global civil society? Emerging evidence from the field of education. *Comparative Education Review, 45*(1), 85–126. http://www.jstor.org/stable/10.1086/447646.

Murray, M. (2012). Social history of health psychology: Context and textbooks. *Health Psychology Review, 8*(2), 1–23. https://doi.org/10.1080/17437199.2012.701058

Nadesan, M. H. (2002). Engineering the entrepreneurial infant: Brain science, infant development toys, and governmentality. *Cultural Studies, 16*(3), 401–432.

Nambissan, G. (2000). *Dealing with deprivation.* Seminar #493. https://www.india-seminar.com/2000/493/493%20geetha%20b.%20nambissan.htm

Navya, P. K. (2018, 14 November). What ails Bangalore's government schools? *Citizen Matters.* https://bengaluru.citizenmatters.in/education-quality-in-bangalore-government-schools-deteriorating-28980

NCERT. (2000). *National curriculum framework of school education.* NCERT.

NCERT. (2005). *National curriculum framework.* NCERT.

National Institute of Educational Planning and Administration (NIEPA). (2016). *U-DISE Flash Statistics 2016–17.* NIEPA. http://udise.in/Downloads/Publications/Documents/Flash_Statistics_on_School_Education-2016-17.pdf

Nawani, D. (2010). School textbooks: Understanding frameworks for analysis. *Contemporary Education Dialogue, 7*(2), 157–192.

Nolan, J. L. (1998). *The therapeutic state: Justifying government at century's end.* New York University Press.

Olssen, M. (2007). Understanding the mechanisms of neoliberal control. Lifelong learning, flexibility and knowledge capitalism. In Andreas Fejes, & Katherine Nicoll (Eds.), *Foucault and lifelong learning: Governing the subject* (pp. 34–47). Taylor & Francis e-library.

Nambiar, D. (2013). *Creating enterprising subjects through skill development: The network state, network enterprises, and youth aspirations in India.* In N. Gooptu (Ed.), *Enterprise culture in neoliberal India: Studies in youth, class, work and media* (pp. 53–72). Routledge.

Nambissan, G. (2010). The Indian middle class and educational advantage: Family strategies and practices. In Michael W. Apple, Stephen J. Ball, & Luis Armando Gandin (Eds.), *The Routledge international handbook of sociology of education* (pp. 285–295). Routledge.

Nampoothiri, D. D. (2013). Confronting social exclusion: A critical review of the CREST experience. In Satish Deshpande, & Usha Zacharias (Eds.), *Beyond*

inclusion: The practice of equal access in Indian higher education (pp. 252–288). Routledge.
National Institute of Educational Planning and Administration (NIEPA). (2016). *U-DISE Flash Statistics 2016–17*. NIEPA.
NCERT. (2005). *National curriculum framework*. NCERT.
Nikson, D., Warhurst, D., Cullen, A., & Watt, A. (2003). Bringing in the excluded? Aesthetic labour, skills and training in the 'new' economy. *Journal of Education and Work, 16*(2), 185–203.
Nolan, J. L. (1998). *The therapeutic state: Justifying government at century's end*. New York University Press.
Ong, A. (2006). *Neoliberalism as exception: Mutations in citizenship and sovereignty*. Duke University Press.
Ortner, S. (1994). Theory in anthropology since the sixties. In Nicholas B. Dirks, Geoff Eley, & Sherry B. Ortner (Eds.), *Culture/power/history: A Reader in contemporary social theory* (pp. 373–411). Prineton University Press.
PAHO. (2000). Life skills. In Tobacco Free Youth. A 'Life Skills' Primer (pp. 29–31). PAHO
Palmer, S. (2006). *Toxic childhood: How the modern world is damaging our children and what we can do about it*. Orion.
Parker, I. (2007). *Revolution in psychology: Alienation to emancipation*. Pluto Press.
Parry, J. P. (1999). Two cheers for reservation: The Satnamis and the steel plant. In R. Guha, & J. P. Parry (Eds.), *Institutions and inequalities* (pp. 128–169). Oxford University Press.
Pathak, A. (2019, 20 November). The threat to the idea of a public university. *The Hindu*. thehindu.com/opinion/op-ed/the-threat-to-the-idea-of-a-public-university/article30019537.ece
Pathak, A. (2020, 15 January). Rethinking education in the age of totalitarian politics. *The Wire*. https://thewire.in/education/rethinking-education-in-the-age-of-totalitarian-politics
Peters, M. (2001). Education, enterprise culture and the entrepreneurial self: A Foucauldian perspective. *Journal of Educational Enquiry, 2*(2), 58–71. http://www.ojs.unisa.edu.au/index.php/EDEQ/article/view/558
Peters, M., & Marshall, J. (1993). Beyond the philosophy of the subject: Liberalism, education and the critique of individualism. *Educational Philosophy and Theory, 25*(1), 19–39.
Phadke, S. (2007). Dangerous liaisons women and men: Risk and reputation in Mumbai. *Economic & Political Weekly* (Review of Women's Studies), *42*(17), 1510–1518.
Philips, D., & Ochs, K. (2004). Researching policy borrowing: Some methodological challenges in comparative education. *British Educational Research Journal, 30*(6), 773–784.
Planning Commission. (2008). *Eleventh Five Year Plan: 2007–2012* (Volume I: *Inclusive Growth*). Oxford University Press.

Popkewitz, T. (1991). *A political sociology of educational reform: Power/knowledge in teaching, teacher education and research.* Teacher's College, Columbia University.

Popkewitz, T. (1998). The sociology of knowledge and the sociology of education: Michel Foucault and critical traditions. In Carlos Alberto Torres, & Theodore R. Mitchell (Eds.), *Sociology of education: Emerging perspectives* (pp. 47–89). SUNY.

Population Reference Bureau. (2017, 14 August). 2017 world population data with a focus on youth. https://www.prb.org/2017-world-population-data-sheet/

Postill, J. (2010) Introduction: Theorising media and practice. In Birgit Bräuchler, & John Postill (Eds.), *Theorising media and practice* (pp. 1–32). Berghahn.

Press Information Bureau. (2012, 19 January). Opening remarks of the prime minister at the meeting of PM's national council on skill development. *Press Information Bureau, Government of India.* http://pib.nic.in/newsite/PrintRelease.aspx?relid=79733

Press Information Bureau. (2016, 12 January). PM inaugurates National Youth Day. *Press Information Bureau, Government of India.* http://pib.nic:in/newsite/PrintRelease.aspx?relid=134401

Press Information Bureau. (2018, 12 January). PM addresses two video conferences on the occasion of National Youth Day. *Press Information Bureau, Government of India.* http://pib.nic.in/newsite/PrintRelease.aspx?relid=175586

Prinsloo, P., & Louw, H. A. (2006). Being educated in the 21st century: An exploration. *SAJHE, 20*(2), 288–298. https://journals.co.za/docserver/fulltext/high/20/2/high_v20_n2_a9.pdf?expires=1569649780&id=id&accname=guest&checksum=2772D43D021753EFBBC9003E98C9A4E0

PROBE Team (India) and Centre for Development Studies. (1999). *Public report on basic education in India.* Oxford University Press.

Rabinow, P. (1984). Introduction. In P. Rabinow (Ed.), *The Foucault reader* (pp. 3–30). Pantheon Books.

Ramanathan, A. (2015, 17 December). Can CSR and volunteering mix? *Live Mint.* https://www.livemint.com/Companies/4IwNhhy9vEdq EFqQ77cs6O/Can-CSR-and-volunteering-mix.html

Rockwell, E. (1996). Keys to appropriation: Rural schooling in Mexico. In Bradley A. Levinson, Douglas E. Foley, and Dorothy C. Holland (Eds.), *The cultural production of the educated person: Critical ethnographies of schooling and local practice* (pp. 301–324). State University of New York Press.

Rose, N. (1999). *Governing the soul. Shaping of the private self* (2nd ed.). Free Associations Book.

Rose, N. (2004). *Powers of freedom: Reframing political thought.* Cambridge University Press.

Rose, N., & Miller, P. (1992). Political power beyond the state: Problematics of government. *British Journal of Sociology, 43*(2), 173–205.

Ruddick, S. (2003). The politics of aging: Globalization and the restructuring of youth and childhood. *Antipode, 35*(2), 334–362. https://doi.org/10.1111/1467-8330.00326

Ruddick, S. (2007). At the horizons of the subject: Neo-liberalism, neo-conservatism and the rights of the child. Part II: Parent, care giver, state. *Gender, Place and Culture, 14*(6), 627–640.

Sadagopal, A. (2006). Dilution, distortion, and diversion: A post-Jomtien reflection on education policy. In R. Kumar (Ed.), *The crisis of elementary education in India* (pp. 92–136). SAGE Publications.

Sancho, D. (2015). Ego, balance and sophistication: Experiences of schooling as self-making strategies in middle class Kochi. *Contributions to Indian Sociology, 49*(1), 26–51.

Santhya, K. G., & Jejeebhoy, S. (2007). Young people's sexual and reproductive health in India: Policies, programmes and realities (Regional Working Papers, South and East Asia, No. 19). Population Council.

Sanyal, K. (2007). *Rethinking capitalist development. Primitive accumulation, governmentality and post-colonial capitalism.* Routledge.

Sarangapani, P. (2003a). Childhood and schooling in an Indian village. *Childhood, 10*(4), 403–418.

Sarangapani, P. (2003b). *Constructing school knowledge: An ethnography of learning in an Indian village.* SAGE Publications.

Sarangapani, P. (2010). Quality concerns: National and extra-national concerns. *Contemporary Education Dialogue, 7*(1), 41–57.

Sarangapani, P. (2011). Soft disciplines and hard battles. *Contemporary Education Dialogue, 8*(1), 67–84. https://doi.org/10.1177/097318491000800104

Saraswathi T. S., & Pai, S. (1997). Socialisation in the Indian context. In H. S. R. Rao, & D. Sinha (Eds.), *Asian perspectives on psychology* (pp. 74–92). SAGE Publications.

Schoenberger, E. (1988). From Fordism to flexible accumulation: Technology, competitive strategies and international locations. *Environment and Planning D: Society and Space, 6*(3), 245–262.

Scroll. (2018, 2 July). Delhi government launches 'happiness curriculum' for school students. *Scroll.in.* https://scroll.in/latest/885008/delhi-government-launches-happiness-curriculum-for-school-students

Seth, S. (2007a). *Subject lessons: The Western education of colonial India.* Duke University Press.

Seth, S. (2007b). Changing the subject: Western knowledge and the question of difference. *Comparative Studies in Society and History, 49*(3), 666–688. https://doi.org/10.1017/S0010417507000667

Sharma, A. (2007). The changing agricultural demography of India: Evidence from a rural youth perception survey. *International Journal of Rural Management, 3*(1), 27–41.

Sharma, A. (2011a). States of empowerment. In Akhil Gupta, & K. Sivaramakrishnan (Eds.), *The state in India after liberalization: Interdisciplinary perspectives.* Routledge.

Sharma, A. (2011b). Specifying citizenship: Subaltern politics of rights and justice in contemporary India, *Citizenship Studies, 15*(8), 965–980.

Sharma, V. (2005). Commercialisation of higher education in India. *Social Scientist, 33*(9/10), 65–74.

Shore, C. (2008). Audit culture and illiberal governance: Universities and the politics of accountability. *Anthropological Theory, 8*(3), 278–298.

Sinha, P. (2013). *Combating youth unemployment in India*. Friedrich-Ebert-Stiftung Department for Global Policy and Development.

Sinha-Kerkhoff, K. (2003). Practising Rakshabandhan: Brothers in Ranchi, Jharkhand. *Indian Journal of Gender Studies, 10*(3), 431–455. https://doi.org/10.1177/09 715215 0301000303

Smyth, J. (2006). Teacher evaluation as the technology of increased centralism in education. In Tom Schuler (Ed), *World yearbook of education 1990: Assessment and evaluation* (pp. 237–257). Routledge (Original work published in 1990).

Srikala, B., & Kishore, K. K. V. (2010). Empowering adolescents with life skills education in schools—School mental health program: Does it work? *Indian Journal of Psychiatry, 52*(4), 344–349. https://doi.org/10.4103/0019-5545.74310

Sriprakash, A. (2010). 'Joyful learning' in rural Indian primary schools: An analysis of social control in the context of child-centred discourses. *Compare: A Journal of Comparative and International Education, 39*(5), 629–641. https://doi.org/10.1080/03057920903125677

Sriprakash, A. (2012). *Pedagogies for development: The politics and practice of child-centred education in India*. Springer.

Sriprakash, A. (2013). New learner subjects? Reforming the rural child for a modern India. *Discourse: Studies in the Cultural Politics of Education, 34*(3), 325–337, https://doi.org/10.1080/01596306.2012.717187

Sriprakash, A., Maithreyi, R., Kumar, A., Sinha, P., & Prabha, K. (2020). Normative development in rural India: 'School readiness' and early childhood care and education. *Comparative Education, 56*(3), 331–348. https://doi.org/10.1080/03050068.2020.1725350

Stahl, T. (2013). *What is immanent critique?* (SSRN Working Papers). http://ssrn.com/abstract=2357957, doi: 10.2139/ssrn.2357957.

Stearns, P. N. (2005). *Growing up. The history of childhood in a global context*. Baylor University Press.

Subramanian, V. (2018, 14–16 December). Parallel partnerships: Teach for India and new institutional regimes in municipal schools in New Delhi. Paper presented at the Comparative Education Societies of India, M. S. University, Vadodara.

Swift, J. (1995) *Wheel of fortune: Work and life in the age of falling expectations*. Between the Lines Press.

Tahir, M. (2017, 24 July). Youth protests in Kashmir. *The Asia Dialogue*. https://theasiadialogue.com/2017/07/24/youth-protests-in-kashmir/

Tait, G. (1995): Shaping the 'at-risk youth': Risk, governmentality and the Finn report. *Discourse: Studies in the Cultural Politics of Education, 16*(1), 123–134, https://doi.org/10.1080/01596309501 60108

Talreja, V., Krishnamurthy, K., Sanchez, D. J. W., & Bhat, V. (2018). *Mapping life skills in India: Research, policy and practice.* Dream a Dream. http://www.dreamadream.org/reports/mappinglifeskillsinindia.pdf

Talwalker, C. (2001). Book review: Nita Kumar, Lessons from Schools: The History of Education in Banaras, New Delhi, Sage, 2000, p. 233. *The Indian Economic and Social History Review, 38*(4), 478–480.

Tarabini, A. (2010). Education and poverty in the global development agenda: Emergence, evolution and consolidation. *International Journal of Education Development, 30*(2), 204–212.

Taylor, A. (1998). Employability skills: From corporate 'wish list' to government policy. *Journal of Curriculum Studies, 30*(2), 143–164.

Thapan, M. (2005). Cultures of adolescence: Educationally disadvantaged young women in an urban slum. In Radhika Chopra, & Patricia Jeffrey (Eds.), *Educational regimes in contemporary India* (pp. 216–234). SAGE Publications.

The Economic Times. (2018, 11 September). Government has brought a new work culture: Narendra Modi. *The Economic Times of India.* https://economictimes.indiatimes.com/news/politics-and-nation/government-has-brought-a-new-work-culture-narendra-modi/articleshow/65772160.cms

The Economic Times. (2019, 7 March). Eight sectors to add over 10 crore jobs by 2025: CII. Author. https://economictimes.i ndiatimes.com/news/economy/policy/eight-sectors-to-add-over-10-crore-jobs-by-2025-cii/articleshow/68303637.cms?from=mdr

The Wire. (2020, 18 April). 'Unending witch-hunt of Muslims': Eminent citizens condemn targeted arrests of anti-CAA protesters. *The Wire.* https://thewire.in/communalism/muslims-witch-hunt-caa-protests

Torrance, E. P. (1966). *The Torrance tests of creative thinking—Norms technical manual research edition—Verbal tests, Forms A and B—Figural tests, Forms A and B.* Personnel Press.

Torrance, E. P. (1974). *The Torrance tests of creative thinking—Norms technical manual research edition—Verbal tests, Forms A and B—Figural tests, Forms A and B.* Personnel Press.

Singh, J. (2014). Criminalising the right to protest. *Economic & Political Weekly, 49*(45). https://www.epw.in/node/130231/pdf

United Nations. (2007). *Understanding youth issues in selected countries in the Asian and Pacific region.* Economic and Social Commission for Asia and the Pacific, United Nations.

United Nations, Dept. of Economic and Social Affairs. (2019, 12 August). *International Youth Day, 12 August 2019.* https://www.un.org/development/desa/youth/wp-content/uploads/sites/21/2019/08/WYP2019_10-Key-Messages_GZ_8AUG19.pdf

UNESCO. (2004). *Report of the inter-agency working group on life skills in EFA.* UNESCO.

UNESCO. (2018). Quick guide to education indicators for SDG 4. UNESCO Institute of Statistics. http://uis.unesco.org/sites/default/files/documents/quick-guide-education-indicators-sdg4-2018-en.pdf

UNICEF. (2005). *Life skills-based education in South Asia. A regional overview prepared for: The South Asia life skills-based education forum*. UNICEF.
UNICEF. (2011). *The State of the world's children: Adolescence an age of opportunity.* UNICEF. https://www.unicef.org/sowc2011/fullreport.php
UNICEF. (2012). *Global evaluation of life skills education programmes*. Evaluation Office, UNICEF. https://www.unicef.org/evaluation/files/USA-2012-011-1_GLSEE.pdf
UNPFA-India. (n.d.). *Adolescent sexual and reproductive health*. www.india.unfpa.org
Upadhya, C. (2007). Employment, exclusion and merit in the Indian IT industry. *Economic and Political Weekly, 42*(20), 1863–1868.
Upadhya, C. (2011). Software and the 'new' middle class in the 'new' India. In Amita Baviskar and Raka Ray (Eds.), *Everyman and elite: The cultural politics of the Indian middle classes* (pp. 167–192). Routledge.
Upadhya, C. (2019). Cultures of work in India's 'new economy'. In Sanjay Srivastava, Yasmeen Arif, & Janaki Abraham (Eds.), *Critical themes in Indian sociology*. SAGE Publications.
Urciuoli, B. (2008). Skills and selves in the new workplace. *American Ethnologist, 35*(2), 211–228. https://doi.org/10.1111/j.2008.1548-1425.00031.x
Urciuoli, B. (2010). Neoliberal education: Preparing the student for the new workplace. In C. J. Greenhouse (Ed.), *Ethnographies of Neoliberalism* (pp. 162–176). University of Pennsylvania Press.
Varghese, N. V. (2010). Review: Karnataka school quality assessment. *Contemporary Education Dialogue, 7*(1), 144–148.
Vasavi, A. R. (n.d.). *Reflexive and relational, empathetic and engaged: A case for 'social transformative learning' in India*. Rethinking Universities for Development Intermediaries, Innovation and Inclusion 66. IDRC-CRDI. http://vikalpsangam.org/static/media/uploads/Perspectives/social_transformative_learning_arvasavi.pdf
Vasavi, A. R. (2008). 'Serviced from India': The making of India's global youth force. In Carol Upadhya, & A. R. Vasavi (Eds.), *In an outpost of the global economy: Work and workers in India's information technology industry* (pp. 211–234). Routledge.
Vasavi, A. R. (2013–2014). *'Government Brahmin': Caste, the educated unemployed, and the reproduction of inequalities* (TRG Poverty and Education Working Paper Series). http://www.ghil.ac.uk/trg_poverty_and_education/publications.html
Vasavi A. R. (2015). Culture and life of government elementary schools. *Economic & Political Weekly, 50*(33), 36–50.
Vasavi, A. R. (2019, 3 May). School differentiation in India reinforces inequalities. *The India Forum*. https://www.theindiaforum.in/article/school-differentiation-india-reinforcing-inequalities
Vasavi, A. R. (Forthcoming). *Differentiation and disjunction: Interrogating India's education system*. Orient Blackswan.
Vasavi, A. R., & Kingfisher, C. (2003). Poor women as economic agents: The neo-liberal state and gender in India and the US. *Indian Journal of Gender Studies, 10*(1), 1–24. https://doi.org/10.1177/097152150301000102

Velaskar, P. (1998). Ideology, education and the political struggle for liberation: Change and challenge among the Dalits of Maharashtra. In Sureshchandra Shukla, & Rekha Kaul (Eds.), *Education, development and underdevelopment*. SAGE Publications.

Velaskar, P. (2010). Quality and inequality in Indian education: Some critical policy concerns. *Contemporary Education Dialogue*, 7(1), 58–93. http://www.teindia.nic.in/e9/pdf/articles/Padma_Velaskar_Quality_article.pdf

Vijayan, P. (2016). Privatising minds: New educational policies in India. In Suman Gupta, Jernej Habjan, & Hvroje Tutek (Eds.), *Academic labour, unemployment and global higher education: Neoliberal policies of funding and management* (pp. 57–78). Palgrave Critical University Studies. https://doi.org/10.1057/978-1-137-49324-8

Vincent, C., & Ball, S. J. (2007). 'Making up' the middle-class child: Families, activities and class dispositions. *Sociology*, 41(6), 1061–1077. https://doi.org/10.1177/00380 38507082315

Visaria, P. (1998). *Unemployment among youth in India: Level, nature and policy implications* (Employment and Training Papers 36). International Labour Office.

Wallace, C., & Cross, M. (1990). Introduction: Youth in transition. In Claire Wallace, & Malcolm Cross (Eds.), *Youth in transition: The sociology of youth and youth policy* (pp. 1–10). The Falmer Press.

Wakefield, A., & Fleming, J. (Eds.) (2009). Responsibilization. *The SAGE Dictionary of Policing*. http://dx.doi.org/10.4135/9781446269053.n111

Warhurst, C., & Thompson, P. (1998) Hands, hearts and minds: Changing work and workers at the end of the century. In P. Thompson, & C. Warhurst (Eds.), *Workplaces of the future*. Macmillan.

WCEFA. (1990) *World declaration on education for all and framework for action to meet basic learning needs*. WCEFA Inter-Agency Commission.

Weber, M. (1930/2001). *The protest ethic and the spirit of capitalism* (Talcott Parsons, Trans.). Routledge.

WHO. (n.d.). *Skills for health. Skills-based health education including life skills: An important component of a child friendly/health promoting school* (Information Series on School Health Document 9). http://www.who.int/school_youth_health/media/en/sch_skills4health_03.pdf

WHO. (1993). *Life skills education for children and adolescents in school. Introduction and guidelines to facilitate the development and implementation of life skills programmes*. Geneva: WHO. http://whqlibdoc.who.int/hq/1993/MNH_PSF_93.7A.pdf

WHO. (1999). *Partners in life skills education. Conclusions from a United Nations inter-agency meeting*. WHO.

WHO. (2009). *Violence Prevention the evidence: Preventing violence by developing life skills in children and adolescents*. World Health Organization. http://www.who.int/violence_ injury_ prevention/violence/4th_milestones_meeting/evidence_briefings_all.pdf

Wong, T. (2017). Developmentalism. In Y. Douglas Richardson, Noel Castree, Michael F. Goodchild, Audrey Kobayashi, Weidong Liu, & Richard A. Marston (Eds.), *The international encyclopaedia of geography*. John Wiley and Sons. https://doi.org/10.1002/9781118786352.wbieg0185

Wyn, J. (2015). Thinking about childhood and youth. In Johanna Wyn, & Helen Cahill (Eds.), *Handbook of children and youth studies* (pp. 4–20). Springer.

Wyn. J., & Cahill, H. (2015). (Eds.). *Handbook of children and youth studies*. Springer.

Wyn, J., & White, R. (1997). *Rethinking youth*. Allen & Unwin.

Young, M. (2013). National vocational qualifications in the United Kingdom: Their origins and legacy. In Michael Young, & Stephanie Matseleng Allais (Eds.), *Implementing national qualifications frameworks across five continents*. Routledge.

Zacharias, U. (2013). To race with the 'able'? Soft skills and the psychologisation of marginality. In Satish Deshpande, & Usha Zacharias (Eds.) *Beyond inclusion: The practice of equal access in Indian higher education* (pp. 289–327). Routledge.

About the Author

R. Maithreyi is currently the Strategic Lead of the Adolescent Thematic in the Karnataka Health Promotion Trust, Bengaluru, India. She completed her PhD from the National Institute of Advanced Studies, Bengaluru. She has a training both in psychology (with a specialization in child guidance) and sociology of education and childhood. Her research interests span childhood and youth studies, skilling and education. Maithreyi has previously worked as a practising child psychologist at the Parijma Neurodiagnostic and Rehabilitation Centre, Bengaluru. Currently, she also leads a national study for the Ministry of Health and Family Welfare and the World Health Organization on 'Mapping adolescent vulnerabilities in India.' Maithreyi has been invited to present her work on youth, skills and empowerment at several international conferences and workshops, and has published papers on the same in several international journals such as *Childhood* and *Comparative Education*.

Index

Acharya, Garima, 94
acquisition of skills and knowledge, 30
Adkins, Winthrop, 56
adolescence
    cultures of, 22
    neo-developmental, 11
Adolescence Education Programme (AEP), 68
advanced liberalism, 53
aesthetic or style skills, 39
Akshaya Patra, 167
Albee, George, 53
Ambani, Mukesh, 22
American Psychological Association, 53
anthropology, 234
Aradhya, Niranjan, 85
Arya, Devesh, 93
assembly-line, 34
Atmanirbhar Bharat, 21
audit culture, 163
autonomous and rational worker/citizens, 42
awareness among students, on strengths, weaknesses and opportunities, 246

Bakhtin, Mikhail, 7
Ball, Stephen, 196
Bavegadi, Chandrika, 151–52, 154–55, 179, 232
Behar, Anurag, 22
Bengaluru government and aided schools
    disciplining interventions within schools, 74–76
    life skills education (LSE), 67–72
    LSP disciplining within school, 76–82
    structural inequalities in schools and LSP, 87
    targets of life skills interventions, 72–74
Blair, Tony, 41
blind drawings, 242–44

capitalist accumulation, 34
Central Board of Secondary Education (CBSE), 46, 68
classroom transactions, 151–60
Clinton, Bill, 33
Cohen, Stanley, 6
colonial education, 65
colonial subjects, 65
commodification of the self process, 31
Confederation of Indian Industries, projection on job creation by 2025, 38
corporate social responsibility (CSR), 22
cultural capital, concept of, 196
cultures of poverty, 237

Dell Foundation, 110
demoralization, 54
Department of State Educational Research and Training (DSERT), Karnataka, 68, 90
deskill workers, 39
Dewey, John, 62
Dhotre, Sanjay, 31

digital technologies, 35
discourses, skilling, 34, 38
division of labour, 34
divisions of labour, 36
Dravida Munnetra Kazhagam (DMK), 83

economic globalization, 35
educated citizen, 39
educated youth, 97
Education for All (EFA), 60
edu-entrepreneurs, 61
edu-services, 61
employability, 33
employable citizen, 57
empowerment, 14
enterprise culture, 31
enterprise culture by skilling young people, production of, 32–33
entrepreneurial mindset curriculum, 67

failed student, 39
Fendler, Lynn, 41
Fordist model of production, 34, 41
Foucault, Michel, 11
Frank, Thomas, 7
free market economy, 44
Freire, Paulo, 62

Gandhi, M. K., 62
General Electric, 167
geography, 234
global governmentalities, 40
Gore, Al, 33
governmentalization of life, 40
government and aided schools, distinction between, 24
government elementary school (GES), 58–60

hard skills, 38
Harvey, David, 34
Holloway, Wendy, 41

housewife, 8
human capital formation, 60
humanistic psychology, 41
hyper-masculine religious nationalism, 21

Imagine Possibilities (IP), 25, 78, 81, 90, 93–110
information and communications technology, 163
information society, 35
institutional ethnography (IE) approach, 24
International Families and Schools Together, 44
invisible pedagogy, 42

jeevana amulya, 91
jeevana kaushalya, 91
Jessor's problem behaviour theory, 132

Kendriya Vidyalaya (KV), 68
knowledge economy, 35
Kumar, K., 64
Kumar Mangalam Birla, 22
Kumar, Nita, 65–66, 72

Larson, Dale, 54
Latheef, Fathima, 20
lifelong learners, 42
life skills education (LSE)
  programmes, 2, 13, 33, 153
  applied to socio-political problems, 56–57
  class, self and strategic opportunity, 195–99
  defined, 45–49
  developed influential social learning approach, 55
  discourse, 49
  facilitators and production of new professional status, 200–10
  in Bengaluru, 90–97

integral to daily aspects of living, 50
middle-class culture, 184–95
need to understand field response, 184
production of culturally better education subject, 210–19
structure of, 52
life skills programmes (LSP), 235–39
cultivation of employment opportunities, 170–77
meeting developmental targets of schooling and education through, 161–170
life skills organizations
Imaging Possibilities (IP). [see Imaging Possibilities (IP)]
Media for Change Limited (MFCL). [see Media for Change Limited (MFCL)]
Viveka Youth Brigade (VYB). [see Viveka Youth Brigade (VYB)]
logic of childhood, 5
LSE as pedagogy of discipline
importance paid to establish relationships of care, 133–39
language role within the programmes, 139–46
need to regulate body, 146–49
structure of, 132–33

Make in India, 21
manager and production of distinction, 219–31
manual labourer, 8
manual or hands on skills, 51
marketization of education, 237
marketization of the self, 37
Mathias, Joel, 94
Media for Change Limited (MFCL), 78, 80, 95, 97, 119–129
oath of behaviour, 240
Michael & Susan Dell Foundation, 167
middle class, 93

Millennium Development Goals (MDGs), 60
Millennium Education Society (MES), 184
Mind Matters, Australia, 44
modern education, 59
modernity, 9, 13, 66, 72, 200
middle class, 23, 197
new, 59
Western, 16
Modi, Narendra, 20
importance to skills development, 30
Myer Briggs Type Indicator (MBTI), 110

National Aids Control Organisation (NACO), 68
National Curriculum Framework (NCF) of NCERT, 64
National Education Policy (NEP) 2020, 22, 31, 67
National Institute of Mental Health and Neuro-Sciences (NIMHANS), 68
National Qualification Frameworks (NQFs), 31
National Skills Qualification Framework (NSQF), 31
National Youth Policy (NYP) 2014, 15
focus areas of, 17–18, 20
objectives of youth development, 17–18, 20
Navodaya Vidyalaya Samiti (NVS), 68
neoliberal governmentality, 32
neoliberalism, 34–35
political and economic issues, 40
neuro-linguistic programming (NLP), 110
new public management (NPM), 61, 163
non-elite youth internalization, 238
non-middle class, 93
normal adult, 39

objectivization of individual subject, 12

policy borrowing, 31
Pongal festival, 83
positive youth development (PYD), 2
post-liberalization, changes in India, 233
privatization of education, 60
provincial other, 72
provincial schools, 66
psycho-education, 33
psycho-educational programmes, 44
psychological knowledges, 40
psychological theory on the management of workers, 41
psychologization of school curriculum, 235
psychology, skills revolution within, 53–57
psychosocial skills, 51
psychotherapeutic education, 233
psy complex, 12

Ramadorai, S., 22
Raza, Aamir, 94
resilient subject, 39
responsibilization, 21
risky youth, 39
RMSA–NSQF Vocationalization of Secondary and Higher Secondary Education scheme, 67

safe space, 135–36
schooling in India
 and government schools, 62–67
 classrooms and learning, 62–67
 culture of, 58–62
school knowledges, restructuring of, 234
self-actualization theory of Maslow, 41
self-governance ethic through freedom, 42
self-help, 53–57
self-maximizers, 42

self-reflexive revolution, 53
self understanding, in relation to gender, 178–82
semi-automation, 34
semiology of skilling, 32, 37–39
Sharma, Aradhana, 14–16
short-term employment-oriented skilling, 39
Singh, Manmohan, 20
skill development/skilling
 education and psychological reconstruction of neoliberal citizen, 40–45
 Education Plan in 11th Five-Year Plan, 31
 national strategy for, 30–31
skilled employee, 39
Skill India, 21
skills turn and new economy, 33–37
Skinner, B. F., 53
Social and Emotional Aspects of Learning (SEAL), UK, 44
Social and Emotional Learning (SEL), USA, 44
social entrepreneurism, 95
social learning theory, 54, 132
social skills training programmes, 55
sociology, 234
soft skills, 33, 38, 46
strengths, weaknesses, opportunities and threats analysis within classroom, 166
Sub-Assistant Director of Public Instruction (SADPI) for Adolescent Education and Life Skills, Bengaluru, 69–71, 91–92
successful worker, 39
Sustainable Development Goals (SDGs), 60

Tadvi, Payal, 20
Taylorist models of process-oriented learning, 42
teacher accountability, in India, 86

Teachers' Training Programme (TTP), 184
Thapan, Meenakshi, 22
training for workforce preparation, forms of, 33
training, technical and vocational education and training (TVET), 33
training websites and programmes on skills, 38
triple helix, 9

UNESCO, 161
unique selling point (USP), 39
United Nations Convention on the Rights of the Child, 3
United Nations International Children's Emergency Fund (UNICEF), 161
The State of the World's Children Report, 10
United Nations Population Funds (UNPFA) Programme for adolescent education (AEP), 45
universalization of elementary education (UEE), 60

Vasavi, A. R., 58
Vemula, Rohith, 20
Vincent, Carol, 196
vital conjectures, concept of, 9
Viveka Youth Brigade (VYB), 25, 78, 80–81, 93–95, 97, 110–19
vocational education and training, 30
vulnerability designation within youth policies, 14

Warm Fuzzy, 150, 152, 228
welfare governmentality, 59
well-being, 2, 13, 57, 92, 134, 173, 237
white-collar professional, 8
whole child approach, 43
working mother, 8
World Bank
  structural adjustment programme (SAP), 61
World Conference on Education for All (WCEFA), 162
World Health Organisation (WHO)
  advocacy for individual skills, 11
  life skills by, 47
  report on *Mental Health Programmes in Schools*, 10
  school mental health (SMH) campaigns, 44

youth
  actors, 238
  and regulation, 10–15
  as discrete developmental phases, 5
  categorization of, 3–7
  cultures and sub-cultures, 7
  discourse in Indian scenario, 15–18, 20–22
  emergence of, 3–7
  in contemporary times, 7–10
  portrait of, 5
  real social category, 8
  risk discourses, 11
  risks, 17
youthhood, 1, 4–6, 8, 32, 235